Charles Forbes Harford

Pilkington of Uganda

Charles Forbes Harford
Pilkington of Uganda
ISBN/EAN: 9783743353879

Manufactured in Europe, USA, Canada, Australia, Japa

Cover: Foto ©ninafisch / pixelio.de

Manufactured and distributed by brebook publishing software (www.brebook.com)

Charles Forbes Harford

Pilkington of Uganda

PILKINGTON
OF UGANDA.

BY

CHARLES F. HARFORD-BATTERSBY, M.A., M.D.

(Principal of Livingstone College.)

Author of "Daily," "Do you pray?" &c.

WITH AN INTRODUCTORY CHAPTER BY

REV. J. H. SKRINE, M.A.,

(Warden of Trinity College, Glenalmond).

London.
MARSHALL BROTHERS
Keswick House, Paternoster Row, E C

TO THE PARENTS OF
GEORGE LAWRENCE PILKINGTON
THIS RECORD OF THEIR SON'S LIFE AND
WORK IS DEDICATED, IN RECOGNITION
OF THE INFLUENCE OF HIS EARLY TRAINING
UPON HIS MISSIONARY CAREER.

CONTENTS.

	PAGE
PREFACE	xi
INTRODUCTORY CHAPTER	xi

CHAPTER I.
HOME - - - - - - - - 1

CHAPTER II.
UPPINGHAM - - - - - - 8

CHAPTER III.
CAMBRIDGE DAYS - - - - - 20

CHAPTER IV.
THE MISSIONARY CALL - - - - 41

CHAPTER V.
A VISIT TO KILIMANJARO - - - 65

CHAPTER VI.
THE LONG MARCH - - - - 80

CHAPTER VII.
UGANDA AT LAST - - - - 113

CHAPTER VIII.
A LULL IN THE STORM - - - 127

CONTENTS.

CHAPTER IX.
Civil War - - - - - - 160

CHAPTER X.
Language Study - - - - 185

CHAPTER XI.
The First Mutiny - - - - 209

CHAPTER XII.
A Revival - - - - - 221

CHAPTER XIII.
On Furlough - - - - - 240

CHAPTER XIV.
Bible Translation - - - - 264

CHAPTER XV.
The Church in Uganda: A Retrospect - - 272

CHAPTER XVI.
The Future of Uganda: A Forecast - - 287

CHAPTER XVII.
By Bicycle to Uganda - - - 302

CHAPTER XVIII.
The Second Mutiny - - - - 319

CHAPTER XIX.
A Last Word - - - - - 339

PREFACE.

This book is an attempt to record the life story of one who, whether as a boy at school, as a Master, or as a Missionary, "tried to do his duty." Wherever possible he speaks for himself, and it will be understood that the majority of the letters are private, and were never intended for publication. The usual allowances must therefore be made for some freedom of style, and for a certain abruptness in passing from one subject to another, which may be noticed in some letters. It is hoped that this memoir may form a fitting sequel to the biography of Mackay of Uganda, which tells the story of Uganda work during the earlier days of the Mission, up to the time when Pilkington was appointed to Uganda. With this in view, a title has been adopted which may serve to connect the two volumes. There is no attempt here to give a history of the Mission, except in so far as it refers to the life and work of Pilkington of Uganda.

The author begs to tender his hearty thanks to the Rev. J. H. Skrine, friend and former master of George Pilkington, for an Introductory Chapter, and for many valuable suggestions; to his parents

PREFACE.

and other members of the family, who have unreservedly placed at his disposal letters and other materials, besides assisting in many ways; to the Church Missionary Society for free permission to use any portion of their publications, and for supplying the maps which are given in this volume, and to which special attention is directed; to Messrs. Lafayette, of Dublin, for permitting the reproduction of the frontispiece; and to] Dr. Cook, for allowing the use of the photograph taken by him in Uganda.

Also to a large number of friends, who have supplied materials or otherwise rendered assistance.

That this book may lead to practical results in the Evangelisation of Central Africa is the prayer of

THE AUTHOR.

INTRODUCTORY CHAPTER.

I am asked to give my reminiscences of George Pilkington as a boy at Uppingham and later. My first sight of him was when he came from Ireland to try for an Entrance Scholarship, which he gained. His look is still distinct in my memory. A solid little figure of a boy, with features promising to be handsome when the nose should rise; a complexion with the bloom on it of a boy from the soft West; and fine eyes, large and deep. But most I remember the steady, purposeful air with a shade of attractive shyness in it. It was the look of a boy who would have, perhaps, genius, but certainly the power of doing something distinctive in life. Most boys at that age (and it is well for them) look as if they were only conscious of being boys; he looked also conscious of going to be a man.

I do not think that I knew him, as a boy, 'all round.' As a pupil in class, I saw much of him, and in another aspect which I am coming to. But he was not in my own House, and I hardly have a view of him in his ordinary life among other boys.

The gravity which one noted in him when 'on duty' did not, I believe, prevent him from being as blithe as the rest of the world, and an eager talker;

INTRODUCTORY CHAPTER.

also, I fancy, fond, as afterwards, of argument. On the football field I remember him distinctly, where his play was solid, business-like, of a good quality, though without genius.

We formed good expectations of his scholarship, which were not disappointed, but classical scholarship, in the strict sense, was not a thing in which the strongest side of his mind was represented. He rather lacked pliancy and imagination in the direction of language; and his success in Latin and Greek was somewhat of a *tour de force*. His friends look back upon his classical studies as the foundation of his linguistic success in Uganda; and so, no doubt, in a sense they were. Yet it was not because he was a 'scholar,' in the literary sense, that he made so great an interpreter and translator: the power of languages is not the same thing as the power of language, and his splendid work on the African tongue is owed, I expect, first to the scientific element in him, and next, to that characteristic of him noticed by those who knew him best from childhood—a power of minding his own business and doing it.

Only one incident of his school life, worth chronicling, recurs to me. But it was nearly being the last. Bathing in the pool under the Welland 'lasher,' at Thorpe, before he could swim, he stepped out of his depth, went under, not once, but twice, within a few yards of his unconscious comrades, and was sighted and saved only as he sank a third time. He told me there was no discomfort or anxiety in the experience. Remember, superstitious mortals, that one may be saved from drowning to die, not by the basest, but the noblest, of all deaths.

But if I recall few incidents, there is a season of his school life which, among my memories of him, is to myself the most worth retaining, for it is the most prophetic of the life which followed. It is the season when he was preparing for confirmation. It fell to me to be his instructor, and as he did not join one of the confirmation classes (his confirmation was at home and at another time than the Uppingham Confirmation), but came to me alone, my observation of him was the more intimate. It is one best recorded, however, by briefly saying that, in the young boy then at my side, with his silent but felt intelligence and shy enthusiasm, I see the man who lived and died for Christ in Africa.

And I ask myself, did he, in the later stress of religious vehemence, tell himself that this young boy was not yet converted, and did not yet know Christ aright?

* * * *

When he left Uppingham, I saw him only once more. He came back there in the summer of 1886. He was much transformed. No wonder, for the tide of that religious impulse which set in during his Cambridge days was now running strong. I felt something of shock at first. The enthusiasm, of course, was boyish, crude as new wine always is, and slightly, though only slightly, aggressive. The strain of what I should have then called Salvationism had, in a man reading for a classical First, much of the unexpected and even odd : it wanted taking in. Then an Uppinghamian of those days could not but feel a shade of regret to notice how the 'old school' sentiment and what we will call the 'Uppingham legend' had been pushed (most naturally) into the background of his mind. But all this went by when we came, as we did at once, to close quarters, and he laid bare the new thoughts at work in him. He talked out the religious movement at Cambridge (which was leaving poor old Oxford a long way behind, I remember), and the group of men who brought the 'new wine' in; and we argued with much fulness, and mutual tolerance, I hope, the theory of Conversion, touching on the question, which some of his Cambridge friends had raised, of the practicability of sinlessness. Then we came upon Missions to the Heathen, and here, I must frankly say, I trembled; for he told me of some one who had gone out to convert China (if I am correct) with no companions, and no appliances except the Bible in his pocket. George seemed to think my demur to this plan had some reason in it: but I trembled, seeing how congenial was the plan to the theories running in his brain, lest another life, and one I had some share in, should be lost in a morass.

That fear of mine was not unshared by other friends. A knightly love of adventure conspired with the disproportion of thought inevitable in a time of religious stress, to push him towards courses which we thought barren, if not dangerous. It was with a sense of relief that we heard later of his destination to a well-organised field of mission work. Meanwhile, the touch of the 'clear spirit,' of the glorious whole-heartedness of him, charmed these apprehensions away. It was hard to do anything but rejoice in him. It was easy to say he was a little fanatical (why not, at one and twenty?), but whatever there was of the fanatic was sweetly redeemed by his sincerity, by a true freedom from self-conceit, in spite of his assurance of mind, and from any harshness, except, again, that which new wine must always have. Pleasant, too, it was to see how the old patriotism of school had only undergone transformation, like the rest of him, and was there again in the desire to evangelise. Two years later, I heard of him as having given the boys at Uppingham a singularly moving address on religion and conduct.

As we walked, we reached the Welland and the pool (it made him tell me the story) where he was all but drowned; and I remembered how, when we had bathed, he discovered on the bank a gypsy camp, and was at once in talk with the wanderers on the greatest matters. Next morning he was away across the hot three miles to endow the camp with a Bible, which they promised him to read.

Where could I leave off better than with these gypsies? For I never talked with him again, and have no further first-hand memories of him, except a letter from Uganda describing some of his doings with a modesty and an absence of colouring which quite disguised the splendid character of his work there; a note on his coming the last time to England with the promise of a visit to me; and another, dated from an unmooring ship, to wish goodbye and speak his regret that his hard work had robbed us of the visit. So I like to think of him last among the gypsies. Are they not named, rightly or wrongly, of Africa? Is not the little scene a picture in small of the scene to come, of the brave, whole-hearted, confident love of his 'barbarian' brother in Christ, which has been so echoed in the wild men's love for him?

And yet that must not be my very last word. For it does not fall to me to write of the Missionary, but of the boy of my 'old school.' So what I would say is this. A chivalrous boy from an English Public School is one of the beautiful things in God's world of men; and, to me, that knightly tale in Africa will be most thought of as the full blowing of a beauty of soul which I saw first and shall last remember in a boy at Uppingham.

JOHN H. SKRINE.

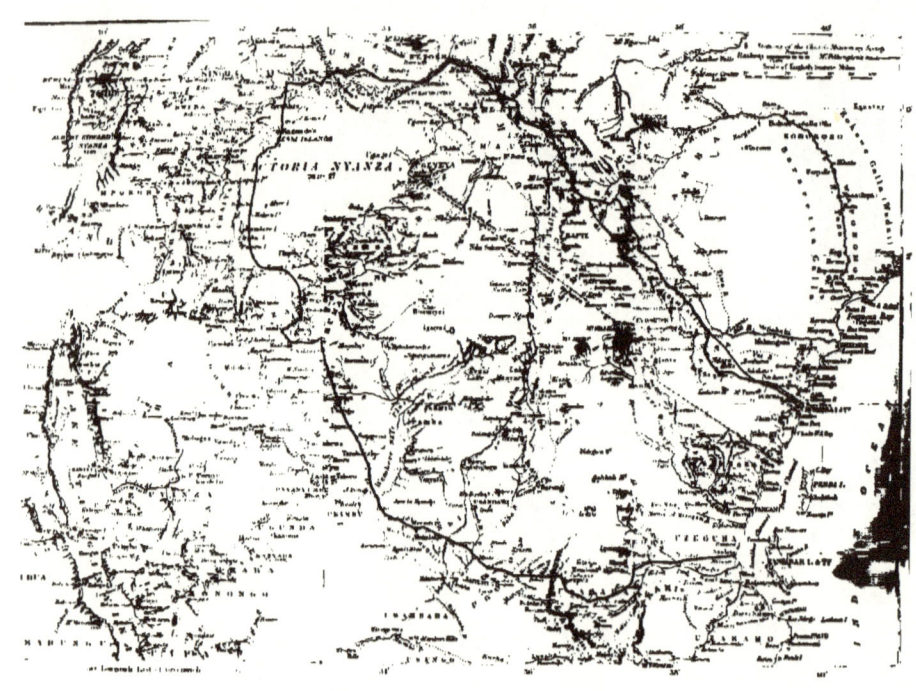

CHAPTER I.

HOME.

> Oh ! 'tis a noble thing to trace
> Our lineage thro' a noble race ;
> But nobler far where lineage leads
> To nobler thoughts and nobler deeds.

GEORGE LAWRENCE PILKINGTON was born on Sunday, June 4th, 1865, at 35, Gardiner's Place, Dublin ; being the fourth son of H. M. Pilkington, Esq., Q.C., of Tore, Westmeath.

It is no mere formality to speak, in his case, of a noble ancestry, and the lines with which this chapter opens, taken from a story in verse, by his father, recounting the brave deeds of some early members of the Pilkington family, voice well the aspirations which have been handed down from generation to generation, and which found a response in none more truly than in Pilkington of Uganda.

To come to more recent history, the family of the Pilkingtons is universally respected in the country side of Westmeath, and amid all the troublous times through which the Irish landlords have passed, they were able to secure the love and affection of their tenants. Though well known as an old Protestant family amid a Roman Catholic constituency, they have been able to over-ride the bitter prejudices which have so often been aroused over religious questions, and by their care of their poorer neighbours, endeared themselves to all, Roman Catholic and Protestant alike.

George's father was a most respected member of the Irish Bar, from which he has now retired, and he is chiefly known in connection with the framing of the constitution of the Irish Church in which he played a prominent part, and, for his distinguished services in this respect, he was awarded the Honorary Degree of LL.D. Trinity College, Dublin.

His mother was a member of the McDonnell family, so well known in Ireland, her grandfather being the celebrated Dr. McDonnell, of Belfast, and her uncle, the late Sir Alexander McDonnell, a scholar of the first rank, and one who, as Resident Commissioner to the Board of Education in Ireland, earned a brilliant reputation. Some words written concerning him at the time of his death, in the *Spectator* of Feb. 20th, 1875, are so striking in their likeness to the character of this Memoir, that they are worth recording.

After a description of his life and work, the article concludes:—"Those who have enjoyed his conversation must despair of expressing its charms. Frank, enthusiastic with the enthusiasm of a boy, full of recollection of the men he had known and of the statemanship of fifty years, yet happiest and most winning in the region of pure literature, and above all, poetry. With his physical constitution, his abstemiousness of habit, and his love of air and exercise, he seemed to bid fair for fourscore and ten, but bronchitis, caught in a season more than usually deadly, carried him off at the age of 80, leaving few like him or approaching him."

With traditions such as these, it is not surprising that Mrs. Pilkington possessed an unusual power in the training of her children, to whose education and development she devoted herself.

One who was a companion of George Pilkington as a boy, and who shared with him Mrs. Pilkington's teaching, says unhesitatingly that "his gift of languages came from his mother." It is remarkable that, in teaching her children to spell, she adopted a phonetic system, very similar to that system which George afterwards so strongly recommended as a basis for the learning of a foreign language, though we are not aware that he himself recognised the likeness to his mother's teaching.

His mother, and those who knew him as a child, noticed from very early days a remarkable power of concentrating his attention upon anything he had in hand, whether it was upon his lessons or the manipulating of a toy. He seems to have had naturally a scientific bent of mind, rather than any particular taste for languages, and he was always anxious to learn about everything.

He had a profound admiration for his uncle, Dr. Robert McDonnell, of Dublin, and was particularly fond of questioning him; on one occasion when he had inflammation of the lungs and his uncle was attending him, his mind was absolutely set on the scientific aspects of his illness. "Now, Uncle Robert," he would say, "I want to know what is giving me this pain," or, "My pulse is too quick, and I'm very hot, I want to understand about it."

At that time, his mother was afraid that, young as he was, he had sceptical tendencies. He would often say when he had been reading in the Bible about some miracle, "I don't believe a word of it." On one occasion, when they were reading the old story of Elisha and the complaint of the sons of the prophets that there was "death in the pot," George vehemently exclaimed, "I don't believe there was death in the pot either before or after."

On another occasion, he came to his mother with the question, "Is every word in the Bible absolutely true?" His mother's answer was one that might well be remembered by others under similar circumstances,—"The Bible is intended to teach you to serve God; read it for that purpose, and in that sense every single word of it is perfectly true."

With the advice of various friends, it was considered best that his attention should be turned to classics, rather than that his mathematical and scientific powers should be too strongly developed.

The basis of his classical training was well laid by Mr. Bassett, to whose school, in Dublin, George went as a day scholar when he was eight years old.

Mr. Bassett seems to have been a schoolmaster of great power, and with an intense belief in the influence of Latin and Greek. He was noted for extreme accuracy, and was a strict disciplinarian.

A former schoolfellow writes:—"He may be said to have been Mr. Bassett's 'white boy,' as he was clever and hard-working, and was always well up in his work. He was often held up to us other boys as an example we would do well to follow. He was by no manner of means, however, a bookworm. On the contrary, he was fond of football and of all other games, and took an active part in them.

He was of a distinctly pugnacious turn, and I remember many a fight in which he played a principal part. I have very vivid and distinct recollections of a terrible encounter I had with him, which ended in much bloodshed. We bathed our bleeding noses in the pond in Wilton Square, Dublin, in the presence of an admiring crowd.

He was chiefly characterised by a certain stubbornness of will and a tenacity of purpose which showed themselves by his hard work at his books, his pluck and doggedness in a fight or in games, and his determination in sticking to a thing, once he had put his hand to it."

Another, writing of the same time, says: "He was always a boy with great confidence in himself. Often he would almost irritate us by the way he would develop a line of his own in any game we were playing. He was always full of spirits."

Although born in Dublin, and at school there later on, he spent the greater part of his childhood at his father's country seat at Tore, in the county of Westmeath. Here he was in his element, revelling in all kinds of outdoor occupations. Here he gained his knowledge of cooking, which was so useful to him afterwards, and he was known, with one of his brothers, to have improvised a rough oven in a field near his home, so that he was quite prepared for the sort of cooking which fell to his lot on the march to Uganda and elsewhere.

It was in the old home that he gained from his mother his knowledge of cows, which gave him the proud position of being in later years the chief Uganda dairyman.

He was fond of all kinds of animals, and had a special affection for pigeons, of which there were a considerable number at his father's home.

George was ready for all kinds of games with his brothers and sisters, and had a leaning to anything of a mechanical nature. Electric bells, telephones, or little engines had a fascination for him, and he was exceedingly fond of watching any kind of machinery.

At the same time he evinced, even at an early age, a remarkable appreciation of books, and seemed to take in the points of a story. When only ten years old, his mother writes of him: "The boys are in immense delight with 'Ivanhoe,' and I, as well pleased to read it as if for the first time. George gave witness to the admirable writing, by springing to his feet and calling out with flashing eyes: 'It's not fair, it's not fair, three of them had no right to come at him at once,' when we were reading about Bois Guilbert, Front de Bœuf, and Athelstane, all attacking Ivanhoe."

Thus, in his early years, he gave evidence of the chief traits in his character, indomitable perseverance, a keen sense of what was right, and a determination to do it, though without much religious impression, and, withal, every inch a boy, with a boy's failings and a boy's instincts, only with some premonition of the man that he was to be.

CHAPTER II.

UPPINGHAM.

A MESSAGE FROM CENTRAL AFRICA TO THE BOYS OF UPPINGHAM.

Here from the land of the sun, of the blazing sand and the plantain,
Write I a letter to you, my brothers afar in the home land,
Written in metre strange, in ancient hexameters, metre
Not unfamiliar to you who, grinding away in your studies
Late on a Saturday night, fill up the due complement weekly.
Brothers I say—not only as schoolfellows—brothers in kindred,
Race, and language; and oh, how dear is this brotherhood only
We who have missed it long can realize. Brothers we have here,
Africans tried and true, who love us, whom we love; united,
Yes, by the mightiest bond, the surest, the dearest, eternal
As is the Lord who binds us in one. And yet there is something,
Something we miss, and our hearts go imagining, wondering, yearning.
Conjuring up old scenes, old faces, old voices, recalling
What we had never prized till we lost them, the blessings of England.
Rich inheritance, known in its fulness to those who in far lands
Mourn at the lack of love, at the lack of joy, at the tedious
Round of a hopeless life, wherein joy-bells are silent,

Joy-bells that only wake at the voice of the Lord of all gladness—
Noisy, but joyless mirth, discordant, meaningless, aimless,
Empty cackling of geese as they splash in the mud of the horsepond;
Not the full-throated hymn, the melody born of the woodlands,
Born of freedom and joy welling up at the bidding of nature,
While pure streams spontaneous sing pæans in harmony with them;
Stagnant mirth of the world, that wots not the joy of the Ransomed—
Yet here joy-bells have waked that will yet end the groaning of ages,
Ages of bloodshed and wrong, of rapine and raiding triumphant,
Oceans of tears wrung out of tortured slaves; that will end the
Long, dark night, that already have ushered in "joy in the morning."
Thus I to you, my dear brothers of Uppingham, home of my boyhood,
Home that I loved, and do love, and will ever love; where yet a vision
Floats of a face I know, whose frown was sore punishment to me,
Whose smile heaven: a face where love and wisdom were blended
With adamantine will; his voice no more through the schoolroom
Rings harshly sweet—the old man—our second founder, my master,
Master, so far as to man that title is loyally given.
You who inherit his name, his work, his zeal, and his forethought,
You who inherit the wealth, the stored-up blessings of ages,
Gathered by saints and apostles, by heroes who suffered and laboured,
Won for us freedom and light, the soul-gladdening light of the Gospel,

What is the issue to be? What legacy, say, to your children
Will you bequeath? What increment added? What further
    example
Yet of noble deeds, what self-crucifixion in laying
All that you have, that you are, at the feet of a crucified
    Saviour?
This my message to you from the land of the sun and the
    plantain,
Borne from far Uganda, where blood of African martyrs
Freely was shed because they accepted Christ's perfect
    Redemption,
Took Him to be their Saviour from sin and from sin's retri-
    bution;
You, the Christendom's heirs, you heirs of England, you sons
    of
English martyrs and saints, you rightful owners of heaven,
Sell not, despise not your birthright, your heritage, heirs of the
    ages.
So farewell, and remember in field, in hall, or in class-room,
You are in training for deeds to be done in the might of the
    Saviour,
Worthy the mighty past and the glory whereon you are
    builded.

                              G. L. PILKINGTON,
C.M.S., Mengo, Uganda,
    Saturday, 8th July, 1893.

THE choice of Uppingham, as a Public School, had already been made in the case of George's eldest brother, largely owing to the advice of the late Dr. Phillips, then master of Queen's College, Cambridge, Mr. Pilkington's brother-in-law. Since then, Mrs. Pilkington had visited the school and was more than ever satisfied that this was the right school for her boys.

    The one paramount consideration which led to

UPPINGHAM.

choice of Uppingham was undoubtedly the great reputation of Edward Thring, who was not only a clever and distinguished man, but what is much rarer, a great headmaster. What Mrs. Pilkington thought of him is well stated in a letter to her husband during the time that George was at the school. She writes: " I am, every time I hear him, struck with how remarkably Mr. Thring is one of those who ' speak with authority.' I never heard anything in the way of reading, to me, so fine as his reading of the Commandments. Every vestige of a thought ' is there any other school I should like better ? ' vanishes the instant I hear him say ' I am the Lord thy God, thou shalt have none other gods but me.' The intense force with which, with his whole being, he himself is loyal to that God comes out, and it is a thing that, in these days of unsettled belief, is invaluable."

In another letter from Uppingham, Mrs. Pilkington writes : " At three o'clock afternoon chapel, we had a beautiful little sermon from Mr. Thring, about ten minutes long, on these words: ' Thy Kingdom come, thy will be done.' I rarely come across anyone who expresses with such force and clearness just precisely my own opinions about religion and education. What we want for our boy is just precisely and exactly what he wants for him. I look with wonder at that large chapel perfectly full of boys, and reflect that, personally and by name and character, that man knows them every single one. ' More than three or four hundred boys,' he says, ' no headmaster can possibly know, and he has no business to have more boys than he can know.' George says there's not a doubt that he does know them, both in their games and their work."

George entered Uppingham at Easter, 1878, obtaining a scholarship of £30 per annum, and so rapidly did he rise in the school, that, by the end of 1879, he was in the sixth form. That he was a very small boy to be in the sixth is shown by an incident recalled by a contemporary of his, who had assisted in putting him into an empty top shelf of the sixth form room (the old library), to remind him that, though he might be the cleverest, he was still the Baby of the Sixth.

His house was Fircroft, and his first Housemaster, Mr. Rawnsley, speaks of him as follows: " He was always a merry-natured boy and ready for fun, and was a boy of genuine courage, always ready to *dare* anything, and would have been pleased to lead any sort of a forlorn hope at any time since I first knew him. His ability there was no doubt of from the very first, he always worked well, and he was always absolutely truthful."

Of his first few years at school there is little to be said, except what has been already mentioned, which could not be said of most boys, unless it were his steady application to his work, and the enthusiasm with which he entered into every department of work or play.

As time went on, however, his work began to be more and more appreciated, and it was evident that his was to be a career of more than ordinary success.

"This boy is going to do us credit, Mrs. Pilkington," was the remark of Mr. Thring, some time in the summer of 1882, and even in the previous Easter, Mr. Thring had written about him, "I am exceedingly pleased with his work . . . and if he, as I feel sure he will, continues steadily on, and stays here his full time, I feel absolutely certain he will win a high place."

During Mrs. Pilkington's visit to Uppingham, in May, 1882, she was staying chiefly with the Rev. J. H. Skrine, who became an intimate friend of the family and took the greatest interest in George, who was ever afterwards greatly attached to him. On this occasion, Mrs. Pilkington spoke to George about his future. She writes: "I told him Mr. Thring hoped and expected he would distinguish himself at the University. He was delighted, and said, 'Now, what do you think of me mother?' I thought, I wonder what you would think of yourself if I told you the half of what Mr. Thring did say."

In the same letter, Mrs. Pilkington speaks of having told Mr. Skrine that Mr. Thring had proposed that George should stay on for two years more, and added, "Mr. Thring found him so young." Mr. Skrine answered, "Well, you see, he is pretty sure to be second in the school next term, that *must* age him a little." The complaint that he was too young seems to have been the chief fault that could be found against him, and his Housemaster, Mr. Perry, complained that he was too fond of the little boys, and allowed them to take liberties with him which they ought not to take with their captain. This love of boys he always retained, and, even as a Missionary, he did not lose a certain amount of almost boyish enthusiasm.

For the last two years of his time, he was captain of his House, and Mr. Perry writes: " I felt that things were absolutely safe in his hands." He continues, " That he exercised a good influence in the school generally, and still more in the House, is undoubted. I may say that I had reason for knowing that there was a certain amount of bad language used in the House soon after he became Head. With the help mainly of Pilkington, I believe we succeeded in stopping this, and Pilkington, later, was able to assure me that for many months he had not heard an evil word spoken in the House. If such words were spoken, it was in secret corners, and not where the public opinion of the House could be brought to bear."

In October, 1882, Pilkington secured another scholarship of £50 a year, which is thus announced by Mr. Thring :—

" DEAR MRS. PILKINGTON,—

Doubtless you have already received the notice of your son's election to a scholarship in the school for two years. I congratulate you heartily. He is doing very well, and giving me much satisfaction. I think he will be a really successful scholar.

With kind regards,
Believe me,
Yours very truly,
EDWARD THRING."

During the next Christmas Holidays, he obtained, largely through the recommendation of Mr. Thring, a holiday tutorship to some boys at Windermere. Mrs. Broadrick, their mother, gives us the following reminiscences of his stay with them at that time:—

" My first recollection of George Pilkington is one winter afternoon in December, 1882, when he arrived at the Windermere station from Uppingham to commence his duties as companion and tutor to my three little boys, during the Christmas Holidays. He was not more than 17 then, and very young and fresh and bright he looked as he stood there on the platform and introduced himself to us all. He came with the highest testimonials. I remember Mr. Thring, the headmaster, said that, if we could prevail upon G. L. Pilkington to take the charge, we might indeed consider ourselves most fortunate. And very soon we found this out for ourselves. A deep friendship sprang up between him and the boys. His scholarly attainments and high position in the school filled them with respect, almost amounting to awe, and his keeness for all games and outdoor exercises was an endless and most delightful resource, during those wintry days and long evenings.

What struck me very specially about him at that time was his remarkable power of concentration. He put his whole heart and soul into whatever he undertook at the moment, both in work and play. If he was reading to himself, no outside noise, or chatter, or merriment seemed to distract him in the least—he was completely absorbed in his book; that accomplished, he would fling it aside, rise up and be the truest boy again, as eager in the successful manufacture of small fireworks and balloons as if that was the highest object of his ambition. Tobogganing down snowy slopes, runs after the harriers up and down the frosty mountains, rowing expeditions on the lake, merry games in the long evenings, made the holidays fly, until, one bitterly cold day, he caught a chill which developed into a sharp attack of pneumonia.

He was ill for a few weeks, but never was invalid more cheery or light-hearted. His mother came, and how glad he was, and how difficult it was to keep him properly quiet. He requested that there might be a special display of fireworks to celebrate his first coming downstairs, and I can see him now, laughing and rubbing his hands with glee as he watched through the drawing-room window, as the little compositions went off with more or less success."

But to return to Uppingham, Pilkington could not be called a distinguished athlete, though he took part in most kinds of sports. Football was more to his taste than cricket, as he considered it waste of time waiting about for his turn to bat.

He was a long distance runner and was keen on paper chases, which gave opportunity for the testing of his powers of plodding, which were shewn in his running as they were also in his work.

In his last year, he was elected a member of the school committee of games, a high honour among the boys, and he was one of the five out of the nine members who were elected by ballot of the rest of the school, a thing which necessarily speaks much as to his popularity. At the same time he was not popular with all, as Mr. Perry writes: "he was too uncompromising for this; he also saw the ridiculous side of things rather too keenly, and did not hesitate to show it: boys don't like being laughed at, even when there is not a trace of unkindly feeling in the laughter." At the same time he could bear chaff at his own expense, and his nickname of "Pilks," which he bore at school, stuck to him through life.

Another point which Mr. Perry mentions is alluded to by very many who knew him, and that is "his really beautiful and melodious reading. In those days, Mr. Thring made a great point of good reading, and Professor D'Orsay used to visit us for three days, twice every year, and every boy in the school used to have to read from the platform before the whole assembled school. Prizes also were given for reading, and Pilkington won several. He was one of the best readers I have ever heard, both in humorous as well as pathetic passages. Of course, this was partly due to his general intelligence, but he had a remarkably sympathetic and melodious voice, and the touch of Irish accent seemed to add to its charm."

His great friend, Mr. Martineau, alludes to this, and adds, "His voice and style were suited to a lady's part; he was very clear and refined in his mode of reading. He was also generally one of those who took part in the school plays given on other occasions."

Referring to his aptitude in this respect, Mr.

Skrine writes to Mrs. Pilkington to tell her how well George had acquitted himself at a Shakespeare reading. "I find George is starting to-day, and will be with you sooner than any note can be, but he won't have told you, what I can, that, in the opinion of good judges, the scene in which Portia figured was the best bit in the play. I don't think they are wrong, and am rather proud of my scholar's distinction in this new field. He has naturally a very good voice, and he put a degree of feeling into his part, which we hardly expect in so young a boy. I wished you had made your visit to Uppingham, and made it just then.

That you may have your due, I ought to add that one of our audience told me that the boy had his mother's voice and manner. Well, it is, perhaps, a little thing that his performance should give the hearers pleasure, and do himself credit, but it is not a little thing that he should have the power of feeling deeply what is noble and beautiful in literature."

Perhaps the most striking testimony to his power of effective reading was given by a boy, who, in telling of the reading by Pilkington of a piece of Shakespeare about the putting out of Prince Arthur's eyes, remarked, "there was not a boy in the room who could help blubbing."

Among other prizes at school, he obtained the Holden essay, but what was of more value than any other was the silver "Good conduct medal," which he received when leaving, with the inscription, "For good work and unblemished conduct."

Whilst at school, he was prepared for confirmation by Mr. Skrine, and he used for some time to attend a Sunday evening New Testament class, which Mr. Shrine held privately at his house for a few boys.

No more fitting close to the story of his career as a Public School boy could be given than the words employed by his House-master, Mr. Perry, as Pilkington was leaving Uppingham. Writing to his mother, he says, " Whatever happens to George in the future, and there is every reason to hope that it will be a worthy continuation of his beginning, the good done by his bright example, and manly and consistent stand on the side of right, can never be blotted out. What he has done for our House has laid me and all its well-wishers under a very deep debt of gratitude." And once more he says,

"I do not think I can say anything more than that his loss to me, as Captain of the House, seems almost irreparable. Few boys, I think, will have left with a fairer record."

CHAPTER III.

CAMBRIDGE DAYS.

In October, 1884, Pilkington came into residence at Pembroke College, Cambridge, having obtained a Classical Scholarship there, and a leaving exhibition from Uppingham. He was quartered with other scholars of his College in the new buildings, and there entered upon his University course, which was to have the most important influence upon his future career. His first examination was the Little-go, which, but for an amusing incident, might have been passed over without notice, but, on his way to Cambridge Pilkington had lost his luggage, and in his portmanteau was the classical author which was set for the examination. As he had depended upon looking it over at the last moment, he was obliged to go into his examination quite unprepared, and, though he was able to do the translation perfectly, he was absolutely ignorant of the subject matter of the book, and so he was ploughed in the Classical part of his Little-go!

It must not be thought from this incident that it was Pilkington's plan to leave all his work for examinations until the last moment. On the contrary, he had an intense horror of cramming, which he had derived from his teachers at Uppingham, who had no sympathy with the modern craze for results in examinations, but sought rather to turn out good men.

Throughout his Cambridge career, he worked steadily about six hours a day, and, as soon as one examination was over, he began to work for the next. He always timed himself when at work with his watch before him, so that he knew how much he was getting through, but he never sat up late to work.

He had definite methods of study which must have influenced largely his linguistic work when in Uganda. One of his contemporaries remembers him saying:—" Many men who are in for the Classical Tripos try to read all of every Classical author that is at all likely to be set. My object has been to get such a perfect knowledge of the root ideas of the language, that I can understand anything at first sight."

He took part in various forms of athletics, but did not distinguish himself particularly in sports; at the same time he fully maintained his reputation for energy and perseverance in whatever he took up. He was fond of walking, and did a certain amount of bicycling.

The College debates, in connection with the Martlet Debating Society, engaged a good deal of his attention, and he was also a member of the Union.

When he first went up, he was very keen on whist, which he studied with the aid of

"Cavendish," and he used to have whist parties in his rooms, probably in connection with an Uppingham Social Club. A member of this club at the same time, who was at another College, remembers playing a rubber in his rooms, but adds, "we played for love at his wish."

His love of argument is well illustrated by a postscript to one of his letters, in which he writes: "Whether has the man who draws first in a lottery, or who draws last, the best chance of drawing the winning lot? I argued this question with the Senior Mathematical Scholar of our year in this College, and proved this morning, to his satisfaction, that I had been right, he wrong."

It was about the middle of his time at Cambridge, that the great change took place which eventually led to his going abroad as a Missionary. In order to understand this aright, it may be interesting to give a short sketch of a religious movement, which at that time was in progress in the University.

In the year 1882, Moody and Sankey visited Cambridge, and held their memorable meetings. By many, the idea of a comparatively uneducated man like Moody addressing an audience of undergraduates was ridiculed, and their first meeting was a most uproarious one. Moody gave his address on the subject of Daniel the Prophet, whom he would persist in calling "Dannel," and when Sankey had given a solo he was encored. Yet, by the end of the Mission, an effect was produced in Cambridge which has never been effaced.

Largely owing to Moody's work in Cambridge, Douglas Hooper (through whom, later, Pilkington was led to offer for service in Africa), was converted, and, as a result of Moody's work in London later on, C. T. Studd, the well-known cricketer, decided to go out to China as a Missionary, and it was in the early part of 1885 that he, with a party, who have been often spoken of as the "Cambridge Seven," went out to China under the China Inland Mission. This party visited Cambridge before setting forth, and their visit greatly quickened the Missionary spirit in the 'Varsity.

It was at this period that the attention of undergraduates at the Universities was being turned to the opportunities for influencing boys and girls of the wealthier classes, during their holidays, by means of seaside services. Mr. Edwin Arrowsmith was the leader in this movement, and with him parties of young men from Oxford and Cambridge visited such places as Scarborough and Llandudno in connection with the Children's Special Service Mission, with which Pilkington was closely identified on leaving Cambridge.

A particularly strong party visited Llandudno in the summer of 1885, including Sidney Swann, of the Cambridge boat, and Tyndale-Biscoe, the Cambridge cox; also Hector MacLean, from the Oxford boat, and Cecil Boutflower, who has since written a sketch of Pilkington's life for the Uppingham School Magazine. Wigram, Carr, Lewis, Paterson, and others, who, later on, went forth as missionaries of the Church Missionary Society, were members of this band, and that happy month, spen in one another's society and in such splendid work, had far-reaching results.

One result of this work was that those who took part in it were led to see that it was not sufficient to bring the Gospel to bear upon the poorer classes of society, but that a great responsibility lies at our door towards those who have been well called the "poor rich," and who have been greatly neglected as regards spiritual things. This led men to see the great opportunities which presented themselves at the 'Varsity to Christian men in seeking to win their brother undergraduates to Christ.

Accordingly, it was decided to hold some special meetings for prayer at Cambridge, at the beginning of the October term, and from these were arranged a series of meetings, held by undergraduates for undergraduates in the Alexandra Hall. Sunday after Sunday, men testified to the great things that God had done for them. There was nothing particularly remarkable about the addresses, but they came from full hearts; they broke down the barrier of constraint which is so often felt in speaking of Spiritual things, and a great impulse was given to the work of God in Cambridge University.

Meanwhile, there had come up to Pembroke, in October, 1884, at the same time as Pilkington, a very remarkable set of men. Their work may be best described by one of them, now a Missionary of the Church Missionary Society in India. The Rev. H. J. Molony writes:—"I cast in my lot at once with the most aggressive evangelistic set; and, perhaps you will understand why moderate men felt it difficult to join us, when I say that four of us, who were nicknamed in the College 'the four apostles,' divided the fifty-two Freshmen of our year between us, and visited every man in his rooms, until we had direct conversation with him on Spiritual matters. To whom Pilkington fell in this visitation, I cannot remember, but very likely it was to Arthur Klein, our leader, a deeply loving and faithful disciple of Christ. In the summer of 1885, we held some meetings for our year, after hall, in the rooms of Mr. H. T. G. Kingdon (of Clare), in Silver Street. I think it was at the first (and whether there was more than this one meeting I forget) to which Pilkington and other men came. One of us (perhaps R. D. Bishop, who lost his life by accident in the summer vacation) spoke on the words, 'when I am weak, then am I strong,' and I well remember that Pilkington stopped behind, and I see him now, as he stood with his back to the fireplace, and rated us well for preaching such nonsense."

At about that time, George told one of his sisters that Klein and his companions were mad, and he probably would have scorned the idea that these men could have any influence upon him, yet, in spite of their unwisdom, as many may think, and the want of tact which may have been shown in some of their methods, it was largely owing to their instrumentality that Pilkington was brought to that great crisis in his life which he always referred to as his conversion.

Letters written about that time by George to his mother, describing this change, are not to be found, but, in answer to a question addressed to him by the authorities of the China Inland Mission, in November, 1887, as to the circumstances and time of his conversion, he answers, "Two years ago, I believe, on taking a Sunday school class; but at that time 'I saw men as trees walking.' Ever since, my eyes have been opening more and more." From his friends at Pembroke we learn, however, some interesting particulars of some of the events which must have influenced him. Amongst others were, probably, some words spoken at a very extraordinary meeting of the College Debating Society.

The meeting had been called for the arranging of the papers which the Society should take in, and it was the occasion when each man proposed his favourite papers, and various men took the opportunity of ventilating their own hobbies. The Sporting section, for instance, would bring forward "the Pink un"; the Ritualistic party, "the Church Times," and so forth.

Klein, and his following, consequently decided to make this an opportunity of addressing men in the College who would not ordinarily come to an evangelistic meeting. They therefore proposed the "Life of Faith," and Klein proceeded, amid some uproar, to give a ten minutes address in which he said there were two classes of men there in that room, those who professed to be Christians, and those who made no profession, and then he gave it as his opinion that those who made a profession of being Christians, were not half so real as those who made no profession, and that if the former would take example from the latter in the thoroughness of their methods, it would be a great thing for Christianity. Three other men followed. Brand, Bishop and John McInnes, so far as they could do so amid the frequent interruptions, and so the meeting ended. Strange though it may seem, it was probably from this meeting that Pilkington was led to see that, though he was outwardly religious, his heart was not right in the sight of God.

Another friend, Murray Webb-Peploe, speaks of the influence upon him of the meetings in the Alexandra Hall. He writes: "There it was that, for the first time, he was convinced of sin, and saw himself to be a lost sinner in the sight of God, without hope, or peace, except that which Jesus Christ had provided on His cross. I cannot say how long he was in this state of conviction, but, I believe, from his own confession, he was unhappy and miserable for some weeks, 'seeking rest and finding none.' Here, however, his godly training stood him in great stead in his need, for he knew something of his Bible, and betook himself to it most earnestly, striving with prayer to God to obtain guidance into the peace of soul for which he longed. I believe it was in his own room, in the New Buildings of Pembroke, that dear old Pilkington at last found that peace and joy of heart, which so characterised him ever afterwards. I know of no human instrument in the matter. I believe he withdrew himself into the desert of loneliness, as it were, alone with God—and prayed until the light came direct from God in His written Word to his soul. I cannot help thinking that this was what made Pilkington such a champion afterwards for the Truth of God in the Bible. His change of heart, his conversion, was not of man, nor by man, but entirely the work of God the Holy Ghost, to whom be all the glory. This one thing he used to tell me, however, that he thanked God for his faithful friends at Cambridge, who, in his own words, 'would not let him alone' until they saw the grace of God working in his heart.

From that time onwards, there was no man at Cambridge more energetic and earnest in seeking the salvation and spiritual welfare of his friends. He attended regularly at the Sunday evening meetings, at the Alexandra Hall, and almost invariably, I believe, brought men with him, that they might, if possible, share the blessing and joy of heart, which he himself had thus learnt to know.

He was a teacher at the Jesus Lane Sunday School most of his time at Cambridge, but his work there became, after his conversion, a new thing altogether, in that he sought the definite salvation and turning to God of his class, as he had not done before. He also joined enthusiastically in the College open-air services, in Barnwell, on the Sunday evenings of the May Term, and whether it was on such occasions, or when he gave his personal testimony at the Alexandra Hall, his addresses always were characterized by clearness and definiteness of Spiritual truth and personal appeal.

It was a great privilege to work with Pilkington. His uncompromising attitude in regard to sin of any kind, and his clear perceptions and definition of salvation were truly helpful and encouraging to those who listened to him. He never hid his light under any pretence of a bushel, and it seemed to me as if he made a special point of telling his friends and acquaintances of former days of his newly-found joy and peace in Christ."

That this was so is fully borne out by an old school friend of his, who writes: " Though at College we were constant friends, in my pigheadedness, when he took to his more serious line, and would discuss religious questions in my rooms when other friends were there, I told him, unless he could avoid that subject, I could not welcome him there, consequently he, for a long time, would not come to see me. I suppose, feeling it his duty to put forward his views on every occasion." At the same time he adds that this had no effect on their friendship. Of his habits, a contemporary writes:—" As a matter of fact, though I pretty often met him and always greatly admired him, I wasn't very intimate with him. I think the very greatness and goodness of the man, perhaps, kept men, with his high objects and thoughts, from getting very near him. His soul was 'like a star, and dwelt apart.' To know him was to condemn oneself. I don't think, with his work and various engagements, he had time for the long hours of idle talk, which may be a waste of time, but enable men to know each other so well. Pilkington seemed even then to have greater things to occupy him. 'Wist ye not that I must be about my Father's business?' You could not meet him and not feel he was different from most men in his purpose and objects. But I think I used to be most impressed by the great happiness he possessed. Another thing was the respect all showed for his goodness and character, how it influenced their conversation and behaviour."

Of the change that took place in his life there can be no doubt; but, it may be asked, what were the great truths which laid hold upon him, and gave him the rest and peace and happiness which all noticed in his life? Of this he shall speak for himself, and two letters—one to his aunt and the other to one of his sisters—give us his answer.

Writing to his aunt, the late Mrs. Phillips, at Queen's Lodge, on March 6th, 1889, he comments on a service which he had attended at Holy Trinity Church, Cambridge, whilst staying with his uncle and aunt, in the following words: "Mr. Sholto Douglas preached about the assurance of forgiveness and salvation in this world, showing that a true child of God is not only saved here, but may, and should, know it. My friend, on leaving the church, expressed much pleasure at the sermon; and I, not knowing the man well, but believing him to be a Christian, began telling him how, when I came up to Cambridge as a freshman, I had been bitterly opposed to any such belief, and considered it absurd presumption for any man to say that he was saved

He answered: 'I should have thought the same before to-night.' However, he had seen from Mr. Sholto Douglas's quotations from the Bible what the true and glorious teaching there is. I was greatly encouraged by this."

It was no doubt the realisation of the great fact of the possibility of having real assurance of salvation in this life that gave to him the peace and joy of which he so often spoke, but there was more than that, and we have a much more detailed statement of his position, in a letter which George wrote to his sister, in continuation of a conversation, as follows: " The first thing (this is to finish what I was going to say in the 'bus) is for a man to realise that he is a sinner, and then, to desire to flee from the wrath to come. This is hateful to man's pride. 'I never intend to be driven to do right from fear: I work from love.' (Just what I used to say when I was unconverted and only working from love of self, and when I was converted, but in the dark, for a year at least.) Let a man once see that he is a sinner, deserving—in the past, in the present, and for ever (no matter how much saved), still always deserving —to perish everlastingly; that in him there is nothing, and can never be anything, which can merit salvation, *then* he can say and understand:

> I ask no other righteousness;
> I need no other plea:
> It is enough that Jesus died,
> And that he died for me.

Seeing that his justification rests altogether on something outside of himself, he can accept the words, 'My sheep shall never perish'; seeing that he can never deserve to perish more than at the present moment, he can believe that he is predestinated unto eternal salvation before the world began. Then he can say 'Abba Father,' indeed, in perfect and child-like confidence. And all this depends on his seeing his own sinfulness. Then gratitude comes in. Now gratitude is not a power to keep us from sin, though many try to make use of it in this way. Gratitude ought to send us to the only true source of power and victory; gratitude ought to make us wish to lead holy and consistent lives, and to win others to the Saviour; but only the Holy Spirit can give the power. By preaching the depravity of human nature; by proclaiming that the heart is desperately wicked, deceitful above all things, that there is *no difference*, for all have sinned; that they that are in the flesh *cannot* please God; that, except a man be born again, he *cannot see* the kingdom of God, then men may be brought by the Holy Spirit to see their utterly lost and ruined condition: then there is no fear of their apparent conversion being a mere passing whim. On the other hand, by urging beyond measure the duty of living morally, men may satisfy themselves by mere moral reformation.

You see, when a man is really converted, being a new creature in Christ, 'he that is born of God doth not commit sin.' The new birth is such a reality that it must produce fruit. A good tree cannot bring forth evil fruit. The new heart must bring forth good things. If we declare these most unacceptable facts of man's ruin, and God's hatred and wrath against sin, and certain and awful punishment of it—emphasizing its awfulness by teaching that without shedding of blood is no remission.

>What can wash away my stain?
> Nothing but the blood of Jesus.
> What can make me whole again?
> Nothing but the blood of Jesus.
> Nothing can for sin atone,
> Nothing but the blood of Jesus.
> Nought of good that I have done
> (or am doing—such as repentance, prayer, faith—or will do)
> Nothing but the blood of Jesus.

Once a man sees the awful danger from which he has been rescued, he won't see how close he can get to the precipice without tumbling over. He will hate that which so nearly ruined him, and which crucified his Saviour—sin and the Devil.

Repentance ($\mu\epsilon\tau\acute{a}\nu o\iota a$) means a change of mind, and doesn't imply sorrow of necessity, true sorrow for sin cannot come, I believe, till after conversion. Regret for its evil effects is quite possible; but sorrow, because God hates sin, is impossible till our heart feels the same holy impulses as God.

Repentance is as much—or a great deal more—an action as a feeling—it is an entire turning away from sin (perhaps only mentally, but still an active thing), because first, sin is deadly and dangerous, and secondly (when converted), because God hates it.

To conclude what's been in my mind all through this letter, doubt of our own acceptance with God, of our everlasting salvation, comes from self-righteousness in the garb of humility. It is because a man imagines that something in himself is necessary to atone for sin, that he doubts whether he is saved. I stick to Leviticus xvii. 2.

> ' For I have nothing (and never shall) else to plead
>   In earth or heaven above
> But just my own exceeding need
>   And His exceeding love.'"

It will be noticed that reference is made in this letter to a time when, as he says: "I was converted, but in the dark, as I was for a year at least." This probably means that he did not at first realise the full privileges of the Christian life, nor the responsibilities which it entails.

Towards the latter part of his time at Cambridge, he entered into all kinds of Christian work, besides that of a Sunday School teacher in the Jesus Lane Sunday School, and especially helping in various ways at Christchurch, Barnwell.

Probably his first experience of special Mission work was in connection with the Navvy Mission, and an account of this is given by the Rev. H. J. Molony. He writes: "In the Easter vacation, 1887, Pilkington came with me to conduct a Navvy Mission in Yorkshire. I had had a meeting in my rooms at College, addressed by Mrs. Garnett, at which he was present, and, needing a companion in the work, I asked him to join me and he agreed. We stayed about a week in a farm-house at Skipton, near which a huge reservoir was being formed by damming a valley. We worked in the mornings and afternoons, he at his classics; and at midday we went out and talked to the men in their dinner hour, and, in the evening, we held Mission services in a small hall in the village, or another on the works. My memory of him at that time is that he wished to learn, and would not take a leading part, but he gave addresses which were of an argumentative evangelistic character.

We had one very definite conversion in the case of a lad named Billy, who decided for Christ as we were walking home one evening. We knelt down and prayed with him in the lane, and he gave his heart to God. He was afterwards an earnest and consistent Christian."

During the next term, which was his Tripos term, he took part in the open-air meetings, which were held chiefly by undergraduates in various parts of Cambridge, and, towards the end of that term, it was laid on his heart to hold some Gospel Meetings in the neighbourhood of his own home. The letters which he wrote to Mr., now Dean Dowse on that occasion show so well the humble spirit in which he sought to undertake such work, that we give them in extenso :—

"Pembroke College,
Cambridge,
June 3rd, 1887.

My dear Mr. Dowse,—

A number of Cambridge men have, this year, been holding open-air Evangelistic Meetings on Sunday evenings in various parts of Cambridge

—in particular, several men of my own College (Pembroke)—about twenty—including our Dean, have been working in this way, with the approval and help of the Vicar of the parish where we hold our meetings. Having seen something of the blessing which can come by means of such work, it has occurred to me that it might be possible to do something of the kind in your parish next summer. Of course, the first thing necessary would be your sanction and co-operation. That is the reason of my writing. I believe I could get several Cambridge men to come over and stop at Tore, in the Summer or Autumn, and take part in the work. We should address ourselves to all, without distinction of creed, who chose to listen, who do not know Christ as their Saviour. Of course, I cannot promise that the men would come, and I consider it wiser to ask your opinion before definitely writing to them; in case of your approval, my next step would be to consult my father, who knows and approves of our work here. Therefore you need not write to him, or speak to my people, before you let me know what you think yourself.

I cannot believe that we can be justified in hiding God's blessing from those about us by our silence; and, in our poor country, how much less, when the knowledge of Christ is shared by so few?

Hoping to hear from you soon,

I am,

Yours very sincerely,

George L. Pilkington.'

CAMBRIDGE DAYS.

"Pembroke College,
Cambridge.
June 8th, 1887.

My Dear Mr. Dowse,—

I am very thankful for your letter. So far, the way is made plain before us. I can answer for myself and, I think, for any men I ask to come, that we shall do all in entire dependence upon God, knowing our own utter inability, and that only so can our weakness be made strong; we shall, I trust, do nothing but lift up Christ, remembering the promise, and I hope that everything may be done in a way suitable to our solemn Mission, and so 'decently and in order.' We shall, I think I may promise, conform ourselves to your wishes, as is only right. I do not yet know whether obstacles may not arise; but I am confident that all will be for the best. We shall have done our part: the rest will be in other hands; so, be the results what they may, we shall be satisfied. Let us all, in the meantime, give ourselves to earnest prayer that God may both direct and bless the whole undertaking.

Believe me,
My dear Mr. Dowse,
Gratefully and sincerely yours,
George L. Pilkington."

It is, perhaps, not to be wondered at that, at this time, there was a tendency for him to despise the acquirements of mere knowledge, just as, before, he had probably unduly exalted it. For a time, feeling that he had neglected the study of his Bible, he thought that he should read the Bible to the exclusion of all other books. And he even contemplated abandoning his Tripos and going abroad as a Missionary.

Of this time, his mother writes: "It appeared to me at that time that his whole mind was absorbed in the one thought—his sins were forgiven—he did not, for the time, see that anything else was worth knowing. He felt, I suppose, that he had not arrived at this knowledge by any intellectual process, and so, got to think intellect of little consequence, and regarded the years spent in learning Latin and Greek as absolutely wasted. I tried to make him see that all knowledge was the knowledge of God, that 'knowledge rich and varied, digested and combined, and pervaded thro' and thro' with the light of the Spirit of God,' is what it becomes a Christian man to have. He could not for a long time see it, and it was, I believe, only in deference to our wishes, that he continued to work for his Degree." Having decided to do so, he steadily worked on for the Classical Tripos, and, in the end, came out in the second division of the first class in the memorable year when Miss Ramsey (now Mrs. Butler) was Senior Classic, being the only one in the first division.

During the Summer, the Meetings about which he had written to Mr. Dowse, were held at Tyrrell's Pass, Mr. Murray Webb-Peploe, who was present and assisted in the services, writes as follows:—

"In organising our meetings, we were advised not to have open-air services on the village green as we proposed, so our efforts were confined to evening meetings in the Hall next the Church, and to personally visiting as many individuals as we could. The Rector, Mr. Dowse, was very kind to us, and, if I remember rightly, took the chair for us at more than one meeting. The attendances were very good, but we were told that numbers of the Roman Catholics, forbidden of course to attend the meetings, used to listen outside in the darkness, and so we arranged accordingly for open windows and a loud voice when speaking. But it was in visiting from house to house that dear old Pilkington shone to my mind. He knew and seemed to understand the people, and nothing hindered him from witnessing faithfully to the consequences of sin, and the love and power of Christ to redeem.

He always had a word in season ready, owing, no doubt, to his continuing instant in prayer, and living in conscious nearness to Christ."

Mr. Hyslop, who was a friend of Pilkington's during the latter part of his Cambridge career, writes of him as follows:—

"To the outward eye, 'Pilks,'—as we used to call him—was then much what he appeared to those who saw him during the last years. I can recall in my mind's eye the tall, stalwart figure, the square head, the broad brow, the brilliant complexion, and the somewhat feminine parting in the middle of his hair. I cannot remember that he showed any marked vein of humour, such as one had a right to expect from his Irish nature. But he certainly used to cause his University friends much amusement by his spirited advocacy of all articles of apparel made on the Jaegar principle. He would show us with delight his patent ventilated Jaegar boots, and explain their advantages; and in many a trudge through country lanes have I accompanied him when he was testing the same Jaeger boots for their African travels."

During the long vacation of 1887, he was at Cambridge for a short time, reading Theology. He was a member of a class of a few men who were studying the Greek Testament with the Rev. C. H. Prior, of Pembroke College. Mr. Prior remembers very clearly Pilkington's unwillingness to accept anything conventional in the way of interpretation. It is interesting to note here what Mr. Prior has mentioned Pilkington's great loyalty to Edward Thring, his old Headmaster, whom he regarded as a hero.

He was up at Cambridge for another term, and many hoped that he would go on and read for the Theological Tripos; among others, Mr. Boutflower tried to persuade him to do this. He writes: "I remember urging him, with his brains, to stay on a year at Cambridge and read Theology. He asked me if I considered Moody a good Theologian. I said I didn't think *he* had a right to expect God's blessing unless he made himself a better one. But nothing would shake his view that he should be content if he could do Moody's work with Moody's equipment."

He held to this view at that time, and at Christmas, 1887, he finally left Cambridge.

CHAPTER IV.

THE MISSIONARY CALL.

FEW men leaving Cambridge have had better prospects of a brilliant career than those which presented themselves to George Pilkington. His friends and relations hoped that he would become a distinguished schoolmaster, or that in some similar way he would make use of the powers which he possessed, and which had been so successfully put to the test at Cambridge.

No better indication of his abilities can be gained than by quoting some of the testimonials given to him when applying for a mastership soon after leaving the University.

Mr. R. A. Neil, Fellow and Classical Lecturer at Pembroke College, Cambridge, writes of him: "His course here was marked by a steady and continuous improvement in scholarship, which is, I think, unexampled in my experience. This improvement was naturally due to an honest and intelligent devotion to work, and was fitly rewarded by a place in the highest division of the Classical Tripos of his year in which men were placed. His place was well deserved, and forms a sufficient guarantee of his capacity to undertake high school work. I believe his scholarship will be supplemented by a very high interest in his pupils, and that, if he is appointed to a mastership, he will have the success to be expected from the combination of most creditable attainments with a high and vigorous personal character."

At the same time, Dr. Verrall, Fellow and Assistant Tutor at Trinity College, Cambridge, writes: "Mr. G. L. Pilkington, B.A., was my pupil at Pembroke College during a considerable part of his course as an undergraduate. He is a good scholar both in Greek and in Latin. His composition was always correct and sensible, and improved steadily with time. Before he went up for his degree it had become often brilliant, and I quite anticipated for him the high degree which he actually obtained.

All I heard and saw of him was to his advantage, and I have much pleasure in recommending him for employment as a schoolmaster, an occupation for which I believe him to be thoroughly fit."

That he would have been fitted for the work of a schoolmaster, his subsequent experience abundantly showed, but there had already come into his life a conviction which he recognised as the call of God leading him to devote himself to Foreign Missionary service.

Some thoughts of this came to him, as we have already seen, before taking his degree, but it was during his last term at Cambridge that he first offered himself for the work. The Mission to which he made application was the China Inland Mission, whose work had been prominently brought to the front through the visit of " The Cambridge Seven." When asked as to the reasons which led him to offer, he answered in the following way: " Because I believe it to be God's will, and I think this because the need abroad is great; we have a sort of plethora at home, and I am free to go, and Mark xvi., 15. The need of Missions has come before me urgently for a year." At the same time, he wrote to his parents asking for their consent. In reply, his father urged a delay of at least two years before deciding such an important matter, and in consequence, although George was accepted by the authorities of the China Inland Mission, he altogether abandoned his project, saying, " What such a man as my father does not wholly approve of, cannot be right for me to do." Thus, for the time, he gave up his cherished plans and set himself to whatever his hand found to do at home.

One more honour came to him, after leaving the University, in the shape of the Winchester Reading Prize, for which he was bracketted first with another candidate.

During 1888, he was chiefly occupied in Mission work amongst boys, in connection with the Children's Special Service Mission.

Missions held by him, in co-operation with other University men, at Newcastle and at Clifton are specially remembered.

One who heard him as a boy at Newcastle, and who from that time became a fast friend of Pilkington's, writes thus of him: "It was his utter manliness that first struck me: here was a thorough man ringing true from top to bottom. Then that he was a man of God: one who knew God and believed in God. So he was a man of power. How well I remember my first glimpse of him, eleven years ago, as he came swinging round the corner—the great, tall, strapping figure; the beaming face—almost as red as his scarlet tie—his hat far enough back to show his broad forehead; a huge, calf-skin Bible under his arm, and a club of a walking stick in his hand. I never saw him without that Bible! But, alas! a Uganda calf ate it all but a few pages of Revelation."

He also visited Durham and held Meetings at the Grammar School, and, at the same time, some Meetings for young men. One young man, brought to Christ through his instrumentality, wished to follow him to Uganda, but, being prevented on medical grounds, is now working in connection with the Irish Church Missions. Of his Clifton Missions the Rev. J. T. Inskip gives us the following reminiscences:—

"In July, 1888, Pilkington came to Clifton with Murray Webb-Peploe for two weeks' work. The meetings were held in a private house in a central position, near Clifton College. The results were, speaking frankly, very disappointing. The time fixed was unfortunate, as all boys, of the class for whom the Mission was intended, were at school. On Sundays, the meetings were very large, but, on week days, very few boys attended. On the second

Sunday morning, Pilkington arranged an Open-air Service on the Downs. He knew that a large number of the College boys would be within reach after their service in the School Chapel, and he hoped to attract some to this service. I had then not long left the College, and, unhappily, courage failed me and I did not attend the service, but Pilkington and several of the workers persevered. He was not discouraged by the apparent failure of the Mission. He saw that there was a grand opening in Clifton, and promised to come again in the following January. In the opening days of 1889, he began work aided by a band of young men. Meetings were held every morning at the same private house, in the afternoon football was played on the Downs, and, in the evening, Drawing Room Meetings were held by invitation. Boys flocked to the Mission this time and the impression made was deep and widespread. I can see him now—his tall, upright figure, his solemn face, standing out against the background of dark wall-paper in the meeting room at Worcester Lodge. Some of his anecdotes and illustrations are still fresh in one's memory. He told the boys how useless it was, and how wearying, to tie fruit on a fruitless tree—the nature of the tree must be changed. He described himself as being not the same person since his conversion—in fact, as almost literally someone else, a new creation. He stated that he had very little conviction of sin at his conversion, but that he had since found out more and more what sin really was. And, in the afternoons, how heartily Pilkington threw himself into the games. One dreary Saturday afternoon, there was a run to Wick—a village between Mangotsfield and Bath. The way was unfamiliar and fog came, and some of the runners began to lose heart. But Pilkington was in the best of trim, and carried one or two boys in turn on his back, breathing perseverance into the spirits of all, till at length a hospitable reception and a hearty meal at Wick Vicarage put everyone to rights. All too soon the mission ended, but not a few will bear through life the impress of Pilkington's influence under the blessing of God. Some few who took part, as boys or workers, have been called away, one worker (S. W. Day) being killed by an accident when riding only a month after Pilkington's death. The majority are now scattered over the world. But none will forget the happy weeks spent together under Pilkington's leadership, or the quietness and confidence which were his strength."

Rev. Murray Webb Peploe, writing of the first Clifton Mission, says:—"At Clifton, there were some five of us Cambridge men taking part in the mission to the Schoolboys, but, to my own mind, Pilkington was a head and shoulders above us all in his power of speaking to boys. This capability he proved himself to possess either in addressing boys publicly or in speaking privately to them alone. His common sense, manly, straight talks were the very thing for boys. He was, as I remember him, like a big, simple boy himself, and as he had a special love for boys, I do not doubt but that he helped many a lad to clearly understand the way of life and salvation."

During the time that he was working as Assistant Secretary of the Children's Special Service Mission he was associated with Mr. Martin Hall who was, in after years, his colleague in Uganda.

As has been already stated, Pilkington felt most at home when he was addressing boys, and Mr. Murray Webb-Peploe adds: "Girls were never in his line at all;" consequently, as he did not find sufficient opportunities for mission work amongst the boys alone, he turned his thoughts once more to school-work.

He spent a few days at Dover College, towards the end of 1888, and, of his time, there a correspondent writes to the *Morning Leader* : " He was a first-rate classical scholar, at once precise and deeply read, almost too much so for school purposes. A splendid figure of a man—well over six feet, and broad in proportion—he brought into the schoolroom the imperturbable sweetness of temper and childlike simplicity—in short, the Christianity —that marked his whole life.

His earnest recognition of such things as services in chapel that boys are only too prone to scamp, the lonely walks, spent in serious converse, that he would take with one or two members of his class who particularly interested him, were thought lightly of at the time. Perhaps they had a more permanent effect for good than the Greek verbs that Mr. Pilkington taught with such conspicuous ability."

One of these boys, now Rev. E. H. Elwin,

Acting-Principal of Fourah Bay College, Sierra Leone, writes of this time: "Pilkington was the first man I remember to speak of Christ to me when a boy at Dover College. He came to take the Sixth, when our Headmaster was ill, in November, 1888, and I well remember him taking me to his rooms and asking me to read a paper pinned to the wall. To my surprise, I read John iii. 16. He then asked me if I knew the verse, and how glad he was that I did in some degree. He stayed with us at the College for twenty days, and, throughout that time, kept asking boys to his rooms to tea, and sought to win them for Christ. I remember what a lift I got during those days, and, after nearly eight years, with what pleasure he heard he had been a help when I reminded him at Oxford, about it just before he last sailed for Uganda."

The summer term of 1889 found him taking temporary duty as a master at Harrow School, and, of this period, Mr. Hyslop says:—"he seemed thoroughly to enjoy his work amongst the boys, and I can remember well his telling me of the various expedients by which he tried to make his boys realise that 'life is earnest,' and to point them onward and upward to the service of his Divine Master. It is clear that he must have spoken to them 'in season and out of season,' and I think of this as one more proof of his whole-heartedness and devotion to the work of God."

The Rev. W. D. Bushell, one of the senior masters at Harrow, who knew Pilkington intimately, speaks of him as one "who loved the school with singular affection from the first day he knew it to the end"; and certainly his correspondence bears witness to the very warm place which Harrow always held in his heart. After Pilkington's death, Mr. Bushell was entrusted with the following message which was conveyed to the boys from the chapel pulpit: "Whilst he was at Harrow, it happened, by the providence of God, that he was led to think of the possibility of sudden, early death; he had no fear of it, nor reason to expect it, then, but he wrote down these simple words to leave behind him: 'If I die here, tell the Harrow boys, especially those of my own form, I sent this message to them: *'Come to Jesus.'*"

It is not to be wondered at that Pilkington's plain and faithful dealings with the boys committed to his charge formed the subject of a certain amount of criticism; he would have been the last to claim infallibility of judgment; but there is no question that many, who were boys under him, will rise up to call him blessed.

The chief reason of his success was undoubtedly the thoroughness and reality of his whole life. If he spoke to the boys about their souls, it was not merely to satisfy his conscience; his whole heart was in it, and his life so bound up with those amongst whom he was working, that their joys were his joys, their sorrows his sorrows. His mother recalls how, one day, he came home with the news that some boy in whom he was interested had gone wrong, and says that he felt it so keenly that he sobbed like a child.

On another occasion, he writes home to his sister telling the good news of two brothers who he had reason to believe had been helped by one of his missions. He writes:—" the younger one in particular sees everything in a new light—he never saw before that eternal life was a gift; he sees it clearly and with wonder now—thank God; moreover, he intends to stand up at school for Jesus; do pray for him, for he will have a hard time; he has announced that he intends to start by burning his cribs.—Pray for him and his brother."

On leaving Harrow, in the summer of 1889, he had in contemplation the possibility of acting as Classical Lecturer in Melbourne University. One of his testimonials was from Mr. Welldon, who wrote as follows: "Mr. G. L. Pilkington, who is a candidate for a Classical Lectureship in Trinity College of the Melbourne University, is known to me as a man of exceptionally strong physique, of high scholarship and of Christian conviction and character. If I may base an opinion upon the printed list of qualifications for that responsible post, I should say it would be hard to find a Lecturer who could render more efficient service to the College than Mr. Pilkington. He was my colleague, at Harrow, for one term, so I have some direct knowledge of his work. I have a sincere respect for him and should be glad to hear of the success of his present application.

J. E. C. WELLDON,
Head Master of Harrow School."

Sept. 12th, 1889.

THE MISSIONARY CALL.

But a wider sphere of usefulness was to open before him than a lectureship in Melbourne University, and it was in November, 1889, when he was acting as an assistant master at Bedford Grammar School, that the call to Africa came to him.

In order to understand this aright, some reference must be made to the plans before the Church Missionary Society, at this time, for extension in East and West Africa.

Mr. Douglas Hooper had returned from East Africa, and Mr. Graham Wilmot Brooke, and Rev. J. A. Robinson, from West Africa, and, in each case, proposals had been made for an advance on somewhat more simple lines than had hitherto been deemed possible, at the same time great stress was laid upon the importance of securing a small band of University men to act as a pioneering party.

Having gained the Committee's assent to his proposals, Douglas Hooper set to work to find companions to join him, and the account of his stay at Cambridge may be given in his own words. He writes :—

" After four years in Africa, I went home and had the great privilege of being at Ridley Hall again. Very many were the talks enjoyed there with men as to Man's claim on God and God's claim on Man, and one day, Ernest Causton, now working at Narowal, said: 'The doctors will not let me go with you, but I know someone who might, he is now a master at Bedford; next Sunday he will be my guest here and I will bring him to call on you,' and so I met George Pilkington, and he told me his sympathies were with the China Inland Mission. Sometime before, he had wanted to go out in connection with that Society, but his parents had asked him to drop the matter for two years. He was struck with the fact of this time being just up. I told him I believed the C.I.M. offered him nothing that he might not enjoy in the C.M.S. My sympathies were then, and are now, very much with the C.I.M., and I venture to think that the missionary cause owes no living man more under God than the beloved and honoured Mr. Hudson Taylor. But, at Cambridge, there was a feeling that the more deeply spiritually taught men must join the C.I.M. in preference to the C.M.S., and one tried to disabuse minds on the subject. From the first Sunday, Pilkington never seemed to doubt once that God had called him to Africa. The idea was that a few of us (the C.M.S. limited us to four) should go to Ulu and live together in as simple a way as possible. The people there were many, the district healthy, and the food plentiful; but it was not to be, for, shortly before leaving, Mr. Wigram asked one and all to go to Uganda. Mackay was pleading for reinforcements."

Thus the call came, and there seemed to be no doubt about it, but, before he would give a final answer, he determined to put the whole matter before his parents. He had heard God's voice before, as he believed, speaking to him through them; he believed it would be the same again; accordingly he wrote to his father as follows:—

THE MISSIONARY CALL.

"Pembroke College,
Cambridge,
Sunday, 3rd Nov., 1889.

MY DEAR FATHER,—

I have a very important matter to write to you about, to-day. I hope we shall all be able to see it in the same light; at any rate, I am not making the mistake of not first writing to you and Mother about my plans, before taking any step or speaking to other people with regard to them.

Douglas Hooper (an old Harrovian and Trinity Hall man) has come home, some months ago, from Africa, where he has been working under the Church Missionary Society for four years.

He has come back with a new plan of work on the East of Africa, which he has laid before the Church Missionary Society, and which they have accepted and promised to supply the necessaries for, if he can find the men. It is to take five or six Cambridge men and make a station on a new route to the Victoria Nyanza, between Frere Town and the Lake: on the principle of living as simply and as much in native style as is possible. There are four points in his plan on which he lays stress:—

(1.) *Not less than five or six men.*—The deadening effect of heathendom is such that isolated men succumb to it.

(2.) *Cambridge men.*—Experience has convinced him that educated gentlemen are absolutely needed for Africa.

(3.) *A new route.*—Virgin soil—because, on the old routes, the natives are so habituated to the old system of buying the chiefs' favour by innumerable presents, that those who go on another principle are not tolerated.

(4.) *Native style.*—As far cheaper and *healthier* —so he says by experience—and also as the right way of getting into touch with the natives.

This is the plan: he has with difficulty succeeded, after some months, in getting three men besides himself; no others seem forthcoming: he considers it wrong to go unless four at least go with him. Most men have ties and engagements which make it impossible, had they the mind, to go. How about myself? If no one comes forward during the next week or two—he wants to start in January—he will give up the plan, and the East Coast will have to be given up to darkness still, for we know not how long, till another opening like the present occurs. Mr. Wigram, secretary of the C.M.S., told him that the Society's prospects never looked brighter than they do at present in Africa: but what if this attempt be given up? What do you say? It probably lies between you and Mother and me whether it will be carried out or no.

May I point out some of the advantages? I know you would like me to go out with the C.M.S. rather than, as might happen, independently, or with an undenominational Society. I am sure you would be glad that five or six of us should be standing together and helping one another to hold fast by God rather than singly, or in twos, or even threes. Again, the climate is not unhealthy for Africa, as the proposed country is high. I know how much you and Mother wish me to be a schoolmaster, but you would, I know, only wish me to be a good schoolmaster; and, when the mind is distracted even by a *mistaken* idea of duty, it is not possible to produce good work. Supposing then, for argument's sake, that I am best suited for a master, even so, would it not be better that I should be a good missionary (*i.e.*, a missionary with his whole heart in it) rather than a half-hearted and dissatisfied schoolmaster—or, if unsuited to be a missionary, should convince myself thereof in the only efficacious, if unpleasant manner, by a sad experience? Neither you, nor Mother, nor anyone else knows how little satisfaction I have had during the past two years—a continual, ceaseless, restless apprehension, 'You are not where God wants you.' Suppose this is a delusion; the delusion itself is a terrible fact which is spoiling my life, preventing me from doing anything with all my heart, and rendering me more miserable than I can describe; I assure you this is no exaggeration. To get rid of this, by buying my own experience at the price of all the pain of going out and the humiliation of coming back 'a sadder and a wiser man,' even so, it would be a cheap bargain. But I don't want you to think of my feelings. I want you to consider the need—one man, a Cambridge man, is wanted: no one is ready to go. How few men there are who have so little to keep them at home; don't misunderstand me—in the way of inclination, from home happiness and friends and love, who have so much—but in the way of duty? No one dependent on me; no one whom I should leave, who would not have more than one to take my place: and the blessings with which God has surrounded me, though making it harder to go, ought, from gratitude, to be my greatest incentives, if He wants me there.

I have said all I can say, and I can only pray that God will guide us all to see and to do His Will, which who yet regretted having done?

Your loving Son,
GEORGE L. PILKINGTON.'

Two days later, he writes to his mother :—

"Tuesday, 5th November, 1889.

DEAREST MOTHER,—

. . . I am wondering how circumstances will strike you and Father and all; just two years ago, if you remember, you said, 'Wait two years.' I engaged up to, but not beyond, the time when it is proposed to start. Harrow left, from which, perhaps, God knew I would not have torn myself away to Africa; my mind for two years in this unsettled condition: my daily and hourly longing 'Only to *know* that the path I tread is the path marked out by Thee.'

You don't know how I long for that knowledge: I believe I should be satisfied to black boots if I knew that was 'the right way,' by which the Lord was leading me. Now, if all these coincidences with the definite need of a definite sort of man for a definite work (which, unless I go, *will*—I may say—

be abandoned); if they strike you all at home with the conviction that the Lord has called your son, then the last doubt will have gone, and I will have the answer to my prayer for definite and clear guidance; to stay at home or to go abroad—mind, I've not asked for guidance to go abroad—but clear guidance one way, that I might *know*, and so DO with a whole heart.

"Indeed, if unuttered wishes are prayers, I've prayed to be allowed to stay at home. Anyhow, dearest Mother, don't be unhappy; if I *do* go, it will only be in the perfect certainty that this is my 'vocation,' in which case, what an honour to be the King's ambassador—and if I stay at home—all right too.

Your loving son,
G. L. PILKINGTON."

On receiving George's letter, Mr. Pilkington said to Mrs. Pilkington, "God has asked for him, and we must give him," and from that time every help and encouragement was given to their son as he prepared to go forth to his unknown work in Dark Africa. The following is George's reply:—

"54 Midland Road, Bedford,
Wednesday, 6th Nov., 1889.

DEAREST MOTHER,—

Thank you so much for your letter, and Father for his. I am glad to have the way marked so clearly now. Not a sorrow, indeed, dearest Mother; and I'm sure we'll all see that some day; but, for the present, we walk by faith, not by sight.

I've telegraphed to Douglas Hooper, whom you would like immensely. You'll tell people how much one man was wanted to prevent the work falling through.

Pray for all of us. One of the men, Cotter, of Trinity, who is coming, was at Scarborough last summer; then there's a Corpus man, whose name I forget.

Your loving son,
George L. Pilkington."

Having received his parents' consent, he at once entered into communication with the Church Missionary Society, and after some preliminary correspondence, he wrote as follows to Rev. F. Wigram, Hon. Sec. of the C. M. S., especially with reference to his call to East Africa.

54 Midland Road, Bedford,
Sunday, 17th Nov., 1889.

My Dear Mr. Wigram,

Thank you very much for your kind and sympathetic letter. May I explain, if at some length, what I feel about East Africa? For two and a half years I have felt the overwhelming importance of Foreign Missionary work: during the whole of that time, I may say, I think, I have not passed an hour without wondering whether I ought not to go abroad. My prayer has been for distinct and definite guidance—'only to know that the path I tread is the path marked out for me.' I undertook school-work because, in spite of these strong feelings, I could not be certain that I was being called to any special foreign work; but neither could I be sure that school-work was 'the right way.' What I longed for was certainty that I was going on a path of God's choosing, not mine. When Douglas Hooper proposed East Africa with his party, a fortnight ago, I was convinced that my prayer was answered, and this conviction was immensely strengthened by the cordial assent of, first, my parents, and then of many others from whom experience had led me to expect at least a mild disapproval. Under these circumstances, I feel so sure of God's leading, that I not only hope that I may, but firmly believe that I shall, be sent to East Africa.

     Believe me,
      Yours very sincerely,
       GEORGE L. PILKINGTON."

The most remarkable testimony to his fitness for missionary work was furnished by the Master of Pembroke, who wrote :—

"I can hardly find words sufficiently strong to describe his fitness for the work which, for years, he has been anxious to attempt. He has the zeal of an Apostle and Evangelist, and, being a highly cultured man, will be an enormous accession to the missionary cause. I have never had any pupil, who has gone out, in my opinion, so qualified spiritually, intellectually, and physically. There is the promise of a Hannington or a Gordon in him. He must not be too much interfered with. Allow him a free hand.

November 19th, 1889."

Pilkington's preparation for missionary work was different from that which is usually recommended for intending missionaries, and, in view of the varied character of missionary work, it is worthy of consideration if it would not be well for some to engage in educational work previous to going forth to the mission field. It may seem remarkable that Pilkington did not seek ordination. On this point, the Master of Pembroke, preaching in the College Chapel after his death, says:—

"With many of you it will not detract from his praise that he was a *layman*—that he joined the Mission as a layman, and remained as such. I never argued with him about his motives, but I think I can fathom them. His mind was of that independent order that does not easily submit to dictation—especially of an absent committee. I made a point of this, in writing to the C. M. S., that they must not worry him with rules, or attempt too much control, and that he would do original things if he were unfettered. He was altogether unprofessional, and you would mistake him if you associate any affectation or sanctimoniousness with his character and conduct. (A frank, genial Irishman he remained to the last, with an overflow of spirit). This is different, I know, from some of our conceptions of a modern missionary.

Being as he was, he can be used as an argument for the freer and fuller employment of *laymen* in the Church, which, I am glad to think, is gaining ground amongst us. We do not now interpret Christ's command to preach the Gospel to all nations to be

THE MISSIONARY CALL.   61

only a *clerical* obligation, we recognise that His Society is of *laymen*, and we have ceased to describe an intending clergyman as 'one who is going into the Church.' That is wrong in thought and expression."

On December 3rd, 1889, George L. Pilkington was accepted as a missionary of the Church Missionary Society at the same time as Baskerville and Cotter, all of whom were destined for Eastern Equatorial Africa, Graham Wilmot Brooke and Eric Lewis being accepted for the Niger on the same day.

From December 3rd, 1889, to January 23rd, 1890, the date when the East African party left London, was none too long for the work of outfitting, and for taking leave of friends, and other preparations for the journey. Since the plans for the East African party had first been formulated, news had reached England which led to a change in their probable destination. The need of reinforcing Uganda, now that it seemed possible to reach it, was felt to be the primary duty of the new band, and they were ready to fall in with the arrangements which were made for them, their instructions being to proceed to the coast and to wait there until the way opened for them to proceed up country.

The public leave-taking was a most impressive occasion, being the first occasion on which Exeter Hall had been taken for a valedictory meeting of C.M.S. Missionaries. Of this, a correspondent of the *Church Missionary Intelligencer*, now a member of the editorial staff, wrote :—

"It was a bold experiment to engage Exeter Hall for a Farewell Meeting to the band of missionaries set apart for Africa, but it was a venture more than justified by its success. On the evening of January 20th, the doors were besieged as at the Annual Meeting of the Society, and, when they were thrown open, the crowd surged into the great hall. Many of the features of an Annual Meeting of even more than usual interest were there—the room full to the back of the gallery and the furthest corner of the great platform; gangways crowded with people unable to obtain seats; and well-known faces to be seen on every side. We were especially pleased to welcome representatives of other Missions, such as Mr. James Mathieson, Mr. Hudson Taylor, and Dr. Pierson of Philadelphia; and also sixty Cambridge undergraduates, who had come up in a body with Mr. and Mrs. Moule.

One is led to ask what was the immediate cause of all this interest. The explanation is to be found in the striking character of the missionaries on the platform. In Bishop Crowther, we have the only non-European bishop that has been consecrated since the days of the early Church, and a man whose romantic career and long services will always command the public attention. In some of the younger missionaries, we have men of marked individuality, of great ability, and of still greater devotion. And the novelty and danger of their plans have attracted the liveliest interest of all friends of Missions."

There were no long speeches at this meeting, but each of the male members of the two missionary parties proceeding to East and West Africa, rose, one after another, and either told of the works in which they had already taken part, or asked for prayer as they went forth for the first time.

After the President of the C.M.S., Sir John Kennaway, had spoken, followed by the Rev. H. C. G. Moule, Bishop Crowther addressed the meeting, and, after him, Mr. Graham Wilmot Brooke, the Rev. Eric Lewis, and Dr. C. F. Harford-Battersby, proceeding to the Upper Niger with a view to reaching the Sûdan; the Rev. F. N. Eden, the Rev. H. H. Dobinson, and Mr. P. A. Bennett, appointed to the Lower Niger; and the Rev. H. Tugwell, now Bishop Tugwell, located to Lagos. This formed the West African contingent. The East African party followed, consisting of Mr. Douglas Hooper, Mr. G. L. Pilkington, Mr. G. K. Baskerville, and Mr. J. D. M. Cotter.

Mr. G. L. Pilkington said he was going out because he knew the Lord had saved him, and that nothing could separate him from the love of Christ; because the Lord's command was laid upon him; and because, since He is King, we have but to do His will and we shall be safe. He had been kept, he said, 'with a light heart,' not that he was going lightly, for he had never given anything such careful consideration. He urged upon those present to forestall the coming of Christ by accepting His salvation and by doing Him service."

A little incident connected with this meeting is recorded by a friend of his, the Rev. R. S. Heywood, now a Missionary in India. Mr. Heywood writes:

"At his first dismissal meeting at Exeter Hall, a number of us went up from Cambridge, and I was glad to come across him at the bottom of the stairs at the Hall, so as to have a last chat. As we stood there, I noticed several people going up and looking with great interest at him, some evidently pointing him out to others. I mentioned this to him, and at once, with an exclamation of distress, he asked me to move with him into a more remote corner, where he would not be conspicuous. This was only one instance of the humility which all my acquaintance with him showed was most truly genuine."

The last night in England was spent under the hospitable roof of the Rev. W. D. Bushell. From there, he wrote to his mother as follows:—

"I am just beginning this letter before going to bed to-night, to finish it in the morning. I can only praise God for His goodness to me during the last few days. He has been so with me both here and in Cambridge. We had 3,000 in Exeter Hall, more than 50 men came up from Cambridge."

Next morning he writes: "Bushell has given me a pedometer and several other things—he is kind. It's all right. I've never doubted that this is *the* way (Rom. viii. 28)."

On the same day, January 23rd, 1890, the East African party left London in the s.s. "Kaparthala," and, after an uneventful voyage, reached Frere Town where they were to wait till arrangements could be made for them to proceed to Uganda.

CHAPTER V.

A VISIT TO KILIMANJARO.

Not long after arriving at Frere Town, finding that there must be considerable delay before starting for Uganda, Pilkington accompanied Mr. Binns on a journey to the neighbourhood of Kilimanjaro, of which he gives the following description:—

> "TARO, E.E. Africa,
> (Half-way from Mombasa to Taita),
> Sunday, April 20th, 1890.

Seated on a box, with two other boxes for a table, our porters squatting or standing all round, just finishing their breakfast of rice and dried fish, Mr. Binns, Secretary of the C.M.S. for the Coast districts, writing beside me on our only little table, ten o'clock this Sunday morning, I am answering your letters.

I want to write a letter which will give you some idea of what an African Safari is like, and so I write to you only, but, of course, you will show it to the rest. If I tried to write a lot of letters, none would be satisfactory. I am keeping a diary, to which I shall refer now, and tell you all that has happened since I left Frere Town. By the way,

Hannington came this way, as he relates in the 20th and succeeding chapters of his life.

We started at 2.30 on Monday from Frere Town by boat up the creek, which stretches up a dozen miles or so inland. "We" means Mr. Binns and his dog Nellie, myself, Edgar and his dog Minnie, whose existence I was, till last Sunday, ignorant of, but on Monday he, Edgar, presented himself with a bit of rope round the animal's neck, and fully determined on having this gaunt, half-starved, and, to me, specially obnoxious beast as his companion to Chagga.

Miss Ramsay went with us to Rabai, to take back Miss Barton to Frere Town next day.

Our porters were to meet us at Rabai.

We sailed and towed up the winding creek, sometimes as much as a mile broad, but narrowing further up between mangrove swamps, and, finally, not more than twenty yards across. I had a shot at a big water-bird with Binns' gun, but missed.

We reached the "banderini," or landing place, about 5.30, where we waited till the dhow containing our loads, *i.e.*, tents, clothes, food, rice for the men, should arrive, to be carried up to Rabai by the forty men or so whom we found waiting our arrival. After a few minutes—during which we drank the juice from some "dafu," or young cocoanuts, which Binns had brought—we heard the panting of the Company's Steam Launch coming up the creek. We hoped it would be tugging our dhow, but it was not; it brought Crawfurd of the Company, who, I told you, was to go with us to Taita. We left the men to bring the loads, hearing that the dhow was only just behind, and started on our way to Rabai. It was a very good road for Africa, European-made, and therefore several feet broad—the native roads just like sheep tracks,—it was very pretty, through undulating, country; we saw lots of orchids. We reached Rabai, which is four miles distant, about 6.30. Passing the fine church, which it was almost too dark to see, we came to Burness's house, where we were kindly received by Mr. Burness and his wife. Miss Barton, of Frere Town, was with them as I mentioned before. After tea, I went out with Burness, but could see nothing for the darkness but fire-flies, of which there are thousands.

Crawfurd had not yet got enough Rabai men to supplement his Zanzibaris up to the 100 he wanted, so we could not start till the afternoon of Tuesday. I walked round Rabai with Binns in the morning; it has a population of 1,500. At Church, in the morning at 6.30, there were 300 or so present. The native pastor, Jones, is often mentioned by Hannington. The population consists half of Waswahili and half of Wanyika, drawn there (for Binns said he remembered when there were not more than fifty or sixty people), by the security of property which a European settlement gives (we heard of an incursion of Masai only ten miles away from Rabai the other day), and, let us hope, some perhaps, by the Gospel. It is, at any rate for Africa, an important place and market. The Wanyika huts are very primitive—from the outside just like a small rick of damaged hay—no windows whatever;

the Swahili huts are very superior. I saw, in Rabai, an India-rubber tree, from which Binns, in a few minutes, by cutting the bark and rubbing the sap on his hands, made a little piece of india rubber.

We started at 2.15, and reached Mwachi (seven miles) at 4.10. These halting places are not towns or villages as a rule, but merely places where water is. The water here (which Crawfurd called splendid) was like the water in the pond at Tore to look at, only covered mostly with green stuff. We boil and then filter all our water; the natives drink it neat. We pitched our tents and set up our bedsteads for the night. Edgar sleeps on my waterproof sheet in my tent; the men sleep out; but since that first night, when there was heavy rain, they have rigged up little tents with sticks and a little cloth or cut grass. The first thing on arriving in camp is, for us, who have carried nothing heavier than an umbrella and a monstrous hat, to rest—for the men, who have carried a load of 50lb. to 60lb. (sometimes more), generally on their heads, to fetch firewood and water. Last night, I counted more than a dozen fires round about. The men sleep with feet toward them, and they keep off wild beasts. And now to make a digression. The contrast will have struck you already. The people, to whom we have come to preach, lie on the ground or in a reed or grass hut, at rice and a bit of dried fish (two cupfuls of rice and a handful of dried fish is a day's ration), carry a load under a burning sun for ten or twelve miles which I should be sorry to carry a mile in England, walk barefoot on the

A VISIT TO KILIMANJARO.

scorching ground, while we live in grand houses or tents (palaces to these people), sleep on beds as comfortable as any at home, eat chickens (carried in a box alive), preserved meat, green peas (preserved), tea, cocoa, biscuits, bread, butter, jam. Necessary for health, perhaps, some of these things may be. It's all very well for people at home, who know that we should have these things and others too, if we had stayed at home; but how are these ignorant people to know or to believe that? They see we live like princes (in their eyes); they cannot but believe that it is for these luxuries we come here: they're not luxuries at home, at least, nothing like to the same extent. Now my feeling at the present moment is that, if it is not possible, or if there is not a prospect of its becoming possible, to live very differently, we might almost as well be at home. Don't think I'm complaining of anything or anyone. I enjoy these things and with a clear conscience at present: the roast chicken we had the other night was very good! so were the peas! and I sleep on my comfortable bed as well as if I were at home: but I stick to what I've said, and say what I think. It's no good coming out here unless we persuade these people (not people at home) that we've come out for something that is not for our own comfort, nor profit, nor sport; and, to do so successfully, it may be *necessary* to do things which would otherwise be foolish and wrong. However, don't be frightened. I take tremendous care of my health, and mean to do so. One more remark about above subject—our life ought to be such as to compel the natives—not Englishmen—to ask, "What on earth brings these fellows out to live like this among us?

There is such a gulf between us already—language, character, thought, and religion: it is terrible if it is necessary to set up another barrier, a physical one, to point all the others out as by an object lesson to these children, such children they are, I think, and so Irish, so like myself, coming in with their loads after a long march, singing and running to shew that they're not tired; taking the tool out of the white man's hand, when he sets himself to some rough work, saying that such is not for the likes of him, an acknowledgement of a social distinction which you will find in Ireland, but not much in England.

We were up about five on Wednesday morning; pack all things in great haste, drink cocoa and biscuit, and start at 6.40 (a late start—the sun always rises at six, and we ought not to start later). We reached Mto Kajembe at 9 a.m. (nine miles); here we had breakfast, pitched tents, slept, etc., till 2.30 when we started, and reached Mto Wa Munyo (Salt River) at a quarter to four (four and three-quarter miles). We stopped here for the night. I had a bath in a portable India-rubber bath, very delightful; we saw a lot of partridges on this and next day; we have also seen several vultures. The general appearance of the country is that of an undulating (or even hilly) plain, well sprinkled with small trees, chiefly mimosa, occasional thick, impenetrable bush —the soil is sandy, covered by coarse grass, as on the edge of the bog at home.

On Thursday, off at 5.50; we had not got far

A VISIT TO KILIMANJARO.

when the men in front stopped and waited for us to come up, as two splendid antelopes, very dark, long, straight horns, big as mules, were grazing about 300 yards ahead. We saw what Binns said was a flowering fungus, and very rare. We saw two small antelopes at a place called Gora, perhaps mentioned by Thomson or Hannington. We reached Samburu at 8.35, ten and three-quarter miles (all measurements by pedometer, given me by Mr. Bushell). On, one and three-quarter miles, in the afternoon, to what Thomson calls, "the stone reservoirs of Duruma." A Duruma man here asked why no Missionaries came among them. Three of Crawfurd's Zanzibaris ran off thi day; they had been paid fifteen dollars (£2) in advance.

Left next day at six; went on, with an hour for breakfast, to this place, Taro, twelve and a quarter miles, reaching this before eleven, the day before yesterday. We then waited for mails which arrived yesterday at 4.30. Forty of Crawfurd's Zanzibaris made their escape on this last march! Seventeen loads are missing, stolen by the men; runaway porters generally leave their loads on the road, but these, Crawfurd says, are a mere pack of thieves. They were engaged for him by a clerk, who got a set of boys to begin with, and besides, the riff-raff of Zanzibar. His headmen accompanied Stanley on the Emin Pasha relief expedition, but he doesn't know whether he can trust even them. He lost, among other things, some most valuable papers, and he is himself now ill with dysentery. The mails arrived yesterday, and with them the news that Mackay was dead! Since he went to Uganda in 1876, he has never come down to the coast. He has left us an example of perseverance.

Crawfurd started back this morning, carried by four men, in a waterproof sheet slung on poles.

Now just a word as to my health; I am thankful to say I am perfectly well; this Safari has cured my prickly heat and trifling tropical rash."

"Frere Town,
June 17th.

We went on again on Monday. The next place where we were sure of water was forty miles away; so we had to push on. We found some water, as a matter of fact, about half-way, but it didn't help us much, as we only rested a little time, while the men re-filled their gourds, dried, in which they carry water. We walked seven-and-a-half hours on Monday, and then slept without water, i.e., at a place where there was no water, and without tents. Off again at 5.20 a.m., still dark, four-and-a-half hours' of hard walking, such a crooked road, ending up a steep hill; under a blazing sun, we at last reached the hill of Maungu. (I forgot to explain why this letter was delayed. Three weeks ago to-day, I wrote to Mother; that evening the doctor sent me to bed in high fever, which continued, more or less, for a fortnight; I am thankful to say it is gone now, but I am still fearfully weak. We hope to start to-morrow week for Zanzibar, *en route* for Uganda. We like the four new men very much, and the Bishop extremely, which, I expect, I said in my last letter).

At Maungu, the unfortunate men, after arriving

some time after us with their heavy loads, had to mount the hill for water, a good hour's walk. It is a lovely place, a high pass between two hills, with a splendid view, filled with flowers; convolvulus creeps over half the little trees. In the afternoon, Binns and I went up to the top, washed (how delightful), and saw a troop of chattering monkeys, and—Kilimanjaro's snowy head, far, far away. Within the last few months, Dr. Meyers, a German, has got to the top; it is almost 20,000 feet high. Mont Blanc with Ben Nevis piled above it.

Next day we reached Taita (Mt. Ndara 6,000 feet high), a C. M. S. station, just given up, for the present at least. We saw the Missionary (who has just left this room, Morris), after that a splendid swim and wash, with soap, in a mountain stream, that was very full after the rains they had had, and filled a fine rocky basin, almost out of my depth.

Next day, on again, five-and-a-quarter hours' morning walk to a populous village—Matali—in a lovely and well-cultivated valley; the afternoon we rested in our tents, eating roast Indian-corn cobs and sucking sugar cane. The people very friendly. On next day, up and around a mountain—lovely view of Kilimanjaro—and down again into a rich and wooded country. Then we started across Seringete, the waterless track of fifteen hours' march. However, we found a fine pool half-way, where we camped. Here, and all this day, we saw animals in great numbers—zebra, ostriches, eland, hartebeest, vultures, giraffes, and buffaloes—very dangerous beasts, (not so many tracks of lions), leopards, elephants, rhinoceros, and, of course, hyenas howling every night. We have them here. Quails there were in endless numbers, also partridges and guinea-fowl. The flowers are often magnificent, but I can't describe them, and, except at Maungu, they were, as a rule, so scattered that there was nothing so fine as a spring or summer field at home.

Next day, Binns shot an Eland as big as a cow, to the men's great delight, for, of course, we could eat only a little of it. We had to camp on the spot while they cut it up and cooked it, and gorged themselves all night long. The cooked, or, rather, burnt morsels they disposed of to great advantage (as I thought, for I wouldn't have touched it) for splendid bunches of bananas and plantains and sugar cane. This was at Taveta, a prosperous village below Kilimanjaro, hidden in the heart of a great forest. It was fine making our way under the great trees, darkened by creepers (not so dark, perhaps, as Stanley's forest), till we came to the "gate" where you have to fire off guns and pay so much cloth to get in. These great log gates, remind one of Irish "gates" on a huge scale. The "gate" consists of a huge pile of logs which have slowly to be unheaped to let you pass. Then through another forest, this time of bananas—a beautiful sight, with the huge bunches of fruit hanging down everywhere. We spent a pleasant afternoon and morning next day buying food and watching the Wataveta. Then we started about one, but alas! some non-Tavetans had barred the road by the other gate, they wanted cloth; this was an imposition we considered, so we came back, re-crossing three rivers, either on slippery, dangerous planks, or rather round poles, at the risk of a wetting, or by wading them. One of the " Elders " of Taveta, on our return, assured us they had no authority at that gate, and advised our taking another road. After losing our way, and having to come back a good bit—three times I think—at last we really started at half-past three. We only got two hours on our way and had to camp in a bad place, where there was no water. Next evening we got within one-and-a-half hours of Chagga; the men, who were behind, thought we had pushed right on, and camped on their own account We were left with boys, cook and guide, no food, no change of clothes, no tents, and it was raining—with a fire, indeed, by which we lay—till the cook and guide, who had gone back, brought up the men with the loads which we wanted. Next day early, we reached Chagga."

The chief object of this journey was to interview the King of Chagga, and to bring him, if possible, to treat the work of the C.M.S. more favourably. Of the interview, and of some further incidents of their visit, Mr. Pilkington writes:—

"The kingdom of Chagga, where Mundara, the one-eyed king, reigns, is a lovely spot on the lower ridges of the great, twin-peaked, snow mountain, Kilimanjaro. Here we found ourselves in the presence of this one-eyed, African despot.

The contrast was strange:—' The palace,' more like a cabin to our eyes: the courtyard, a horrible quagmire of filthy mud; and there sat, in a full-length shirt—that ought to have been white, but it wasn't—Mundara, the dreaded ruler, the ambitious conqueror, whose evil fame reaches to the coast. And another contrast: so polite he was, his words 'smoother than oil,' and yet he is the man who has exterminated whole tribes; has depopulated mountain sides, killing many of the people, and selling the rest into the miseries of slavery. This is human nature as it is, before it knows Jesus, the Saviour of the world.

Mr. Binns' words had a good effect; the attendance of twenty-one boys at the Mission House showed that the king had withdrawn the opposition to that extent, at least. He had been under the impression that, the boys once taught, we should want to carry them off to the coast.

Most interesting our 'safari' was: the natives were sometimes (as we were told), so superstitious that, when our missionaries at Taita went up to the top of the mountain for a walk, they were unpleasantly surprised by a crowd of angry men, armed with bows and poisoned arrows, who insisted that they had gone up there to make 'medicine' to keep the rain off! The Missionaries' assurances were at last believed, and they were allowed to start homeward, followed, however, when they had gone a little way, by a shower of arrows. On the other hand, at Taveta, that Arcadian paradise as Thomson calls it, in the heart of the forest, we found the natives so friendly and interesting. Some of the customs were so odd: beads and cloth are the money of the country—but beads, which are greatly prized at Taveta, are just a shade too blue and a trifle too large for the fashion at Chagga, where, accordingly, they are valueless! How I wish I had had the skill to depict the features of the chief of Matati, when Mr. Binns induced him to try his bottle of smelling salts! At this place, too, we found a huge demand for common salt; a few spoonfuls would buy three fine sugar canes, each ten feet long. In Duruma, nearer home, a man asked us why no missionary was among them: perhaps he only wished for the temporal advantages which come with the white man; but the question stands, why is it? Because, if five times as many men were at work here, they could find work to spare in the stations already occupied.

A few days later we started back; we got drenched for the first four days regularly, and had to sit waiting once, foodless, fireless, in drenched and muddy clothes, lying tired on the wet ground, under a sort of improvised arbour to keep out the drizzle, for two-and-a-half hours till the men came up, with hyenas yowling round. A day or two later, one of our boys walked with us all the way, down with small-pox, covered with the rash: he has recovered, though one of Binns' boys caught it and died here ten days ago. The last of the four days on which we got drenched, sitting by the fire, with the small-pox boy on the other side, I reflected on what the Greeks called the 'irony of fate,' that in my coat pocket on the same 'safari' should be a letter of Mother's beseeching me to take care of my health; so I do, but—well, I shan't describe our return in detail; we reached Rabai, after tremendously hard marching; on the way in, Edgar said to me, 'Have you heard the news?'

'What news?' said I. 'Mr. Cotter's dead.' And so it was, two days before.

And so I have got here again—to be laid up ten days with my foot, and then, just this day three weeks ago, by fever; and I've not been out yet—am very weak, but the Doctor says it's all right; can't expect to get up one's strength at once after a sharp attack of fever; and to-morrow week, please God, we shall start for Zanzibar on the way to Uganda, the change will do me good.

June 19th.

We hear this morning that the ship from Bombay, by which we expect to travel to Zanzibar, will not be here till Friday or Saturday week, which gives me two or three days extra to mend in. I have just re-read my last mail and proceed to answer one or two things. You know that not only Hill, of Corpus, but three other men whom we like very much, have come out; they are not Cambridge men. By the way, you say in one letter that I belong to a superior race to the Africans; do you know I doubt it? Physically, much inferior, except in appearance. I cannot notice that they are intellectually inferior; inferior in knowledge, indeed, because this country provides them (as the ancients said of the golden age) of itself with all they feel the need of; they are, therefore, indifferent to what we call progress, or the knowledge of nature, and the turning her to our uses.

Glad to hear Aunt B's interest in this most interesting of countries. D's assertion, which puzzled K, is most presumptuous. How can any man say of a country, of which four-fifths, if not nine-tenths, are utterly unknown, that there is this or that? The fringe on which his own eyes have rested, he may partly know, but the rest——

June 20th.

I was much stronger yesterday, and went out for a ride on a donkey; a splendid beast; to-day, I feel stronger again. The rest have been terribly busy packing loads, all to be made up to 70 lbs.; how would you like one on your head?

By the bye, you will be glad to hear that to have had a severe attack of fever—and mine was a very severe one—is considered a good thing; in fact, the doctor told me to-day that he did not think it likely I should ever have so bad an attack again.

June 21st.

Douglas was ordained the other day: three of the new men are to be to-morrow.

Monday, June 23rd.

The mail may be starting to-morrow, so this letter goes in to be stamped to-night.

CHAPTER VI.

THE LONG MARCH.

"Ye have need of patience" is a maxim constantly to be remembered by the African traveller. More than five months had passed since our party left England, and it was only after this long delay that they were able to start on their long journey.

Pilkington describes the first stage of their journey in the following letter:—

"Criterion Hotel,
Zanzibar
Wednesday, July 9th, 1890.

Here we are, started at last, I am glad to say. We left Frere Town at 3 p.m., on Monday; after a little tossing about, and a night on deck (we travelled as deck passengers), we got here at 10.30 a.m. yesterday, and, since then, I have been resting, and hope to do so till early to-morrow morning, when we are to leave for Saadani, by H.M.S. 'Redbreast,' and start, I expect, with Stokes next day. You'll understand why I need resting, when I tell you all the news. It has been wonderful how God has brought us all (except one, and there are four in his place) to the start. About a fortnight ago, I began to feel something like myself; but Douglas and Mrs.

Hooper began to be ailing, Douglas with fever, and Mrs. Hooper with overwork: it would have greatly increased the hardness of leaving one another had either been ill. Well, they both recovered before the end of last week—worn out a good deal indeed, but neither ill. But with myself it is even more striking; my foot is only now, two days before starting, recovered; it has been healed for a week or so. Then my fever: I had a sharp attack last Friday for twenty-four hours, then again, on Sunday morning, my temperature was 105°: I was three times awfully sick, and felt as ill as I could be, and I believed, as I lay in bed that morning, that the steamer was to leave at 6 a.m. next morning. We should have had to be up at four, and breakfast, and get our personal luggage (I had still two-and-a-half loads, 70 lbs. each, *unpacked*, and accounts to be settled) on board in the dark. Was it possible, I thought? And the horrors of a steamer, too, with the Monsoon dead against us, all night as deck passengers. But it was all made quite right and pleasant—pleasant surprises coming continually."

"By the way, another horror I forgot, the passage, and if I did reach Zanzibar alive, to Saadani by dhow eight hours at least, and very likely becalmed indefinitely halfway, there would have been no time for rest here: we might have gone on immediately yesterday. Well, on Sunday at midday, I began to improve; then we heard the steamer was not to start till 2 p.m. On Monday, I was a good deal better and just managed my packing, etc. The 'Yuba' and our deck quarters turned out infinitely better than I had expected. I got better and was not sick on board. The Bishop (who, expecting us to follow in two days, came here a fortnight ago) met us with the good news that the Admiral, who is here on the 'Boadicea' with a fleet altogether of ten ships, and two transports expected, had promised to send us across in the 'Redbreast,' a fast vessel, though not a large one, whether strictly a man-of-war or a gunboat, I don't know; this gives one-and-a-half days' rest, and spares us the dhow journey, to God be the thanks.

I'm quite well, but still weak; anyhow, its all right, we have been joined at the last moment by Hunt, of the Company, a delightful fellow and, perhaps, the Mombasa doctor, Dr. Edwards, who was so good to us when ill, sending Douglas and me his own milk, may come too. The Bishop telegraphed yesterday, Emin Pasha has reached Mpwapwa three weeks ago; he has been fighting: of course, in the present state of things, without Stokes we could'nt go."

"Saadani,
14th July, 1890.

Here still! We had a delightful crossing in the 'Redbreast,' the Commanding Officer giving us his own cabin, where we had breakfast. On arrival we found the start put off until Monday (to day): now it is off again till Wednesday: Shall we really start then? Our first communication long ago with Stokes made us expect to start nearly two months ago.

We are camped here in our tents by the sea;

THE LONG MARCH.

Stokes a hundred yards away (to hear him talk Swahili, with an Irish brogue!), and his men in a regular town half-a-mile off, but extending a mile or more beyond that. My loads are all satisfactorily made up, and have been accepted by the porters. On Saturday morning, we had a trying time, finally packing our loads, which the porters then inspected, choosing each man one to suit him. Mine went immediately, though each of two was ½lb. or 1lb. over the regulation weight—70lbs. Besides this, the poor men carry 35lbs. of cloth, their own pay, and water and cooking pots for themselves! The men are very capricious about their loads—some shapes are objectionable, so some of our men had difficulty in getting their loads accepted. It was a trying time, because the tents, too, had to be made into loads, so shelter from the blazing sun was hard to get. But none of us, I think, were any the worse. The same evening we got our mails.

We have a Bible reading, every day after our midday meal, each choosing and starting a subject by turns."

"Sunday, August 3rd.

Two-thirds of the way to Mamboia, near the Mbula Mountains.

At last, an opportunity of writing, or rather starting, a letter ; perhaps it will go from Mamboia, which we hope to reach in a week or so. To-day, being Sunday, we rest as usual.

You have heard of Hill's death : he left Saadani for the hospital at Zanzibar, early on Sunday morning, and died that night. We started next morning, so we did not hear of his death for a few days.

Baskerville has had fever: temperature 105° just now. I wonder whether he will be able to go on my donkey to-morrow? I don't think he is as ill as his temperature seems to make him. However, his illness is too like Hill's not to make one feel that there is danger.

Now about myself. I'm quite well, but still weak. We have two donkeys, and I generally ride half the march. We go an average of nine miles a day, and I assure you I find half that plenty. Isn't that a confession? Then this is Africa.

Baskerville and I in one tent, Dunn and Dermott in another, Smith and Hunt in a third, Douglas in a small one, and the Bishop in a big one by themselves. This is the way we travel. We divide the work as follows: D. and D. (as above), the canteens, packing and unpacking for meals; B., the food boxes; Smith, filtering water; Hunt, making the tea; Myself, the cooking; Douglas, everything. Stokes is a most pleasant man and extremely kind to us.

We are getting among some fine mountains, but hitherto there has been little striking in any way, hardly any flowers, lions or beasts of beauty or interest that I could see. My chief interest is learning Kiganda. No one else has begun it. I have really got on lately. I've been able to get some of the main things of the grammar out of my friend Noah, who seems to enjoy teaching me. We walk together on the way, and sometimes I find an opportunity of establishing myself in a tent with pen and ink and my old Harrow bank book (which is being transformed into a Kiganda grammar) while Noah crouches on the floor and is pumped as to singulars and plurals, futures and perfects, though I need hardly say, I don't put it that way. Indeed, it has interested, though not surprised me to see how utterly foreign and puzzling to N's ideas any thought of grammar is. He has never given me a rule; he never generalizes. You would think that any one—especially a very intelligent man like N., anxious to please me and teach me—would give me some general formula for making the future, when I ask him, say, ten verbs, in the form ' I shall go,' ' I shall send,' but no, he doesn't see what I'm driving at a bit, but fills up my ' I shall see ' into a complete sentence, which he urges me to write down, assuring me that his words are ' very good.'

Then again, when I notice what seems an irregularity, say in one of these futures as compared with the others, and ask him why do you say so-and-so, whereas in the rest you say so-and-so, why don't you say this instead, he answers, ' Oh no,' its not that, and repeats it as he said it before. If you urge him for an explanation, he says it's words only, ' don't you see, of course it's this,' and repeats it as if you were deaf, or very stupid.

I've got one or two tiny books with prayers and the Commandments, and Bible texts, which are a great help, but no grammar. Noah knows Swahili, but no English.

The Germans sent us twice this week a leg of beel

or veal. Besides this beef, we buy chickens from the natives, eggs sometimes, and we use tinned meats when we can get nothing else.

We have for our first meal, oatmeal and Indian meal porridge, tea or cocoa, hard biscuits and butter (tinned), at 5.30 in the morning. Awful scramble while beds, tents, or other loads are being, or are to be, packed and sent off, everyone shouting for something or someone, all in the dark, made visible by one lantern. March before 6. In camp, 8, 9, 10. Food:—Chickens, rice, biscuits, native beans, perhaps dried potatoes, jam, any native vegetables; we are looking forward to sweet potatoes (on Sundays, apple rings), at 4.30. Same with soup (pea generally), at one or other meals."

"Mamboia, E. Africa,
Tuesday, August 12th.

We got here about nine o'clock yesterday morning, the day before, Sunday (our usual practice is not to march on Sunday), we had a long march of six hours, most of which I did on Stokes' donkey: the Bishop had hurried ahead a few days before to be at Mamboia the longer, taking the larger of our two donkeys. Baskerville, who is still weak from the late fever, was riding the other. So, of late, I've been borrowing S.'s donkey, for I'm not quite myself yet; though, on the whole, with occasional relapses, I've been getting stronger ever since we left the coast.

We stay here (a lovely place, of which more anon) till Thursday or Friday. Messrs. Cole and Beverley

THE LONG MARCH.

and Price (of Kisokwe, first two men, and Mpwapwa) are expected here to-morrow, for a conference with the Bishop, who is not very well.

My last letter didn't enter into details of the march as much as I intended, so here goes :—We get up some at four, others a bit later, invalids perhaps not till five; then comes a scene, some washing in the bucket or basin outside their tent (unless they think that an evening wash is enough, for the early mornings are very chilly, and the whole thing is a rush), others calling for their boys to pack up their camp-beds, that the tents may be pulled down, which is sometimes done while, if late or lazy, one is still inside. Douglas calling out that the man for the loan of buckets and basins has come, and will everyone send the same at once to his tent. Meanwhile, others are seeing to the food, porridges, Indian and oatmeal, tea and biscuits. At last a whistle is three times blown, and we assemble round the cook's fire for Swahili prayers; then the rush is resumed, increased by the food being ready, as everyone is anxious to get some and be off, if the march is to be long and the sun likely to be hot later on.

Then comes Dunn and Dermott's turn, who have to pack the canteens from which we eat, and which it is well to get off early, as we shall want them for our next meal. Douglas stays last of all and sees that the men take their loads, often carrying what is left behind. More than twenty porters have died since leaving Saadani, dysentery chiefly. Remember, there are 2,200 odd.

Then comes the march. Quite cold at first, the grass, perhaps, dewy. On past the porters, who walk quite slowly with their loads of 70lbs. for an hour (the men have been so ill), two, three or four hours, as the case may be. Some of our men go ahead and choose a camp well in front of the rest. Then the question is, when will this load or that load come in? Is my tent in? Have they brought my bed in, or left it down among the other loads? How about the canteens and the food boxes? Shall we have anything to eat before twelve? (11 a.m. is the hour we aim at.) Has the man we sent, two hours ago—immediately on reaching the camp—to buy chickens and eggs and sweet potatoes, come back yet? Have the boys drawn water yet, or have the buckets not come in yet? Here's my tent, but has the man with the pegs come? The sun's so hot, and there's hardly any shade—where's my boy with my water bottles? etc., etc., etc.

At last, several tents are pitched, and in one of them we get the table ready for food and have our second meal. Then we have our Bible reading: then we read, rest, wash, etc., as we severally please. Meanwhile food has again to be seen to. This comes off at 4.30. Then Swahili prayers, which Douglas and I take by turns. Then, after everything which can be packed in the evening is done with, to bed. It is an interesting and a novel way of life, but it would be a stretch to call it a pleasant one, and a pause in a house, as here, is a great relief and a rest.

Now, about the place. Mamboia is a collection

of villages, some of only a dozen beehive huts, lying in a broad valley, among beautiful mountains, rising not high above the valley, though 4,000 feet or so above the sea. The hill-sides, too, are crowded with villages. Wood, the C.M.S. man here, says you can pass thirty-two villages in an hour's walk. The valley is extensively cultivated—Indian corn, millet, sweet potatoes, banana, and pine apples, etc. The mission station is situated most beautifully, high above the valley, 3,960 feet above sea level, commanding a grand view of it. It is built on a comparatively level slope. There are two houses, three rooms in each, besides store rooms (the Roscoes, whom C. and S. met at Cambridge, were here.) Below the house is a garden, where, beside native things, English flowers and vegetables are grown. It is wonderful to see the geraniums and petunias in full bloom in Africa (it is so cold here); carrots, too, and potatoes. A church is being built—stone walls; for mortar, the ordinary earth, which is better than our mortar, for it has all been worked by white ants; walls three feet thick. It is paid for by Wood himself and the natives, who give either in kind or in labour. We had service there this morning; thirty natives or so present. They speak a language which is called Kimegi, which bears resemblance to both Kiswahili and Kiganda.

This is a splendidly healthy place and we hope to gather health and strength here. I wish I could tell of anything encouraging in our work. The Lord is with us, and to Him all power is given in Heaven and in earth, even in Africa. Pray that this power may be shewn, and that nothing in us may hinder it."

"Kisokwe (six miles beyond Mpwapwa), E. Africa,
Friday, 22nd August, 1890.

Here we are at Kisokwe, rather over two hundred miles from the coast, not quite so far as Chagga, from which we came back in ten days, and yet on Monday, when we expect to start again, it will be five weeks since leaving the coast. We arrived early yesterday, 7.15 a.m., from Mpwapwa. Here I was met by Mwaka or Andreya (Christian baptismal name) the boy who taught me on the steamer. He came running to meet me. I gave him some chocolate, and hope to give him a piece of cloth before I go. He has been preaching to the people since he came back. His mother comes each Saturday to the Mission to be taught; this means a walk of three hours over the hills with a child on her back. She goes back on Mondays. This is the most encouraging thing I have heard or seen in Africa. I hope and believe we may say in both cases, 'This hath God done.'

You will have heard what is at present uncertain news about Uganda. The Germans, in the fort at Mpwapwa, have received news that the English Company's expedition to the lake (we know they are five hundred rifles strong, and are even now followed by probably a second party eight hundred strong) have combined with the Protestants in Uganda, and ousted Mwanga and put Kalema, the Arab nominee, upon the throne. Likely enough, too, if the jealousy between the Roman Catholic chiefs and the Protestants comes to a head. We heard of the growing jealously in Zanzibar, but why Kalema? Surely the Arabs are not in league with the English Company! Was it in default of any other of the blood royal, or has he turned Protestant (I don't say Christian) on the chance of a crown? Had Mwanga favoured the Roman Catholics or even taken to Protestant persecution again? Or is it all a lie? I daresay we shall all know when you read this letter.

By the way, I'll say here that I've not ridden a donkey since Mamboia and am strong and well; Baskerville is still rather feeble. The house at Mpwapwa was burnt down by the Arabs; all agree that it was a very good thing; the house was so grand as to be a hindrance to the work. Mpwapwa is a very populous place. Lately, Price, the Missionary there, has been encouraged by the increased numbers coming. Here they have three hundred in church on Sunday and seventy every day. Kigogo is the language here. Cole, the Missionary, was nearly killed by a buffalo not so long ago.

We have come through some magnificent valleys—some of them populous enough; the country, from Mamboia as far as this, is the mountain region of Usagara. On Monday, we start into a comparatively flat though elevated country. Just beyond Mamboia is the pass of Rutako, 4,700 feet higher than Ben Nevis. You ought to look all these out in the C.M.S. Atlas."

"Sunday, 24th August, 2 p.m., Kisokwe.

We had a confirmation this morning. Fourteen from Mpwapwa, and I think twelve from Kisokwe; some big men, rough and wild looking. Three hundred natives or so were present. Our visit here has been encouraging."

After leaving Kisokwe, the roughest part of the journey began, and is graphically described by Bishop Tucker in a letter from Unyanguira, about one hundred and twenty miles beyond Kisokwe.

The Bishop writes as follows:—

"Unyanguira, E.E. Africa,
September 6th, 1890.

"As you will see from the above address, we are getting on. We are now, I suppose, within six weeks of the Victoria Nyanza. Our progress has been slow, but not the less sure on that account. I believe Africa is one of those countries in which it is essentially true that it is the pace that kills. The tortoise very frequently wins the race here.

The solemn services of Sunday, August 24th, over—that is to say, the ordination of Messrs. Cole and Wood, and the confirmation of thirty candidates—we prepared for an early departure on Monday, 25th. We left Kisokwe at 6.30 a.m. Mr. Cole accompanied us as far as our first camping ground. We there bade him an affectionate farewell, and, as a party, were once more alone.

To get water entailed a journey of three hours, and, when obtained, it was found to be distinctly brackish in flavour. The night spent at this spot we

THE LONG MARCH.

shall not easily forget. It was an open, sandy plain, across which the wind rushed with unobstructed force. Our tents, happily, had been pitched in good time, so that, when the wind arose, we had some shelter, however precarious. Every moment we expected our tents to be blown away. Not one of us got a wink of sleep that night. As we were to make a long march through a porri or waterless desert the next day, it had been arranged to start at 3.30 a.m., so, at two o'clock, I gave the signal to prepare for the march. The wind, a few minutes later, dropped in a very remarkable way. We were thus enabled to pack, and prepare breakfast in comfort. Most providentially, the day proved to be cloudy, so the march was robbed of half its horrors. None but those who have experienced it can understand what it is to have a burning sun beating down from above, and scorching heat rising from the burning ground or sand at the same moment. This, happily, we were spared in going through this porri. We marched for six hours, and then halted to prepare some food with the water from our water-bottles. After an hour's rest, we resumed our journey, and, in a couple of hours, reached our camping-ground ; but here again, alas! the water was brackish. Still, we had to drink it, and were very thankful for it. It is wonderful the things you take kindly to when there is no other alternative. During the last two months, I have swallowed more mud in water than in all my life previously. And not only swallowed it, but swallowed it thankfully.

Another day of brackish water had to be endured,

and then we started on another long march through another waterless tract of country. We were now in Ugogo—which is indeed a weary land—a land which seems stricken with a curse—even the forests are leafless and bare. Here and there, out of the sandy plain, rises a conical hill, 200 or 300 feet high—whether volcanic in its origin, I cannot tell—probably the ants have had something to do with the work of raising them. About these hills, a few huge boulders have been tumbled. How grateful their shade—'the shadow of a mighty rock within a weary land.' Of a truth, with the exception of these few hills and rocks, the country is a sandy waste. The inhabitants of the few villages we came across have to dig for water in the earth. Some of these holes are thirty feet deep. These holes are our only hope of water. You can imagine how eagerly we look down into their depths. This second long march in this waterless district was distinctly more trying than the first. Still we held upon our way, upborne with hope of fresh and sweet water. This, happily, we found as we halted at Mizanza.

Here we spent two days, in order to bring up the rear. Our rear was in a considerable state of excitement; a straggler had been speared by the Wagogo, and his load taken from him. The surgical skill of Messrs. Dermott and Dunn was again put to the test. Of course he had been speared in the back. The wound was a bad one, but still not fatal. The best was done for him, and he is now, I am glad to say, all right again. This incident was a disagreeable reminder that we are now in a country in many

respects hostile. The Wagogo are great thieves and
bullies. We have just received the startling news
that they have almost utterly destroyed an Arab
caravan of 500 porters—within a few miles of where
we now are—men, women, and children, all
massacred. Two or three of our own mail-men have
also been murdered. This very serious business will
probably delay us a few days, as the German commander is going to punish the chiefs of the tribes
implicated. This will probably mean burning
villages and hanging one or two of the chiefs. Oh,
when will this country—this land of misery, and sin,
and death, emerge out of its utter darkness? Truly,
to pass through is oppressive to the spirit in the
highest degree. Owing to the state of the country,
the German commander has intimated to me that
he will not be responsible for my safety (not that I
regard him as in any sense responsible), if I do not
keep nearer the main body on the march. Usually,
I am in the habit of going ahead with our fastest
donkey, so as to be in a position to choose the most
favourable site for our camp, when the kiongozi—or
leader—has indicated the spot where water is to be
found. Of course, when a large number of Natives
are travelling together, this is a most important
matter. I generally try to get to windward of their
camp. I suppose now I shall have to be a little
more careful. Yesterday, for the first time, I made
the acquaintance of zebra-steaks. We passed a large
herd of zebras whilst on the march, and one of the
Germans managed to shoot one at long range; this
was brought into camp later in the day, and the

successful marksman very kindly sent us a joint. We found it very good—quite an acceptable change in our diet."

"September 9th, 1890.

" The air for the last few days has been full of war and rumours of war. Saturday night was a night to be remembered. After we had pitched our tents near Unyanguira, and were preparing for our meal, we were startled by hearing that two German soldiers had been murdered at a village hard by, whither they had gone with cloth to buy food.

" Some time previously—that is, almost at the time of our arrival here—I informed the German officer, Lieutenant Siegel, that I had seen a number of Wagogo marching off from a neighbouring tembe (or village) with shields and spears, apparently in military order. He seemed to attach no great importance to this fact. To my mind, it seemed an indication of the state of the country around. After events proved the correctness of my surmise. The moment the news arrived of the murder, Lieutenant Siegel called his men together and marched off to endeavour to bring in the dead bodies, with the arms and ammunition with which the men left the camp. In about an hour's time he returned, bringing in one dead man—the other body he was unable to recover. One of the men died very nobly. When he left the camp, he received strict orders that on no account was he to fire on the natives. When he approached the village, he held his gun in his left hand and his cloth in the right. He said, ' I have come to buy food.' The natives threatened him with their spears. He answered, 'I am not going to fight with you. My orders are to buy food, and not to shoot. You can kill me if you like,' and held out his arms. Immediately the spears were plunged into his body in half-a-dozen places, and he fell, in obeying orders, as nobly, it seems to me, as ever any soldier fell in battle. The other poor fellow had no rifle; he immediately took to flight and endeavoured to escape. He was pursued for half an hour through the porri by these Wagogo bloodhounds, and fell, pinned by a dozen spears. The Lieutenant also informed us that the country was swarming with men in arms, and that evidently they meant fighting; that, in all probability, an attack would be made upon us some time during the night. We at once set about making as good a disposition of our men and loads as possible. At the moment, they were actually in as bad a position as they could be—scattered about in little camps over a wide plain. Word to concentrate was sent round, and soon we had the Wanyamwezi camped all around us. Our force was, unfortunately, divided; Mr. Stokes, with several hundred men, was some miles in the rear. Messengers were sent off to him with information as to the serious state of affairs. (We afterwards learned that these runners did not leave the camp until five hours after they had been ordered to leave). The German officer in command had only seventeen soldiers now left. It is true they were armed with breechloaders, but it was a force altogether insufficient to deal with the mass of men which filled the country in front.

Our trust was in the Lord God Omnipotent. We placed men to watch during the night, and committed ourselves into the hands of our Keeper—the Keeper of Israel—who neither slumbereth nor sleepeth. I could not help being struck with the evening portion of 'Daily Light,' which I read as I turned into my tent: 'Watchman, what of the night?' I slept from nine till four in the morning, and then rose. The Lieutenant was of opinion that if an attack came, it would be about half an hour before sunrise, that is to say, at about half-past five a.m. We were on the alert, but, happily, no attack came, and, as the sun rose above the level of the plain, we felt that we, through the goodness of God, had escaped a great danger. Of course, you know that we missionaries, as a party, are entirely unarmed. There is no doubt at all that, had the Wagogo chosen to attack us during the night, they could easily have massacred the whole lot of us—even had we been armed. I do not regret in the very least coming without arms. We should not have used them, and they would only have been a temptation to the men and boys.

A little after eight o'clock, on Sunday morning, Mr. Stokes arrived, and I felt at once that, humanly speaking, things would be arranged. He is a man of great influence with the natives—a man who keeps his word with them, and who has never done an unkind action with regard to them. Besides all which, he has travelled up and down and through this country for years. He at once sent out men to try to get hold of a native through whom communication could be opened up and the matter arranged. In this they were successful, and, in an hour or two, words were spoken between the parties. The chief of the country disavows the action of his people. The men, he says, were killed contrary to his orders. This disavowal is most satisfactory, as it puts a different complexion upon the matter. The death of these men was therefore murder, and not an act of war. Mr. Stokes thereupon demanded that the murderers be given up for punishment. Whether this will be done or not it is impossible to say. I cannot help feeling, myself, that the chief is merely excusing himself and trying to put the best possible aspect upon the matter. There is no doubt in my mind that the Wagogo would destroy us if they could as completely as they have destroyed the Arab caravan. What they fear is the presence of many white men. When they came into camp, they said, What can we do against 100 Muzungu, or white men? (We are only fourteen).

A letter has just arrived from Dr. Wolfendale, who is some miles away, stating that he is in difficulties, and asking for assistance. Dr. Wolfendale, you will remember, is a brother of Mr. Wolfendale, the Congregational minister in Durham. He has come out in connection with the L.M.S., and is travelling with a caravan of his own, and is bound for Urambo. It seems that a Wagogo chief has stopped or barred his passage until he has paid heavy hongo. He hears, moreover, that there is another chief, a little way in advance, who is waiting to make a still heavier demand upon him, and so he has written asking if we can help him out of his difficulties. This we are very glad to be in a position to do. We have sent off armed men, who will, in a few hours, we trust, bring him on here, and then we shall travel on together until we get out of Ugogo. Dr. Wolfendale's kind attention to poor Hill, who died at Zanzibar, I shall never forget, and I am only too thankful to be in a position—in some degree—to requite that kindness. Dr. Wolfendale in his note says that so far he has had a pleasant and prosperous journey. We expect him to arrive at about four or five p.m. I trust there will be no fighting in getting him here. I do not anticipate it."

Later.

"Dr. Wolfendale and his caravan have just come into camp, escorted by the German soldiers sent by Mr. Stokes for his rescue out of the dangerous position he was undoubtedly in. Lieut. Siegel thinks that, without question, he has escaped a great danger. The country is simply swarming with armed Wagogo. A single act of imprudence will be like throwing a firebrand into a powder magazine. May God give patience and wisdom to those who are concerned in the arrangement of this matter!"

"September 10th, 1890.

"I am thankful to say that all danger of a collision with the Wagogo seems now to be over. The chief has sent in the murdered man's rifle and ammunition, but declares his inability to produce the murderers, as they have fled out of his country.

THE LONG MARCH.

He is willing, however, to pay the blood-money in ivory and cattle. He says he has no cause of war with us, and desires peace for himself and people. I believe, myself, that he simply fears our strength, and that, had we been a small caravan, he would have smashed us up without mercy. However, 'all's well that ends well.' We shall probably take him at his word and go on our way. Mr. Stokes will probably leave the Germans at Mpwapwa, on the coast, to call the Wagogo to account for the destruction of the Arab caravan. I am thankful to be able to report the safe arrival of our mail men at Usongo. They escaped the massacre, and are now, in all probability, at Usambiro."

"September 11th, 1890.

We left our camp in front of Unyanguira this morning, and a two hours' march brought us to an abundance of water and food. We shall evidently get through Ugogo without any attack by the natives. They seem thoroughly to respect our strength. An Arab caravan, bound for the coast, has just come in, and I must send this and other letters by it, so must close. We are all in good health and full of hope, greatly cheered by our near approach to a country more hospitable than Ugogo. The Master has indeed been with us, guiding, keeping, strengthening, and comforting us at all times. All being well, we hope to be in Uganda before this letter reaches you. We expect to reach Usongo about the end of September, and to be at

Usambiro about October 21st. But we are in the Lord's hands, and can calculate on nothing; content to live a day at a time."

On October 3rd, 1890, Pilkington continues, writing from Byaba, 12 miles South of Usongo.

" Here is another chance (sooner than we expected) of writing. Mail men have just arrived from the Lake; they go on to-morrow. I was not expecting to have an opportunity of writing till we had reached Usongo, so you must excuse a scanty letter. Usongo is Stokes' village; the chief, Mtumginya, is his ardent friend and supporter. We hope to get there at 8 a.m. to-morrow, after a four hours' march through a ' porri,' or scrubby forest (nothing but scrubby little trees, fairly close together, nothing grand), these ' porris ' are uninhabited tracts, in fact, where there is a village, a clearing is made for cultivation; uninhabited, I should say, but for robbers, who catch stragglers with loads of cloth and kill or disable them. We got through the ' Mgunda Mkali' at last; we had a two days' halt on the verge, owing to difficulties with our Wasukuma porters, which made it especially trying to the men, whose cloth, for food, had to last all the same. My cookery has, of late, been greatly helped by quantities of native butter and honey. I have just borrowed, to my great joy, a Kiganda Grammar in French, by a Priest, from one of the German party, a Dane; it will be a great help and most interesting, after I have tried to make things out for so long without such help.

THE LONG MARCH.

Have just come back from packing my bucket, or rather arranging for packing in the morning—getting out loads and stowing in tins, native meal, rice, milk, honey, butter, pea-flour, etc., etc—not quite all these to-night. We shall be called about 2.30 a.m. to-morrow—the loads will go off to-night now that I have done with them. I am writing, through the Bishop's kindness, in his tent, and on his materials.

You will have heard, by telegram perhaps, a month before this reaches you, the news of general interest which goes by this mail, the various incidents in Uganda; Emin Pasha, just beyond Usongo, unable to proceed because of war in Usukuma—we are thankful to hear that now this is at an end; the death of four French Priests. Anyhow, the upshot of all this, as far as we are concerned, is this: that we hope and believe at the present moment we shall be able now to go right on into Uganda without delay, except four days or so at Usongo to settle about the carriage of forty or fifty C.M.S. loads (left there long ago) to Usambiro (the C.M.S. station at the South of the Lake, where Deekes and Walker, of the C.M.S., and Gedge, of the British Company, are at present trying to buy from the Arabs), and such further delay at the latter place as may be thought desirable, or may be necessary, for preparing the boat or boats to convey us and our effects. The C.M.S. boat was soon to go back with Gedge; it will now, no doubt, wait if possible for us, as they ought to have received the Bishop's letter from Mamboia some days ago, just after the departure of their mail men, who arrived here to-day, having passed our mail men a few days only from Usambiro.

We are now in a land of plenty, such a relief after Ugogo. Usongo is a goal we have long looked forward to. Our rest there will give an opportunity, much needed, of washing and mending our clothes, our bodies and other effects, *e.g.*, my camp bed, which is rather out at elbows. We are all quite well and strong, and so we can see a great deal for which to praise God, not that this is not always 'comely for the righteous,' 'it becometh well the just(ified) to be thankful.' We have long hoped in vain for letters: there'll be the more when they do come. We got our last at Mamboia.

Douglas has just come for letters, and for buckets, the porter whereof wants to do them up for an early start; nobody knows where they all are—I chiefly use them for the kitchen—so I have promised to hunt them up, and, as it is pitch dark, I had better set to at once, as it is now 7.10 p.m., and we are to get up at 2.30, and lots of other things are to be done."

"Nera (two days from Usambiro),
Saturday, October 18th, 1890.

We expect to start on Monday from here, and reach Usambiro early on Wednesday. The C. M. S. boat, we heard yesterday, started, a fortnight ago, for Uganda, with Walker. The Bishop will be greatly vexed at this, for it means our stopping at least a month at this end of the lake. Two men of our party are going to stay

THE LONG MARCH.

at Nassa with Deekes for the present, and Usambiro will be given up; this is not certain, but only very probable. Nassa is four days from Usambiro to the West, on the Lake, Hooper's old station, very good for the work, except for a cantankerous chief. We had a note from Emin Pasha yesterday, asking for letters to be forwarded; he is four or five days from here.

We are all, I am thankful to say, perfectly well. We arrived here, after some hard days, very tired; so the rest is very acceptable though tantalizing, when so near the end, but unavoidable, as this is the home of most of our Wasukuma porters, and they have nearly all run off and left their loads, declaring they only agreed to carry them as far as this.

We have lately had lots (well, comparatively speaking) of milk, much of it sour, which we all, myself not least, appreciate very much.

This is a very populous country—people very friendly—I should think as populous as a great part of the country in England. We are stopping a mile or so from the Capital, where the chief lives, at the village of a Mwanangwa (or village chief), who has been with us from the coast. We killed a bull yesterday, given us by a chief some way back, so the cooking department is busy, and boys and all are in clover. How pleasant the prospect of reaching a station is, I can't express, except by asking you to imagine reaching Dublin or Kingstown by steamer after a stormy crossing:—No more cooking, no more marching, no more resting (?) in a broiling tent!

At Usongo, where Stokes had a place of his own built for him by the chief, we found among a lot of C. M. S. property stored, most of which is to follow us, a Kiganda grammar in English, a very poor one, still a great treasure, and a cookery book! both of which were presented to me. I succeeded in making a very good sweet omelette the other day, but *good* eggs are scarce; out of 38, the other day, less than ten were eatable. They were a present; I weigh them in water before buying. Yesterday and to-day I tried and rejected 20, I daresay.

No mail from the coast yet.

It has been decided to send mail men to Stokes to get our loads taken on from here; we shall go on, we hope, with a few of our personal things.

"We also got a French Kiganda grammar at Usongo; it is a far better one than the English; it was published three years later.

Did I tell you that the Latin word 'mensa,' 'table,' has passed through Portuguese into Swahili in the form of 'meza,' and thence by a reverse process into Kiganda, as 'menza'? I am afraid I shall find it hard not to go on with 'menzam, menzæ, &c., &c.'"

Two days later the party arrived at Usambiro, and thus came to the end of the long march from the coast.

A member of that party, Rev. F. C. Smith, gives some interesting reminiscences of this journey. He says that Pilkington was specially noted for the keenness with which he would urge the claims of

THE LONG MARCH.

his favourite hobbies, whether it were superfatted soap, or Jaeger boots, or, it might be, his methods of language study.

When he got hold of a man who would help him in his language, he almost made his life a burden to him, and it is said that some of the Baganda, on the way up, shunned him if they thought they were going to be catechised.

He was always great on controversy, or on the solving of problems. Bishop Tucker once set a problem on political economy which Pilkington would not leave till he had solved.

He strongly contended with his fellow Missionaries that the worth of a thing was the amount that it would fetch at a particular place.

"Usambiro, E.E. Africa,
Saturday, November 1st, 1890."

We got here ten days ago: Wednesday, the 22nd. Douglas arrived the evening before, by an afternoon march; the Bishop and Dermott on the Saturday mid-day, having gone ahead from Nera. On Thursday, *i.e.*, the next day, the Bishop and Hooper and Deekes went on to Nassa, to see about re-establishing a station there. This place is to be given up as a Missionary Station, and Deekes and Dermott are to go to Nassa. They left me with the five other men in temporary charge of this place, where there are about twenty boys and eight girls on the station: most of them, including two dwarfs, left here by Stanley. They had been seized by his men during the wars in the interior, and were redeemed from them by Mackay. Seeing after them and our own boys, and the household arrangements, as well as school in the afternoon—besides trying to buy a good supply of meal, rice, honey, etc., to support us here and to carry on to Uganda (where the late disturbances have caused great scarcity)—makes me busy. Besides, I want to do Luganda and read all day, what seems, after Safari, the endless wealth of books that we find here. I sleep at night on a bed made by Mackay, on which both he and Bishop Parker died. The graves of these two and Blackburn (who formed three of the party of six who were here when Hooper was last at Usambiro), are within a stone's throw almost.

The reading sheets we use, each afternoon, were printed—at least the large letters—with wooden type cut by Mackay with his knife. We have this type in the printing office.

The C.M.S. boat, as I think I told you, has gone on to Uganda. Stokes' boat we expect here any day, but how many of us will be able to travel by her we don't know yet. The Bishop and the two others may be back in three or four days, now. By the way, I had a day-and-a-half's fever soon after we got here (temp. 103°) but not much, and it is gone now."

Here, two subjects dealt with in this letter may be mentioned, showing that, although deeply occupied with his own Mission work, he kept up a deep interest in the spheres in which he had worked, and especially in Harrow, and also in other Mission Fields.

"My letter's in *The Harrovian*! It tickles my foolish pride to know it, and it is pleasant not to be forgotten. There are so many at Harrow of whom I think continually, that it is only fair that they should have been reminded of me. It was interesting seeing the pictures of Harrow in *The Illustrated*, which has just arrived.

I have just written a note to Mr. Broomhall, in which I promise him £10 for the work in China, which he says is to help 'an attempt to evangelise, in the course of the next ten years, the whole of China.' To give £10 for such a purpose looks almost like a joke, but every little helps, and it will be accepted according to what I have, not what I have not."

"Sunday, 11th.

More than a fortnight since I began this, and much has happened. I have not written because, during that time I have had two more attacks of fever (Temperature 105° and 104°), both short and not serious. But I have sad news: another of our company has been taken to rest. Hunt, who joined us at the coast, having been in the service of the Company, died on Friday, after six days' illness, of fever, and finally we thought we saw symptoms of typhoid. We buried him that evening. I was asked by the others, Deekes—who had returned from Nassa—and our men, to read the service in English. He was buried beside Mackay, near Parker and Blackburn. That evening, the

Bishop and Hooper came back; the Bishop not yet well from two attacks of fever he has had at Nassa. Hooper had had fever too. Deekes had come back a week before. Dunn has had fever twice here, and is seriously ill still. Baskerville is just recovering. Myself, three times; everyone of our coast boys too. The latter we have sent back to the coast now, and very glad they are gone. Coast men and boys are the worst in all Africa, they combine the vices of European and Arabian civilisation with those of Africa.

We have divided up the boys here among ourselves, each man undertaking to provide for his three or four, and to take complete care of them. In fact, we adopt them, as they have no relations or other friends for such time, at least, as we shall be in the country. I've got three intelligent and very willing boys, Nasitu, who came with Stanley (say 14 years), Matruki, about the same age, and Kitera, 12 years. I expect I shall now have one of Hunt's.

We expect the boat every day. I'm particularly well now; these touches of fever for two or three days are totally different from what I had at the coast. I'm thankful for that now, both because I probably escaped thereby having a bad attack on the road, or here without a doctor, and other things, and also without the experience of myself which I have now. We had Communion this morning at 7 a.m."

"21st November.

More sad news. I told you Dunn was ill. He died last night very quietly. I've had wot more quite slight attacks of fever; they are good things, as taking the place of a heavy attack. Hunt had been in Africa a year without a day's illness. His first attack carried him off in six days. Dunn had merely a touch of fever two or three days before, and then, in a week, he is taken. Most thankful I am that my first and serious attack was at the coast. We hope to be off soon for Uganda."

At last, after six weeks delay fraught with such terrible disaster to the party, the long-looked for boat arrived. Mr. Smith tells us that, when the natives sighted the boat, they called out in Luganda which Pilkington was the first to understand, and danced about in glee at having been the first to bear the good news.

"Usambiro,
Tuesday, December 2nd, 1890.

I am thankful to say the boat arrived a few days ago, and we hope to start on Thursday. We shall be glad indeed to get out of this poisonous place; I've had my sixth dose of fever since I came here, and am seedy now. Baskerville was ordained deacon and Hooper and Dermott priests, yesterday."

"Christmas Eve, 1890.

On the boat among the Sesse islands, Victoria Nyanza. Within a day or two of Uganda (or rather Mengo, the Capital) we have met canoes on their way to bring up the rest of our loads— so I write a line. We have had, on the whole, a pleasant voyage. I've had fever four times, but am particularly well. We shall miss Christmas in Uganda; I'm to try with bananas, Mtama flour, &c., to make a pudding for Christmas. On Sunday, I spoke, through Noah, and a little on my own account, to twelve Waganda in the morning and fifty in the evening, sitting outside my tent. I've also spoken to little knots on islands and mainland since we reached the Uganda country. Captain Lugard has reached Uganda, so the place will soon be settled."

So he thought, but the settlement was not to come so soon as he expected.

UGANDA & NEIGHBOURING DISTRICTS.

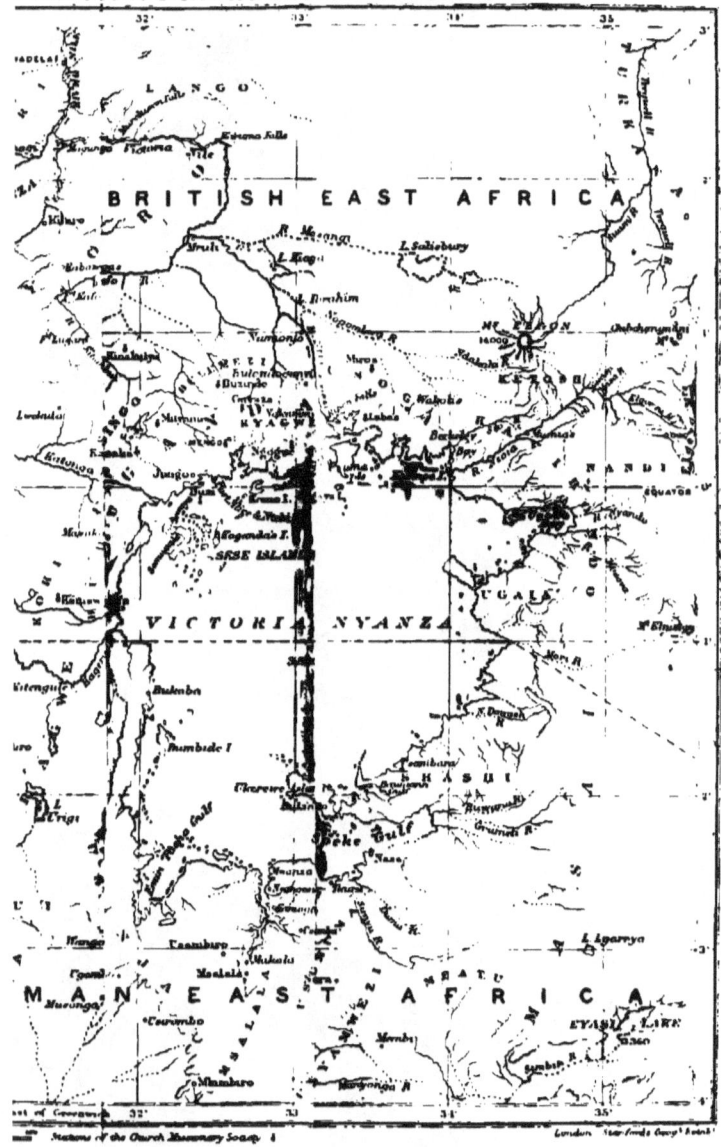

CHAPTER VII.

UGANDA AT LAST.

On the threshold of Uganda, it may be well to pause for a moment in order to remind ourselves of some of the events which had taken place since Missionaries of the Church Missionary Society first entered on work in this great district of Central Africa, and also to gain an idea of the meaning of some of the terms which will be used in this and succeeding chapters.

It was in November, 1875, that Stanley's memmorable letter to the *Daily Telegraph* appeared, telling of King Mtesa's willingness to receive teachers, which led to the sending forth of the first band of Missionaries. Since that time, in spite of disease and death, and in spite of the fickleness of Mtesa, the work was maintained.

Mwanga succeeded his father in October, 1884, and then indeed, a reign of terror began. Persecution tried to the utmost the early Baganda converts, some of whom were tortured and burnt to death; then followed the murder of Bishop Hannington, the excuse for which was that the bishop had approached Uganda from an unlucky side. Still, Mackay and Ashe kept the field, the former for a considerable time alone. Gordon and Walker took his place in the summer of 1887, Mackay retiring to the south end of the Lake. The following year they were obliged to leave Uganda owing to a revolution in which Mwanga was driven from the country.

He was, however, re-instated at the end of 1889 and Gordon and Walker returned with him.

Meanwhile Mackay, who had been a member of the first Missionary party and had never left Africa, died at Usambiro on February 8th, 1890, at which place Bishop Parker had also died. Mr. Jackson had entered Uganda as a representative of the British East Africa Company, followed a little later by Captain Lugard. Such was the condition of affairs when Bishop Tucker and his party arrived. It may not be out of place to explain here that the term Uganda is a word used by English travellers and others as a name for the country to the north of the Victoria Nyanza, which is known by the natives as Buganda. Still, the name Uganda is so familar to English readers that its use is justifiable. The inhabitants of Buganda are known as Baganda, or, as it is in Swahili, Waganda; a single native of Buganda is known as a Muganda, whilst the language is termed Luganda, or, as the Swahili have it, Kiganda.

The Victoria Nyanza is the largest of the chain of lakes which extends in a broken line from the Nile Valley to the Zambesi. Its area is rather greater than that of Scotland, so that it may almost be called an inland sea.

UGANDA AT LAST.

Reference to the map of the entire lake will give the best idea of the position of Uganda, and it will be noticed that there are a large number of islands in its immediate vicinity, and closely identified with it in politics and religion. The land is said to consist of a succession of hills and hollows, and the soil is exceedingly fertile, so that the hillsides are, in many cases, covered with rich groves of plantains and bananas.

The climate is an unusually healthy one for Africa, and, when the railway is completed, it is hoped that the risks to health may be still further diminished; as the trying journey from the coast, through belts of the most malarious country, has been responsible for much of the sickness and death of members of the Uganda Mission.

The most interesting geographical boundary of Uganda is the River Nile, on the east, which flows out of the Victoria Nyanza over the magnificent Ripon Falls.

The appearance of the country has been changed by the laying out of roads in the neighbourhood of the capital. In other parts, there are only the ordinary African paths.

The capital of Buganda is generally known as Mengo, though that word is more accurately applied to the hill on which the king's residence is situated, which is only one of about thirteen hills of which the capital is composed. The best known of the other hills are Namirembe, the centre of the C. M. S. Mission; Rubaga, of the Roman Catholic Mission: Kampala, at that time the head-quarters

of the representatives of the British East Africa
Company; and Natete, where the Mohammedan
chiefs have settled.

With this short preface, and with the aid of the
maps and plans which illustrate these points, we
may pick up our travellers where we left them pre-

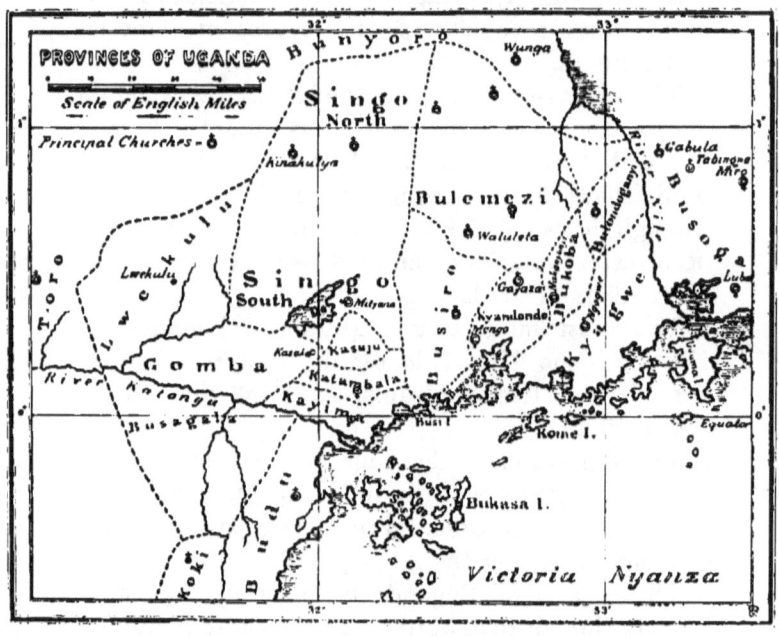

Map of Uganda and surrounding districts.

paring for a voyage across the great inland sea of
Central Africa.

Of this, Pilkington writes: "We coasted round
the lake in a small sailing and rowing boat of the
Mission, camping in our tents at night, or, indeed,

owing to head winds, by day and sailing by moonlight. We had to leave most of our things behind *pro tem.*, and still with three loads, five Europeans, men, boys, and sailors, we were all squashed like sardines in a box."

The voyage was not without incident, and here we may quote the story told by Bishop Tucker. He says:—

"We were sailing with a fair wind, but there were signs of a coming storm. The thunder was behind us, and dark clouds were crowding up; the water was becoming disturbed. The boatmen thought it a good thing to spread the awning—a most dangerous thing to do under the circumstances. The main-sail, instead of being held loosely in the hand, was tied to the side of the boat. Hooper shouted, 'Loose the sheet!' but before the words were out of his mouth, the storm struck us. The boat heeled over in such a manner that it seemed utterly impossible she could right herself again; but just at that moment, most providentially, the sail gave way, it split, and we were saved. Had it not done so, it is almost a matter of absolute certainty we should all have gone down like a stone."

Continuing his story the Bishop remarks:—

"After paying a visit to Emin Pasha on the western shore, we approached the confines of the country of Uganda, and it was truly wonderful the evidence we saw, from day to day as we camped, of the intense desire of the people for Christian instruction. Within a few minutes of our landing, quite a crowd came about, and those who had books would bring them and ask to be further instructed, whilst those who had none, begged and implored us to give them some. Mr. Pilkington, who was the only one able to speak the language of Uganda, would frequently have within a few minutes, quite a crowd round about him, who would be engaged in learning and repeating texts of Scripture; and by simply giving notice that, in an hour or so, a service would be held, some fifty or more would come together for prayer, &c. Of course, all this filled us with great hope and increased our impatience to reach the capital. At length, after many delays caused by light and variable winds, on the twenty-third day of sailing, and on December 27th, we reached the capital. And how shall I tell of that warm welcome given to us by the Natives of the Church and by Brethren Walker and Gordon, who for so long have so nobly held the fort?"

"On Monday, December 29th," Bishop Tucker writes, "we paid our respects to the king in open court. At about half-past nine, a messenger came from the king to say that he was ready to see us. So, setting off, we reached the royal residence at about 10 a.m. Our party consisted of Messrs. Walker, Gordon, Pilkington, Baskerville, Smith, Hooper, and myself. Outside the palace, another messenger met us, his work being apparently to conduct us into the royal presence. I suppose he must have been the Chamberlain. As we came near the reed gate which separated us from the audience or reception room, drums were beaten and trumpets blown. The gate was immediately thrown open and we were in the presence of the king and his court. The former at once rose up to greet us, shaking each one by the hand. Our seats—for we had taken the precaution of bringing our chairs with us—were placed on the right hand of the king. He at once inquired about our journey and made various inquiries about our ages, &c., &c., at the same time making remarks as to the colour of our hair, our height, &c., &c. With regard to the king himself, his appearance is certainly not prepossessing. The impression he gives one is that of his being a self-indulgent man. When he knits his brows, his aspect is very forbidding. During the whole of the time we were there, he kept giving his hand either to the Katikiro on his left hand or to the Admiral on his right, or to anyone who amused him and was near at hand. I had intended to bring with me one or two presents for the king—not on the old scale or principles, but as a simple acknowledgment of his courtesy in sending canoes to Usambiro for our goods. But his unfaithfulness in regard to his promise recoiled upon his own head. Thinking that the canoes would follow us from Usambiro in a few days, I left the presents for the king to be brought on later. No canoes appearing, no presents were forthcoming. I thought the king seemed quite angry with those about him who were responsible for the delay in the departure of the canoes. At any rate, he asked several very sharp questions with regard to the causes of the delay. The atmosphere of the reception-room was oppressively close, and so we were not sorry when the king rose up from his seat as the signal that his audience was at an end. Instead of retiring to the rear, as his custom is, he followed us to the front of the barraza, not merely, I think, as a matter of courtesy, but in order to inspect us a little more narrowly."

Pilkington's early impressions of the position in Buganda are given in a letter to his friend, Mr. Martineau.

"C. M. S. Station, Uganda,
January 4th, 1891.

This is a wonderful country and a wonderful people; war has ruined the country for the present; the bananas, which, with sweet potatoes, form four-fifths of the food of the country, won't be bearing again, barring the few spared in the war a year ago, for two more years; what with war and disease, there are hardly any cattle left; in fact, we are only just now coming out of the famine. In spite of this we have been amply supplied, seven of us, and our 'boys,' with bananas, sweet potatoes and meat from our native friends here, as presents, for which they expect no return in material things; we live mainly on green bananas boiled. Three houses, in native style though of English cottage shape, have also been built to receive us; we shall give the builders a present, but not the value of their work; and very likely they are not expecting anything. So we needn't cost the C. M. Society much. The houses are built of a strong and tall grass cane dried in the sun, and tied firmly in regular lines with strips of bark (if you can call it so) of the banana tree; the grass roof is supported by stems of a palm that grows here (no eatable fruit, however). The doors are made of the same as the walls, and are at present just leaned in the doorway. The windows are holes, over which we are putting blinds of native bark cloth. These houses keep out rain and sun, but not wind and cold; however, I think them very comfortable and pretty to look at; the floor is earth beaten down, rather damp as yet.

A thousand or more come to our service on Sunday; half of these at least can read, though some would be only beginners; the Church is overcrowded. On week days, 500 or so come to 'read' (i.e. to worship and to be taught) from six to nine in the morning. The keenness to learn is incredible. Many, I believe, would keep it up all day long if you let them; how far and in how many cases this is a sign of real Christianity in them, I can't say at present.

The state of the country is still very unsettled, though much improved. There are five *political* parties in the country (to none of which do we, the white men, belong—politics are not our business):—
i.—The English Company, with Capt. Lugard at present at its head. He has not strength enough yet, or thinks he has not, to take a strong and decided course. ii.—The Roman Catholic Party, headed by the King and half the big Chiefs. The King hates and fears the first and following party. iii.—The Protestant Party, headed by the biggest and wealthiest of the Chiefs, the 'Katikiro,' and the remaining Chiefs. iv.—The Heathen party,

which is not a party, but the great majority of the population, who have lost nearly all political power. v.—The Mohammedan party, which is no longer in this country, but in the neighbouring and once subject State of Bunyoro, whither those who have not been killed have been driven. The Christian parties have all the guns, 2,000 each perhaps, hence their exclusive power.

The people are like children, or like tinder, and the least excitement sets them in a blaze. The other morning they had come to Church here with their guns, of course, when a report got about that the Roman Catholics were about to attack—all a lie. Immediately, they all rushed out in tremendous excitement into the main road, and had the Roman Catholics had time to collect, they might have caused a fright. A night or two later, the Roman Catholics got a similar scare. All through the night they were assembling at the King's. In the morning, the Protestants gathered at the Katikiro's. They were at last calmed with great difficulty; now each party has sent in to Captain Lugard a list of grievances against the other; I hope he may settle them justly and wisely, and be able to have his decisions fairly carried out.

This is a beautiful country, very hilly, covered with banana trees (our houses are in the middle of a banana 'shamba,' or garden, which is the Mission's), 10 miles or so from the lake, and a good bit above its level, very healthy, we are told, for Africa; we are just north of the Equator.

This place is to my mind a fresh proof, or I should

say, confirmation, of the living power of the Word of God; it has turned the world upside down here. They are ready to pay as many cowries, 1,500, as would amply feed a man for two months, for a New Testament in Swahili; of course, we don't give them away, for many would take them only to sell them again; and we are out of books at present, we can't supply the demand fast enough.

My work here, if God lets me work here, is to be chiefly in the language; the four Gospels are nearly finished; nothing else; so plenty is left for me."

Thus early, Pilkington was marked out for linguistic work, and in this connection the following letter from Bishop Tucker is of great interest, particularly as it refers to others who had already done splendid work in reducing Luganda to writing and producing the earliest translations:—

"Buganda,
Jan. 1891.

My. Dear Mr. Pilkington,

It seems to me to be clearly pointed out by Him, who never leaves his Church without guidance and direction, that the special work to which you are called in Buganda, is translational and linguistic; in entrusting to your care this important part of the work of the Mission, I do so with the utmost confidence, believing that the Word of God will have in you, one who, as a Christian, will handle it with holy reverence, and who, as a scholar, will translate it with accuracy. I am, however, not forgetful of the fact that at present you have scarcely done more than make a beginning with the language. I am, therefore, glad to know that you have, in Mr. Gordon, one who will greatly assist you in your studies, and in every way co-operate with you in your work. For some time to come you will naturally seek Mr. Gordon's help, and consult him in matters in which his experience and linguistic attainments will qualify him to express an opinion. He is at present engaged—as I dare say you know—in the completion of an important work commenced by Mr Mackay: this will, of course, remain in his hands until its passage through the press. After this, it is Mr. Gordon's own wish that the translational and linguistic part of the work should be placed in your hands. I am sure you may depend upon his hearty support and loyal co-operation in all that is undertaken for the Glory of God, in the spread of the knowledge of His word. This translational work will not, I am sure, prevent you from engaging as opportunity may present itself from time to time, in the more directly Spiritual work of the Mission, for this, you will place yourself at the disposal of those who have charge of that work. Praying that a great blessing may rest upon your labours, and that you may have health and strength given to you for all that you undertake, and that much joy and peace may fill your own soul. I remain,

   Ever yours in Christ,
 Most faithfully and affectionately,
    Alfred, Bishop, E. E. Africa."

"P.S.—I cannot help thinking that one of the most useful pieces of linguistic work to which you can put your hand would be (as soon as you feel yourself qualified to undertake it) a simple Grammar. Its usefulness to those coming up country for the first time would be simply incalculable. I commend it earnestly to your attention."

Early days in Buganda were not idle ones. Pilkington writes to his mother on

January 3rd, 1891.

"We've had a lot to do, the houses to rig up, get the floor pounded down, get a trench dug round it to keep off the rain, rig up a shift for a table, etc., etc. Then I've had to set a Swahili paper, and shall have to look over it for ——, who is to be examined for orders, to be preparing Noah for confirmation, besides getting oneself and one's clothes washed, learning Luganda, etc., etc.

Then, on Monday, we're to start classes for confirmation, about fifty candidates to be taken in Swahili by four of us. So I've plenty to do."

Later on, writing to one of his sisters, he describes his surroundings as follows:—" I'm sitting on a native stool, cut out of solid wood. As my table, I have put my large tin writing desk on my native bed (a strong wooden framework with a cowhide stretched tightly), my table is too high for the stool. On my right side against the wall is my camp bed, whose canvas is greatly torn in the middle, and which I use only as an untidy table to put things on. By the way, one of the chiefs lent, and then gave, the native bedstead. Then comes a basin, supported on a four cross-legged stool made by my Muganda boy, Erasito; intended to make a stool for myself, but unsatisfactory. Then I have a table behind me, strewn with books, standing on four legs that are fixed in the ground, and the top formed, like the walls of the houses, of the grass cane tied to the frame with strips of banana bark—this is only temporary. Over the windows and door I have curtains of bark cloth. On the pole which stands in the middle of the room and supports the roof, I have two bags of clothes hanging.

Above my head I have a large package—a yard long, six inches in diameter—of native salt done up in banana leaves—salt is very scarce here. For this salt—10 lbs., perhaps—I paid four yards of the miserable white calico which is called cloth here; this is equivalent to 20,000 cowries, or, as we say, 20 strings, which, in normal times, would buy 40 huge bunches of bananas, each with 100 or 200 bananas on it; or three fat goats or sheep; 40 strings would buy a cow. A string of shells costs us, including carriage, about a shilling."

CHAPTER VIII.

A LULL IN THE STORM.

For some little time there was a cessation from those violent outbreaks of hostilities which had so often interrupted Missionary work, and though, to those who were familiar with the situation, it was evident that this was not likely to last, opportunity was afforded for considerable progress, especially in translational work, and on the part of the people in their desire for books.

Pilkington felt the need of more books most keenly, and his letters about this time are full of schemes for expediting the production of books.

On February 24th, 1891,
He writes:—"In the loads came books, which went (at least the New Testaments),"—no doubt these were in Swahili—"like wild-fire at 1,000 cowries apiece; 200 cowries buy ample food for a man for a week. Only 120 New Testaments or so came; after a day and a half all had gone, and many people had to be sent away disappointed. We want thousands of books and hundreds of men.

"February 25th, 1891, 4.30 p.m.
I've just finished a spell of writing translation: this is, of getting a Muganda who knows Swahili to

translate from that language into Luganda. I am doing the Acts in this way, every morning, for three hours, with Henry Wright Duta, the most educated of our people. In the afternoon, I am doing some Bible stories from Swahili. These translations won't be perfect when they are done, but I think they will be correct and intelligible, and the need of Luganda books is most pressing. Matthew, and an abridged prayer-book, and a reading sheet with the Commandments and Lord's prayer, are the only Luganda publications we have or have had, for as soon as we get any they go like the wind. . . . The four Gospels have been translated. Now to have them printed and sent here, there's the rub! We got the other day the first copies of Matthew that reached Uganda, and they were printed in '88, two or three years' delay. I can't imagine how it was, and the people here dying for books and ready to pay for them. Now what I want to do is this, only I want your help: I want friends at home to subscribe money to get these books printed, and want you, that is my family, to get them printed, and to look over the proofs, because you know my handwriting; to have a proof out here means a delay of six months or so. Do you think you could manage this? The need of native books is enormous. We should sell them here for cost of printing and carriage, and send the money home to get more printed. You, that is all you who are familiar with my writing, could look over the proofs more satisfactorily than anyone else. I've no doubt Father knows a good printer in Dublin. If I try to get them printed in any other way, I am sure it would only mean endless delay. Where each book had been thoroughly revised (and to do this printed copies here would be an immense help) I should send it to the Bible Society. But this wouldn't do at first, and we must have an immediate snpply. The natives here are ready and fit to teach a great deal, only they want books. The first thing is to gather some money together. I shall write to a good many people, and I am sure this will be no difficulty. But still, if you would write to anyone who would like to help, it would be a great thing. I don't think you would find it either very difficult or very tedious looking over the proofs, because all you could do would be to compare them with my copy, original corrections you could'nt make. What do you say?"

"Sunday, March 1st, 1891.

I shall write more about the above matter when Gordon has come back from Busoga, and I have consulted him; whether that will be before this letter goes (we expect him for Easter perhaps) or not, I can't say. I can't bear to think of delay of six months at least, perhaps a year, while the proofs could come and be sent back, when the people are so eager for books. At the same time, I don't wish to burden you at home; however, I am sure that my sisters would think it a great privilege to have a part and a very important one in so grand a work. I believe that the results of having a Luganda Bible here would be amazing.

The position of Uganda, within easy reach by

steamer of all the country that fringes the lake, a central position too, in Africa, generally commanding further the South end of the Nile valley, makes me think the events of the last dozen years :—Stanley's visit, the Missionaries coming, the great movement (whether you think of it as religious, intellectual, or political), the persecutions, the coming of the English Co., the death of Mackay, and Stanley's return to England (because of the interest in this country aroused by these two events), all these things coming together, seem to me in a most special way to be providential. In other words, I think all these things point to the fact that 'Ethiopia shall soon stretch out her hands unto God,' and that Uganda will be a great centre of light.

Henry Wright Duta, whom I mentioned as my translator, is a very clever man. He might have been a big chief, Katikiro had he chosen, but he preferred the position of a simple teacher; others have made the same choice.

We had the Lord's Supper in Church to-day. Captain Lugard (theoretically the King, but it was Captain L's advice that prevailed) has decided that the Sesse islands are to be divided as originally agreed between the Protestant and the Roman Catholic parties. The Roman Catholics have hitherto held them to the exclusion of all other parties; this has been decided. When will it be carried out? When that happy time comes we shall be able to get canoes for our loads from Usambiro. The canoes are now under the control

A LULL IN THE STORM.

of Roman Catholic chiefs and the King, who promises anything but performs nothing.

We expect De Winton to afternoon tea to-morrow afternoon. I've undertaken to make the bread. I've made very fair bread from native materials lately; rice, plantains, potatoes, milk, and pombe barm, but now I've got English flour, butter and cake, with raisins and currants, of which we have a few. So with translations, etc., I'll have a busy day to-morrow. So good night, it's 9.15 now."

"Sunday, 8th March, 1891.

We are getting canoes sent. We hope to-morrow to send to Usambiro for loads, so the letters are to start on Tuesday and catch the others up. The political state of the country is still very unsettled. Smith and Gordon are still in Busoga, at least, so we suppose, we have not heard of them since they crossed the Nile.

With Henry Duta, I have now translated nearly half the Acts. I hope to send to the Bishop by this mail, short translations of Bible stories, Adam, Noah, Abraham, Isaac, Moses, Samson, Jonah, Nebuchadnezzar, etc., which would be very useful while we have no Old Testament in Luganda, and especially for teaching children both the Bible and reading. They have been translated by different natives who know Swahili. In another fortnight or so, I hope to finish the Acts, and in another month, perhaps, the Grammar which the Bishop suggested. All these things will, of course, at first, be very imperfect, but I want the Grammar to be ready, if possible, to give what help it can to the 20 men the Bishop hopes to bring out soon.

Do you know the picture leaflets which are published by the Children's Special Service Mission? I am going to write to Mr. Bishop to-morrow to ask whether he could get some in Luganda printed for us, and I mean to send him, in case he can do it for us, the story of Naaman with a few words in explanation of its typical meaning. The last part of Revelation VII., Psalms LI. 1, 2, and 7, 1st John, I. 7, and a hymn, of which this is a translation . . . . It is very doubtful whether the C. S. S. M. can undertake to do them, but I think it worth trying. The rains are on now, which makes it much cooler and pleasanter, to my mind. My boys, who came from Usambiro, are thriving fearfully here. One had dysentery when he first came, he was dangerously ill, nearly as bad as Edgar on the road (to whom I am writing by this mail). In both cases, ipecacuanha was successful. Now this boy, who was a skeleton, is as fat as may be; so is Najibu. whom I hear in the next room practising ta, to, te, ta, to, te, from his reading sheet. He has the reputation of being the cleverest of the boys whom Stanley brought to Usambiro. The other boy who was ill, was Emin Pasha's, Erasito. My Muganda boy is 17 or so, and can read perfectly, and knows Swahili well; he is the brother of the Katikiro, the 'Lord Chancellor,' as Ashe calls him in his book. Have you read it? 'Two Kings of Uganda.' The smallest of them is Kitera, who arrived here with the last mail.

In writing to Mr. Bishop about the picture leaflets he says: " I have been thinking lately of the picture

A LULL IN THE STORM.

leaflets of the C. S. S. M., and wishing very much to get some for our people here (who would appreciate them immensely and buy them with shells); and wondering whether it would be possible to get some in Luganda. . . . .

I think this country has a particular claim on you, because the oldest of its people are only overgrown children."

This request was gladly granted by the Children's Special Service Mission.

"April 5th 1891.

Nearly all the Waganda have gone out to fight the Mohammedans, who were ravaging, a week ago, only six hours' march from here. The Katikiro is 'Mugate,' *i.e.*, General, and Henry Duta is with him as his Secretary. Samwili (who went as a sort of Ambassador to the three Consuls, English, French and German at the coast, who has just come back), was to have taken Henry Duta's place in helping me, but he has fever. The Waganda have driven the Mohammedans off, they are retreating to their stronghold in or near Bunyoro, the Captains are soon to start with seven hundred men and two Maxim guns in pursuit; they will offer them terms, and, if these be refused, will take their stronghold.

The Acts, Henry and I finished a week ago, but I must still revise it. I am working hard at the grammar now, making vocabularies just at present. I hope to be able to send something in the way of a Grammar and general Handbook to the language in two months more, but I shall have to work hard. This might be ready to help the men coming out in the Autumn. I have written ten Luganda hymns to the tunes, and to some extent following the words of the following: 'Art thou weary?' 'There is a fountain,' 'There is life for a look,' 'Onward Christian Soldiers,' 'Look ye Saints,' 'I heard the voice of Jesus,' 'Grace, 'tis a charming sound,' 'I lay my sins on Jesus,' 'Just as I am.' I intend to send a copy of this to Deekes at Nassa; he may be able to print us some. This, and Grammar, and translations, making bread, butter, and pancakes (you should see me toss them before a group of admiring black boys) have chiefly occupied me since I last wrote.

Gordon is back from Busoga. Smith is still there. Walker went the other day to Budu, the Pokino's country, to make a start there. Kitera, my small boy, was Gordon's originally, so Gordon has taken him. He starts home in a month or two. I have an odd bit of black mortality in his place called Kisasiro, a very odd little boy. Nasitu told me to-day that one of Stanley's porters bought him for a doti, that is four yards of calico; he seemed rather proud of having been worth so much. One of Walker's boys was bought for an old tin cannister; to remind him of it is a favourite method of teasing him. I think he tries to make out it was a biscuit tin."

"April 12th, 1891.

I've been particularly well lately, and accordingly my Grammar makes good progress; the whole thing is to consist of grammar, syntax, notes on pronunciation, specimens of Luganda, especially

A LULL IN THE STORM. 135

conversations, Luganda-English Vocabulary, and English-Luganda ditto. I hope to finish it by the end of next month; a good deal is done already.

De Winton has asked us all to tea this afternoon. Lugard and Williams and the Doctor are out at the war; no fighting yet. The enemy shewed some desire to fight before the English came up, but I expect they are retreating now.

We have planted beans, Indian corn, guavas, pawpaws, lemons, peas, and radishes; cabbages we have had several of lately. There are four fresh eggs on this table waiting for me to cook. I have made some excellent bread lately. A good deal of wheat has been planted, but not by us. The country is rapidly improving; perfect quiet now and confidence in the English Company."

In a letter to Mr. Martineau he remarks:—"Sugar here is a great luxury; we have some left, but only use it on great occasions. I daresay you look on saccharine with scornful eyes: but as articles cost about 2s. per lb. to bring up here, or sometimes 5s., lightness is a very valuable quality for us. The Society pays for our loads, but of course we all try to cut down expenses as much as possible (you see at the present moment we could find ample work for twenty Europeans here and this would cost, to bring them here, £5,000 at least); so there is every reason to economise: accordingly, I've only ordered saccharine for next year, a couple of little bottles. If you could tell me any simple process by which sugar-cane (which we grow, but not much, here) could be used for sweetening things, it would be very useful. Slicing it and putting it in hot water makes no earthly difference, I find: indeed, it's of very little use to us. The people chew it largely, spitting out the fibre, but we don't care for it. We get honey from the South end of the lake occasionally."

With reference to the demand for books, Mr. Walker writes from

"Namirembe, Buganda,
March 9th, 1891.

Just lately we sold 4,000 Luganda reading-sheets and about 200 Swahili New Testaments, as well as other books. The demand is very great for the New Testament, but Ezekiel and Jeremiah are not much cared for because they are not understood. Could you have sent up of the Luganda reading-sheets, 10,000 copies; of St. Matthew in Luganda, 3,000 copies; of the Prayer-book in Luganda, 3,000 copies? I should like to ask for more, but the above will make $22\frac{1}{2}$ loads. We do not intend to charge the actual cost-price here in Buganda necessarily, but so near to this that there should be no great loss on the books. For a Swahili New Testament we have charged the people 1,000 shells, and these we have sold for 3s. 6d. The book in England is sold for 2s. and weighs one pound. There must, therefore, be a small loss on each book, but it is only a small one. On the Luganda reading-sheets we have made a little profit, as we sell each for thirty shells.

The French priests are here in great numbers and are very active. Surely many people in

England, who cannot come to help us themselves, would like to help on the work by sending the Word of God here in its written form."

Pilkington writes to Bishop Tucker on the same date—

"The other day the first instalment—only 100 or so—of the Luganda St. Matthew, which had been printed in England, arrived at last. We are naturally extremely anxious to get anything that we can manage to get translated, printed and sent back without loss of time. I have begun the attempt at a grammar which you recommended me to make, and in another month I expect to have ready what would, I think I can say, (though, of course, it would have many little faults and deficiencies) be a great help to new men coming out. I have got Natives to translate from Swahili (making use both of the Bible and the 'Picture Bible' in Swahili) a good many Old Testament stories; these are meant especially for teaching children, although, while we are without an Old Testament in Luganda, they would be also generally useful. Henry Duta and I have also begun and nearly done half of the Acts. In another month I hope this will be finished too. I believe we could dispose of 2,000 at least of any small book in Luganda at cost price. The books which have hitherto come have quite failed to satisfy the demand. We ought to aim at having the books as small and light as is consistent with good printing and binding, both in order to save cost in carriage and because the Waganda are far readier to buy a neat book and one which they can easily carry about with them, than anything large and clumsy. If you could see the eagerness of this people for books—I am glad to think you did see something of it—how they swarmed round us day and night while the books lasted and after they were all gone, and would not believe that there were no more New Testaments or St. Matthews or reading-sheets to be had, you would be as anxious as we are to see them satisfied at last. Even the Roman Catholics buy our books. Even the sending out of more missionaries is, to my mind, at present scarcely so important. With native books, so many here are already capable of teaching a good deal."

The next letter tells of a visit to one of the islands rendered necessary by an attack of fever.

"Island of Sowe,
V. Nyanza,
4th July, 1891.

I had an attack of fever for a week, and so De Winton asked me to come here for a change, which I did, and it has done me a lot of good, only, alas, we've missed the mail and my vocabulary is here. Capt. Williams assured me that the mail would pass here, but it did'nt. We are negotiating for a canoe, and I heartily hope we'll get one, but the prospect is dark.

I've started the Galatians with Henry. Walker we expect back from Budu every day; he wants Baskerville to go back to Budu with him. We hope to have the Church started now, the new one, large enough to accommodate with comfort our large and increasing congregations. Smith is back in Busoga, Gordon on his way to England. We have had no mails yet, and so we don't know any more about Ashe's coming. The Waganda are tremendously fond of Ashe.

I got fever going through a marsh on my way with Baskerville to the Mumenga, a big chief, who had had ulcers, and who refused to use medicine on the ground that God could cure him without. We did'nt know of this abominable marsh, and I had hardly reached the Mumenga's when fever came on, and I had to be carried back. The Mumenga still refused medicine, but agreed to use water for his ulcers. I have not heard since, except that the poor fellow has now got small pox; but his faith is encouraging to see, even though we may think it mistaken in a way.

We intend to go back to Mengo on Monday, and then I hope I shall get on with translation all the quicker and better for this rest, but if we can't send off these letters and my vocabulary, it will be a great disappointment. I should not have dreamt of coming here at such a sacrifice.

De Winton has been shooting at hippos and crocodiles, which abound here; we believe he killed one of the latter, he was hit and careered about, lashing his tail and showing his great jaws, but we could'nt actually get him. If we had a good boat's crew, we could get hippos, but our paddlers are afraid to go near enough; they are hideous monsters,

I have seen them quite close. We have wanted to shoot and eat some parrots, which abound here, however we've been unsuccessful as yet. The butterflies are wonderful; there are honeysuckers here, green and red and black; also a fine osprey. Mosquitoes are terrible, but De Winton's description of the same in Canada throw our mild experience into the shade."

A letter to his mother, ten days later, speaks of another attack of fever, and in it he gives his opinion on a variety of topics. Of religious papers, he prefers *The Christian*, as he finds that it is not bitter. He adds: "*The Christian* deserves its name."

His order for articles of clothing and other things gives some idea of his views as to dress in the Tropics. It is evident that Jaeger boots must not be confounded with Jaeger slippers!

"14th July, 1891.

If you could order me a fairly decent suit of clothes, not too heavy, but fairly warm and large enough—I don't mind if they are a size or two too big; but tight clothes in this country are an abomination. Also a couple of football sweaters—R. will tell you what they are—and a couple of Pyjama (is that right) suits, rather warmer than the last (which were just what I wanted, only I like warmer things now), and a few pairs of socks, a pair of slippers (leather wears better than Jaeger), and six pocket handkerchiefs. Could you get these things packed, and sent out to Boustead, Ridley and Co.; also some rennet powder and baking soda."

The doings of the next few months are well

A LULL IN THE STORM.

described in the following series of letters, some to Mr. Eugene Stock, and some to his mother:—

"Namirembe, Uganda,
August 11th, 1891.

The mail arrived this afternoon. I am alone (of our missionaries) here.

Baskerville went to Budu, intending to come back for a while, at any rate, in a month. The month will be up in a week or ten days, but, in a letter I got from him on arrival at Masaka, he spoke of staying longer, as he would be delayed in visiting Zekariya's place, because the petty king of Koki, Kamswaga, had come into Budu, and, being joined by the Roman Catholics, had burnt and destroyed several houses and gardens, including Zekariya's. I was alarmed by the first reports that reached us of this business: 'The Pokino killed! Three of Walker's boys, whom he left at Masaka during his recent visit to this place, murdered!' This would have been terrible. Walker is very fond of his boys; so are we all, but Walker especially, perhaps. But, thank God, things were, as usual, immensely exaggerated.

Now about things here. Politics (how I hate them, but I suppose they are necessary evils!) hinder the work more than anything. When I came back from the island of Sesse, after a week's change to try to shake off fever, the country was terribly excited; we all of us (Walker and Baskerville were here then) really apprehended war, or, at any rate, that the Protestants would leave the country. This was caused by a proposal from Captain Williams to abolish the agreement made between the two parties, and to permit chiefs (all of whom now hold office *qua* Protestant or Roman Catholic, appointed by one or other party) who change their religion to retain their chieftainships. We should, of course, be delighted to see full religious liberty, but the people do not understand it, and the Protestant party was very resolute against accepting the proposal; this was because, whereas the Roman Catholics, in the choice of their chiefs, had been guided by the priests, and had appointed consistently the most thorough-going Roman Catholics, our party, on the other hand, were guided by general, at least as much as by religious, considerations (e.g. hereditary claims, fitness other than religious)—Gordon and Walker refusing to choose the chiefs. Well, the other day, the Roman Catholic Bishop claimed 'religious liberty' from Captain Williams, on the ground that the country was under the British flag; our party answered that if that were the case, and we were really under British government and therefore we could have British justice, let Captain Williams hoist the English flag, and let us follow British customs; he tried to do so, but the attempt did not succeed, the Roman Catholics and the king refusing point-blank.

Well, this, and the division of the islands, and the innumerable cases of men turned out of gardens, houses destroyed, goods stolen, &c., &c., has occupied every one for weeks past. At first, the church was empty on week-day mornings, but a day or two after Walker and Baskerville went, I made a round of visits to various chiefs, urging them to be patient and aim at 'peace at any price,' and to come and bring their people in the mornings. Since then we have always had fair and sometimes very large (500 or 600) congregations —on weekdays, I mean; on Sundays, the church is crowded out. During this time I have started giving them Bishop Ryle on St. Matthew every morning after the 'reading' is over; the 'reading' means that the people are divided into classes, each with a leader, who translate the Swahili of various books of the New Testament into Luganda, with exposition (as far as they are able). When I come into church after my breakfast, between seven and eight o'clock, I attach myself to the senior class, of which Henry Wright Duta is the leader (when he is here; he has just gone off to a garden lately received). My arrival is the signal for the class to turn from St. Matthew to Romans, which we read and translate. Someone first reads it in Swahili, the reader then reads it clause by clause, and the first reader translates into Luganda, corrected by the leader. Then they appeal to me for explanation, which I attempt to give, but most of them find Romans 'kizibu nyo' (extremely hard).

Ten days ago, Duta and Sembera came to me on a Sunday to say they could not preach in church (I generally preach at one Sunday service, and one of the six who have the Bishop's license at the other); they had 'not been taught to preach; what was the good of preaching if they had not proper words to preach?' To tell you the truth, I think them quite fit to preach, but I did not say so exactly (though I showed it by still asking Henry to preach as arranged that afternoon, and Sembera the next Sunday), but told them that a knowledge of one's own ignorance is the beginning of knowledge (and if Socrates is to be trusted, the end, too), and we arranged an afternoon daily class for these two and Johana Mwira, to which also Nataneli Mudeka came, a very nice young fellow, just made a church elder. These meetings are rather handicapped by politics just now, and by Henry's departure to the country. We started on Romans again; the first eight verses of chapter iii. were a terrible puzzle. They could not grasp them, so we left them for the next day; I in the meanwhile to make a Luganda translation, much amplified and simplified, which I did with the help of Conybeare and Howson, and I believe they understood them the next day.

I started translating Galatians two months ago with Henry: fever and politics interrupted me, after finishing the first chapter, till to-day. To-day Sembera and I started again. I am translating Genesis with Noah (here called Nuwa), who came with us from the coast. These things, and looking after the boys and place, and visiting for an hour or two most afternoons, keep me very busy. I visited two of the Roman Catholic chiefs lately, who gave each a goat. I have since been given two more by the Roman Catholics, to the great delight of my boys, who eat the lion's share of it.

We have some melons coming on in our garden; also wheat and potatoes! We have great reason for thankfulness for the healthiness of this country, greatly owing, I believe, to the comparative variety and excellence of its food, and clean water.

I have the names of *thirty-six* chiefs, who have offered to build for and feed a European residing at their place. I could easily add to this if I tried, but surely this is enough to show what is wanted. At most of these places, a good number of the people have already learnt, or are learning, to read. The outlay would be (the missionary once in the country) next to nothing, and who can estimate the returns? The Baganda have already begun to go out to preach in other countries (in Busoga and Usukuma). I believe that, with God's blessing, this ought to be the centre of African Christianity, sending the messengers of peace east and west, north and south. We have here, I believe, the fulcrum by means of which to work Africa (and is it not Archimedes who could move the whole earth, if only he had a fulcrum?), but the lever must, in the first instance, be Europeans, men of God, who do not mind being used as levers in Africa or elsewhere in God's hands. —I wrote, 'who do not mind,' but when I read it, it sounds almost blasphemous; 'not mind' being in God's hands for His work! Could there be a safer, a happier position? Could there be a greater privilege?"

"September 14th, 1891.

A long time has passed since I began this letter, and a lot of things have happened. News came yesterday from Captain Lugard, and the Company are sending a mail to-day, so I must wind up as shortly as possible.

On the day after I wrote the beginning of this letter, I saw, in the *Intelligencer*, that Ashe was translating Genesis; so I left the eight chapters I had done, and went on to Exodus. I hope to send by this mail, and indeed with this letter, the Galatians; I have no time to write to Gordon or the Bishop. I also enclose a table of Luganda concords, which I hope will be printed soon, and a few copies sent to us here.

Smith is here now; he was ill on the road. Captain Williams was extremely kind in fetching him, also in visiting me when I had a week of fever, a fortnight ago. Baskerville has had fever three times in Budu. My last was my twentieth attack in fifteen months. Smith brings a much more encouraging account of work in Busoga; I hope one of the new men will go there till Ashe's coming (which we expect in about a month—he is due at the south of the Lake to-morrow). Smith is going to a place on the Busoga road near the Nile, and therefore in the Buganda province of Kyagwe—about three day's from here; they have offered to build him a church there. The elders are choosing four Waganda Christians to go with him and occupy this place and three others, all within three or four hours of each other. Smith will superintend, going from one to the other. I hope to have a sort of dismissal service before they all start. Smith now says the people of Busoga are anxious to learn, and

A LULL IN THE STORM. 147

friendly, and even Wakoli is friendly. The Church agrees to support entirely the Waganda working in Buganda. When Ashe comes, I hope it will be possible to do the same as in Kyagwe in the country between this and Budu, the provinces of the Katambala, Kasuju, and Kayima. There will then be left the province of Singo, and with it that of the Kitunzi, and the province of Bulemezi: these two provinces are to the north, and have no lake-shore, and are therefore most exposed to the Mohammedan attacks, and, at present, are not thickly peopled. Four more men are needed for them. Suppose six men come in a month, we might have three in Budu (Walker and Baskerville have their hearts set on Budu), one in Katambala's country, three in Mengo, one in Kyagwe, two in Busoga. Sesse should be occupied. We ought to have twenty men. Kavirondo might be occupied soon; Smith is longing to go there."

Later in the same day, he writes to his mother:—
"This morning, two Waganda came to me to offer to teach in the Katambala's country; two more for Bulemezi. These were men selected by the church elders. They are looking out men for Singo. Praise God! They have been clearly told to expect no wages except from God. They are to be fed, housed, and clothed at the expense of the Church here. There are besides four men for Kyagwe, where Smith goes in a few days. But we must have Europeans to superintend. Baskerville has had three attacks of fever in Budu. I had my twentieth dose a fortnight ago; now I am looking, everyone says, and

feeling better than I have been since my fever at the coast. Any amount of work to be done. Every morning, if I can manage it, I teach in the church. Deekes has printed ten of my hymns, and I am teaching them these. I visit a great deal and am received with the greatest kindness and hospitality by all. The other day, I went to the king to ask for canoes. On his promise of thirty, I sent nine cakes of Pears' unscented soap and about two pounds of the commonest washing soap—this as an earnest of what would come if our thirty canoes really appeared. To-day, he sent me down ten magnificent bunches of plantains, weighing, I suppose, 3cwt., and a magnificent fat sheep (in the last few days, by-the-bye, the leopards have taken a goat, a kid, and a sheep of ours). The sheep must have had 2lb. of fat (splendid for frying) in its tail. I shall boil it down and bottle it. I have quantities of milk and butter. I have bought up cows in expectation of Ashe and his party. Every European in this country should have a cow. You might send me a small box of very strongly scented soap, also some intensely powerful scent. With two such cakes of soap I could buy a cow. . . . I want maps of Bible countries, Africa, and large pictures for hanging up; all for teaching a large number at the same time. Oh! for a magic lantern. Ashe is due at Nassa to-morrow. One of the chiefs began his house to-day. My house has just been altered, and is now most comfortable and healthy. . . .

I am drinking tea and eating Indian meal bread—while de Winton smokes (alas! he goes

A LULL IN THE STORM.

to join Lugard to-morrow). Emin has dodged past to Wadelai, after ivory no doubt. . . . .

I have several new boys now, one of them the naughty little Bobby Kayinga, mentioned in 'Two Kings of Uganda.' Ashe to come in a month. I am very well indeed."

"Namirembe,
8th October, 1891.

I'm by myself still, as I have been since July 20th, but for Smith's short visit. I have a kind of kitten (a 'mondo'—it will be nearly as big as a leopard), three grey parrots (which I have been given and have passed on to my boys), and a monkey, with which the boys are playing now in in this room. He is a great delight to them, most human and ridiculous, awfully afraid of me, but bites the boys; desperately fond of sugar-cane.

I have been teaching the hymns which I have written, and reading Jeremiah, in church, with some of our people. I have written to Mr. Stock, pointing out how absurdly few we are in this country for the vast work there is to be done. . . . .

Our potatoes are doing well. I enclose a copy written by Mackay, probably a good many years ago, when he was at Natete; also a letter written to me by the Mugasi, the chief of the soldiers, a Roman Catholic, in which he calls me Père Kitene, being accustomed to Pères among the French priests; also a letter written in the King's name for him, by the same chief, asking for paraffin oil, the first in Swahili, the second in Luganda. Observe the

Royal signature, 'Kataka Mwanga' (King Mwanga); also a letter from Sembera Mackay, a most excellent man. . . . .

This climate is *not* perfection. I call no climate perfect wherein, if you stand outside for five minutes while sun is shining, with double felt hat on and umbrella up, at any time between 9 a.m. and 4 p.m., you feel (if you are G.L.P., or like him) the effects of it for an hour afterwards in faintness and headache. . . . You might just as well be in a Turkish bath all day as to be here, or, rather, a great deal better, for here decency demands clothes. It's a grand farming climate I've no doubt, damp and broiling."

For some time Pilkington had been feeling urgently the need of more workers. This is summed up in a letter to Mr. Eugene Stock.

"Namirembe, Mengo, Uganda,
October 2nd, 1890.

I sit down to utilize a few moments this evening by writing, in the hope that I may be able to say something that may show people in England how much we want men here. You see I write in the hope that you will be able to find something in this letter which, if put into any of your papers, might induce some at home to come to the help of the Lord against the mighty.

And let me first say that for more than ten weeks I have been here now by myself, except for Smith's short visit, which lasted a fortnight only, and he was half an invalid. People may blame us for leaving one man (and he not in orders) here alone for so long. But, in the first place, Baskerville was to have come back in a month, but was hindered by fever, &c. Secondly, how can we stand by and see the whole country occupied by the Roman Catholic priests (there are eleven of them, besides '*frères*,' I believe; and ten or fourteen coming), especially when a previous occupation is a ground which the Company will recognize for refusing permission to the opposite party to go into any territory?

At the same time, here am I alone here, with work enough ready to hand for ten men in England, not to say here, where hitherto about one day out of every four is lost owing to fever, and the remaining three none the better in consequence. We have every morning in our church from 100 to 300 *eager learners*, for *three* hours, from 6 or 7 a.m. to 9 or 10 a.m. Most of the teaching is done by Natives; I drop in for an hour or so (and they are grateful for this) towards the end; with my other work I can't do more. I am reading Jeremiah with them now, some of them only. If we had, say, a couple of Europeans, with time enough at their disposal to prepare the morning's lesson thoroughly, and to wind up with a general address, I have no hesitation in saying that these numbers would be doubled. After this school and service is over, I am translating each morning till mid-day Romans with Henry Duta; then, after a hasty meal, I sing with all the boys who care to come (teaching the adults to sing I have given up as hopeless, so have the French priests); I am teaching them hymns I have written, and which Deekes very kindly printed at Nassa. In the afternoon, I translate Exodus (two-thirds are done) with Noah. In the cool of the day I visit, and this is, perhaps, the pleasantest work one could have; everywhere I meet with the warmest welcome. I visit Protestants and Roman Catholics alike. Yesterday, the Kimbugwe, the biggest of the Roman Catholic chiefs, gave me 'bugenyi,' or a guest-present of a goat; the second he has given me. In all this work I feel as if an ocean lay before me to be crossed, and I were paddling on the edge of it.

Let me put down what I think we really want, and I don't want to exaggerate in the least. I put down so many men for each sort of work, not that one man would be confined to any one work, but merely expressing by the number of men the amount of work urgently needing doing:—

For Mengo—

Services on Sunday, class for teachers, and communicants' class	1
Class for catechumens and teaching daily in church	1
Visiting and teaching in houses	1
Doctor's work, accounts, &c	1
Translation	1
Itinerating in the neighbourhood within two days	1 (? 3)
Substitute in case of fever either at Mengo or in the country	1
Total for capital	7

Kavirondo	2
Busoga	2
Budu	3
Kyagwe	1
Kalambala's	1
Singo	1
Bulemezi	1
Islands	1 (? 2)
Total for elsewhere	12
Grand total	19
Now in Uganda	4
Expected	6
	10
Extra men urgently needed	9"

The above figures might easily be revised and largely added to in view of recent developments. It is, however, exceedingly interesting to notice the careful way in which Pilkington planned out the field, as he often did later on, in view of the needs of the time. Commenting on these figures he continues :—

"This is without counting Koki and the countries to the north, or Kikuyu, &c., to the east. Besides, the Committee ought to send an extra number of men here, in view of illness and consequent early returns home, and deaths. Walker, I expect, will have gone by the time the next lot of men after Ashe comes.

The expenses, once a man gets here, are next to nothing; the eagerness for learning is the most remarkable thing I have ever seen or heard of in that line.

This country has had hitherto, since the work was started, possibly an average of one Protestant European with a knowledge of the language; one book only of the Bible, St. Matthew, has been hitherto put into the hands of the Natives in their own language, and yet God has used such very small efforts in an amazing way, so much so that I fully believe that if a number of missionaries at all approaching what this country has a right to expect, considering what these men have borne for Christ's sake, and their eagerness to be taught, and their readiness to welcome and support teachers—if this were done, I believe we should soon have Waganda missionaries working throughout Central Africa. To occupy completely this country now is to put out the resources of the Society at 100 per cent. interest; to miss the opportunity of doing so is to allow this country, and with it, perhaps, the whole of Central Africa, to become (God forbid!) Roman Catholic. I remind you that I have the names of 39 chiefs (and if I tried I daresay I could make it 100) who are ready and anxious to support with native food and build for a missionary. Having eased my mind by writing this letter, which I hope you will believe keeps clearly on the near side of exaggeration, although I am an Irishman, I'll stop for to-night. No more news of Ashe; Baskerville expected."

"Sunday, October 4th, 1891.

It is about twelve o'clock, and I am just out from church, where Henry Duta preached an excellent sermon to our usual congregation of a thousand or so; 'the roaring lion conquered by, and to be conquered through, Jesus alone.' I write now, just while I feel strongly what the sight of that congregation and the hearing of Henry Wright Duta's sermon roused in me.

I am astonished that more men haven't come here, considering the opportunities. Where are all the Christian men I knew at Cambridge? I look for their names in every mail, but they are few and far between. Why don't men such as Mr. ——" [here Pilkington mentions several well-known Evangelical clergymen] ? "They would find here as fine a field for work as in the whole world. Our work here is the evangelization of Africa, and how can we, young and inexperienced as we are, take proper charge and direction of a work so difficult and so vast? When I think of myself here by myself, with a large church, needing teaching and guiding and correcting, with hundreds reading daily and bringing all their 'knots' to be 'untied' to me, with marriage difficulties naturally arising in a country just reclaimed from heathenism, and then think of all England's resources for Christian teaching, it does seem, I was going to say, ridiculous, but I would rather say, a cause of wonder, and shame, and tears.

The two facts that impress me most strongly in this country are, the smallness of England's efforts for this country, and the greatness of what God has been pleased to do in spite of it. Why, if Spurgeon or Moody were to come here, they would soon have audiences of immortal souls (faces black, no doubt, if that makes any difference) as large as any they address in England or America, and more receptive, and less hardened, and far more grateful.

I had hoped that the example of Mr. A. O. Williams, a vicar in Leeds, who went out to China, would have been largely followed. To tell you the truth, I was thinking the other day of writing myself to Mr. ——" (one of the clergyman Mr. Pilkington had mentioned above), "and suggesting that he should come here; but perhaps that would seem to him a piece of interference and impertinence. But all the same, I can't but believe it would be a cause of rejoicing to the Church on earth, and to God in heaven, if he, and such as he, did come.

There are several of these Waganda now, who are fit, with a little systematic teaching, to go out as missionaries far and wide. What we want is that (i.) these men should receive the teaching they need, and (ii.) that the whole spiritual tone of the Church here should be so raised as to press out these its best men to far countries. If there is any truth about Missions which all parties accept as an axiom, it is 'Africans for Africa,' and here are men all but ready to supply this long-felt need; and what makes it more urgent still, is that, if these men are not soon working for us, or rather for the Gospel, they will be against the Gospel in the ranks of Roman Catholicism. Of course, in this last sentence I refer to the Waganda generally, not to the few to whom I referred above."

Thus for the greater part of 1891 the mission work at the capital was carried on with only temporary interruptions, due to political difficulties. Meanwhile, events were being enacted in other places which have had a profound bearing upon the subsequent history of Uganda.

Captain Lugard, upon whom lay the onerous task of administering the government of the Uganda district, as the representative of the British East Africa Company, found himself severely handicapped, owing to the want of suitable soldiers.

At the same time, he knew that there was within no great distance from Uganda, and within the territory which had been secured for British influence, a large body of Sudanese under the command of Selim Bey, who had formerly been in the service of Emin Pasha, and who had been left behind when Mr. Stanley's expedition started for the coast.

Not only did Captain Lugard feel that they might form a valuable acquisition to his fighting force, but he considered that it was absolutely necessary to do something to provide for these men, who, if left to themselves, might prove a source of great danger within the British sphere.

He therefore entered into negotiations with Selim Bey, whom he met at Kavalli's on Lake Albert Nyanza, and eventually came to an arrangement with him, by which he and his men were to serve under Captain Lugard, provided permission were accorded by the Khedive, as he regarded himself as pledged to continue in the service of the Khedive, and he refused to enter into any binding contract without leave from him.

Another difficulty arose from the fact that Selim Bey, as Captain Lugard tells us, "wished to stipulate that he should remain in absolute control of his men." This, however, could not be allowed, and eventually "Selim had to give in."

The number of Sudanese left in Selim Bey's force was about 600 fighting men.

Of these, some were distributed throughout a chain of forts established on the border of Unyoro, whilst others were brought on to Uganda for garrison duty there.

On his return to Uganda, Captain Lugard found heavy news awaiting him, to the effect that the British East Africa Company had decided to withdraw from Uganda.

To be obliged to repudiate the solemn treaties which had just been concluded, and to abandon the country to anarchy, was felt by those carrying on the government in Uganda to be as dishonourable as it would be disastrous, and, happily, the matter presented itself in that light to people at home. Missionaries had not sought the protection of the arm of flesh, but now that a civilised government had undertaken responsibilities with regard to the country, it was felt that it could not so lightly dismiss them.

Bishop Tucker was in England at the time, and lost no opportunity of representing the true state of the case, and much sympathy was aroused, and the conscience of England was touched. It was, however, given to the friends of the Church Missionary Society to afford more practical proof of their sympathy than mere paper resolutions, and when, on October 30th, 1891, Bishop Tucker had told his story at the annual meeting of the Gleaners' Union a fund was started by the friends of the C.M.S. gathered at that meeting, though not officially connected with the Society, which produced a sum of no less than £16,000. This, with a sum of £20,000 contributed by the Directors of the Imperial British East Africa Company and their friends, enabled them to continue the occupation of Uganda for another year, the British name was saved from what would have been lasting disgrace, and one more step was taken towards the consolidation of that part of the British Empire, which lies in Eastern Equatorial Africa.

CHAPTER IX.

CIVIL WAR.

"We are living on a volcano," writes the Rev. G. K. Baskerville in his journal on December 4th, 1891—"the whole country is in a ferment. The Roman Catholics started all the trouble by sending men to destroy the Melondo's place in Kyagwe. He is one of our biggest and most respected chiefs. Wisely, he, before taking any hasty measures, went to consult Captain Williams, who told him to go and defend his property. Accordingly yesterday he went, and the king (i.e. the Roman Catholics) has sent four Roman Catholic chiefs after him to *kill him!* Here our friend Mwanga has put his foot into it, and deserves no mercy at the hands of the Company. Well, Williams went to the king and told him that unless he sent counter-orders to stop these men he would fight with him. Our people have acted nobly and kept from violence; we went to see one chief who was for fighting at once, but he promised to refrain out of respect to our opinion and advice. If the Protestants throw themselves upon the Captain and do nothing rash, they will win; but if they act independently they will lose. They are now waiting to hear from the messengers

CIVIL WAR. 161

sent after the chiefs who had gone to fight the Melondo. If he has been killed there will be war, and it will mean the expulsion of the Roman Catholic party, for Williams will aid the Protestants as being the aggrieved party. To-morrow will bring us news. If there is fighting we are to go up to the camp, leaving only one of our number here to protect the property. Our going will show the people that we have no wish to meddle. Pilkington, knowing the language and people, will stop if it is necessary for us to go. Dear plucky old Sembera Mackay, he has visited the king when no one else would go! He has gone unarmed. One of the big Roman Catholic chiefs ordered his men to fire on him, but no one dared to do so, and he walked past all into the king's enclosure. Then he went to see the Kimbugwe, the chief of the Roman Catholic party, and got him to call in his men; he then went to the camp. Captain Williams has been this evening, and expressed himself greatly pleased with the conduct of the Protestants. Being prohibited from walking out, we spent an hour in sowing vegetable-seeds in our garden. 'In Jesus' keeping we are safe and they.' Good-night.

"Dec. 5th.—The morning rose tumultuous; murmurs of war and incessant noise and parading of men. Of course no work could be done. About noon we could hear the Mujasi's war-drums. He is a Roman Catholic, and was the first on a former occasion to commence; then, he pleaded drunkenness as an excuse. Our people have behaved grandly. They have taken no step without the

Captain's permission. One chief of ours was on his way quietly home at about four o'clock, when we, from our garden where we were walking, saw a Roman Catholic chief fire four times on his men. One man was clubbed in the jaw, and a general mêlée seemed unavoidable. The people, however, saw the folly of leaving the immediate vicinity of the capital to avenge a petty insult, and resolved to wait till Williams could be consulted. My man, Tito, was asked to go off to the camp, which he did, and saw the Captain. The Roman Catholic chief is to send his guns to the camp. But the people are still waiting news of Melondo's fate; this will bring matters to a crisis. If he is killed, nothing, it would seem, can avert terrible war. We hear that Martin has crossed the Nile, and should therefore be here by Wednesday. We can have no public services to-morrow, for it would never do for the people to assemble as a body."

The next letter from Pilkington, written on December 7th, 1891, shows how, amid all the turmoil, the work steadily progressed.

"We have just avoided war by the skin of our teeth for the third or fourth time. I am thankful to say the provocation (as Captain Williams admitted) was mainly, if not entirely, on the Roman Catholic side this time. Had there been war, Captain Williams would have helped the Protestants.

Till this disturbance, our work was going on, to all external appearance, splendidly, ten or twelve classes each morning (Roscoe was able to start one with Sembera's help, in Swahili, as soon as he

CIVIL WAR. 163

came), and between 500 and 700 people in church each morning, then a class for teachers and others at 2 p.m. for *Pilgrim's Progress*. I had sixty people (twelve boys, the rest adults) who want to be baptized. I hope some of these will be baptized next Sunday. The intelligence and the earnestness of some of them, and of others who were baptized a fortnight ago, has struck me very much, and given me great encouragement and pleasure, not for their own sakes only, but because, being all pupils of our elders, their clear knowledge in many cases of Gospel truth, and evident earnestness, are the surest evidence of the fitness of those who taught them. I wish I could send you in full some of Henry's sermons. Some of them have been logical forcible, interesting Scriptural explanations of the work of Christ for sinners. He is a very able man; he would be above the average in Europe. I doubt that he has his equal in ability in Africa. How far his superiority is due to the Universities' Mission (he was with them at Zanzibar), I do not know; but certainly his sermons are compositions, not rambling discourses, and are delivered admirably.

Ephesians and Philippians, and some of Colossians and 1 Timothy, I have translated with Henry and Sembera; I am waiting to finish Genesis and Exodus, in order to get all the New Testament done first. If that could be printed and sent out quickly we would thoroughly revise it. I want to get time for studying the language more thoroughly than I have yet been able to do; perhaps I may be able to succeed in this when Ashe comes, of whom we know only that he left Usambiro about a month ago. I hope to enclose two grammatical sheets which I have made, and which Collins has copied two or three times, so that the men have a sort of substitute for a grammar. Martin's caravan is expected in two days; Captain Lugard by Christmas.

Oh, for books and reading-sheets! and slates and slate-pencils! and MEN! It is delightful beginning to be able to teach these people who are so eager to learn, not by pouring a flood of wisdom over them, as one might pump water on a duck's back, but by question and answer (teaching, when one has anything worth knowing to teach, is the noblest calling in the world). To preach in a language is easy comparatively, but to teach in it—but, till one can do that, it is not much good. But are there not many in England who love teaching, and, above all, teaching the truth of God, who have but little scope at home? They would find a field here, teaching young, teaching old, teaching morning, noon, and night; and oh, so warmly appreciated, so attentively listened to, so gratefully remembered as Mackay, and O'Flaherty, and Ashe, and Gordon are."

"December 14th, 1891.

Mail goes to-morrow; I have addressed Ephesians, Philippians, Colossians, and my two sheets to you.

Henry, in preaching yesterday on the loaves and fishes, said that, really, for those who think, the growth of the plantains on the tree is just as wonderful; 'fools say it grows, because, I suppose, it is its nature'; but really it is a miracle. And, if a miracle is a thing which we cannot in the least understand, he was right, and I believe that this thought was original on his part.

Forty-seven persons—thirty-three men, four women, and ten boys—were baptized yesterday. I had had classes for them for some time, and finally examined each one separately (six I told to wait till I could teach them further); the forty-seven seemed to me to have an intelligent trust in Christ as their own Saviour, and an honest desire to lead a new life by His help: pray for them especially, and for us.

The 'Nalinya' (queen-sister) brought four girls yesterday, whom she asked me to prepare for baptism. I am wondering whether Henry's wife could help in this work; it shows that ladies are wanted here."

The next development of the political situation is described in private letter from Pilkington.

"Namirembe, Mengo,
December 27th, 1891.

I am writing to-day (the anniversary of our arrival in Buganda) to tell you, while I remember clearly, some events of this morning which will interest you. This morning . . . . about 6.30 a.m. . . . . I heard Henry calling to one of my boys. I answered him, and, getting out of bed and putting on some clothes, called him in. He and Sembera, Samwili, Mika, and Stefano had come to tell me that the king wished to become a

Protestant, having quarrelled with the Roman Catholics. I took them into Roscoe's house and we consulted about it. The king had sent them to us. We told them finally to tell the king that, in so far as the matter was a political one, it was none of our business. . . . We further advised them to do nothing till they had consulted with Captain Williams. We then had prayer with them and they went to Captain Williams. He, we hear, will not allow the king at present to become a Protestant, as it would, he says, mean war, and an alliance between the Roman Catholics and Mohammedans. We shall do nothing more in the matter at present. The king's proposal comes, I suppose, only from political motives. Really we have not much to do with it."

"December 28th, 10.30 p.m.

I am sitting up to-night till midnight, when Collins is to relieve me, and then Roscoe him, because threats of burning our houses down have been made by the Roman Catholics. Last night, their temporary Church was burnt down, we suppose most likely by some of the king's people, six of whose houses the Roman Catholics have lately burnt down, besides killing four men. . . . . The Pokino has just been round to see our guard, and he brings the news that the king has returned to the Roman Catholic side, having received a present. . . . . His people of the capital, thirty in number, have, however, determined to join the Protestant side. . . . . It is a terrible pity that, at this critical time, we have not more men, and especially more men who know, if not Luganda, at least Swahili. . . . . These houses, if fired once, burn, every scrap of them, like tinder, only more so; hence our precautions. A chap can steal up and throw on a smouldering torch, and your first warning is the smell of smoke and the crackling of the fire, which is almost inextinguishable."

"January 20th, 1892.

. . . . I ought to have told you how I went to the king, after the events I started with, and asked to see him alone, as I had things to speak of which I thought he would rather hear in private. He turned out all his chiefs, keeping one man only with him. I then explained what we thought of his proposed turning Protestant; I told him his soul was of no more value in our sight, or in God's, than the meanest of his subjects, and that we wanted real, not nominal Protestants. I reminded him of his father Mutesa's opinion, that 'the English had the truth.' I began this by saying, 'Your father, Mutesa, was a clever man,' to which he answered the single word, 'Kitalo,' which means, a marvel. I finally told him to do what he believed God wished him to do."

On January 19th, Pilkington gives voice to the great desire for further books and reading-sheets in a letter to Mr. Wigram, of which the following is an extract.

"I cannot express the earnest longing we have for these books: what I feel is, that the whole future of Africa is in the balances here now, and delay in the arrival of these books may tell fatally. I believe *any* expense ought to be incurred to deliver these books at the very earliest opportunity. It is terribly trying thus writing for books which don't come, or if they do, come in driblets of 200 or 500, when we want thousands; 500 Gospels sell off in two days at a price which, at any rate, fully pays for carriage.

The Roman Catholics are rushing in in the meantimes. We pray every day for books; really, I think that men are less important.

The new Church is very fine: the labour, I calculate, would have cost £1,000 at threepence per man per day. I don't think people at home at all realize yet what a fine people the Waganda are, and what an opportunity there is here to advance God's Kingdom."

A few days later, the storm-cloud, which had been so long gathering, suddenly burst, but, before giving the graphic and temperate description of the conflict and the circumstances which led up to it from the pen of Mr. Baskerville, it may be as well to remind ourselves of the description of the political parties in Uganda which have been already mentioned. We use the word "political" advisedly, for, though they bore religious names, their aims were political rather than religious, and, as a further confirmation of this, we learn that the Roman Catholic party on the one hand, and the Protestant on the other, were known as the Wa Franza and the Wa Inglesa.

The cause of this unfortunate division of two

professedly Christian parties is not far to seek.

Picture a small body of men at work in the centre of gross heathenism, seeking to lead the people to a knowledge of the true God and of His Son Jesus Christ.

Just as they are beginning to gain an influence over the people, another party of men appears on the scene, of a different nationality and teaching a different creed, and bearing in their hands large presents with which to ingratiate themselves with the chiefs and people.

Is it a wonder that the people of Uganda were bewildered, and that between the followers of each Mission there grew up a rivalry which permeated the whole life of the people?

None could regret this state of things more than the Protestant Missionaries, and, as far as possible, they tried to steer clear of such controversies. It was impossible, however, not to be affected by such a state of things as Mr. Baskerville describes.

"Namirembe, Uganda,
January 31st, 1892.

I know you will like some particular account of the terrible events of the last few days. I wrote to you a long letter when in Budu, telling you something of the state of the country with reference to the work of the Company, and also with reference to the position of the two great religious parties. Some six weeks ago, I think anyone who had been in Uganda, during the first twelve months of the

Company's administration, would have said that the country was rapidly quieting down again after its past troubles. The policy of the Company had been one which, taking the goodwill of the Protestant party for granted, had always rather favoured the Papist party; most careful had both Captains Lugard and Williams been to let no national or religious prejudices seem in any way to influence them in their administration. A year had passed since the expedition commanded by Captain Lugard had arrived here at the capital, just a few days previous to the arrival of Bishop Tucker and his party. War had been staved off from time to time, the Company contriving to balance the parties; meanwhile, the Protestants ceding point after point for the sake of avoiding collision. The Resident has certainly done all in his power to avoid war—even swallowed personal insults rather than undo the work of twelve months—and it has been with the greatest regret that he has been forced into violent measures. Troubles began to brew about the middle of last month, just after the Company's new steel boat had left for the south end of the Lake, commanded by Mr. Bagge. But, before this, it had been proved on some four occasions that the Protestants were the aggrieved party. First, some six months ago, in August, a number of houses in the capital were burnt wantonly by the Roman Catholics, including the place of Ham Mukasa, a man who was wounded in the battle of Rubaga Hill. Second, in Budu, Kamswaga, King of Koki, a country south-west of Budu, was sent for, it was

CIVIL WAR. 171

said, by the king, to turn the Protestants out of Budu ; this was done to a great extent, and, because of the unsettled condition of the country, I was unable for a month to move on from Walker's place at Masaka. Third, with regard to Kaganda, one of the islands which had been secured to the Protestant party, the Roman Catholics sent one hundred guns to turn out the chief sent by the king. Fourth, about the middle of December, the Mulondo, a prominent Protestant chief in Kyagwe, hearing that his place was likely to be attacked, asked leave to go down and protect it. Leave was refused by the king, but Captain Williams told him to go. On this, the king despatched four leading Roman Catholic chiefs, with five hundred guns, with orders to kill the Mulondo wherever they found him. This angered Captain Williams, and he told the king that he must at once send off messengers to stop these men ; and further, he told us that if the Mulondo were to be killed, that the camp would be forced into war, which meant taking the Protestant side and probably driving out the Papists from the country. The messengers were recalled, and so the affair blew over. On December 9th, a large caravan for the Company had arrived, bringing a great quantity of ammunition. This had put the king into a great state of excitement, and the day after Christmas Day, the king sent a message to the Katikiro, saying that he wished to become a Protestant. He saw that the power was on the Protestant side, a large caravan had arrived, Captain Lugard had returned as far as Budu with a large number of Sudanese soldiers, recovered from the two regiments of Emin Pasha's, left after Stanley had passed on to the coast. And he had been put in a further state of alarm by the Kimbugwe, the leading Roman Catholic chief, sending a party of men to destroy all his *bhang* pipes. These men had burned one of the king's houses and killed four men. That night, he asked for a Protestant guard to stand over his place. The Roman Catholics then came to our party, proposing to depose the king and put one of Kalema's sons, his nephew, on to the throne. To this the Protestants would not agree. Mwanga was bad, but what could they hope from a boy who had been in training at the Roman Catholic station of Bukumbe, near Usambiro? Accordingly, the king saw that the time was come for the weather-cock to shift. He was not, however, to be allowed to change his religion so easily. The French Bishop, the plan of deposing him being frustrated, thought that it would never do to lose the king from the Papist party, and went out and put the enormity of his sin before him, exhorting him to come to confession. 'First,' said Mwanga, 'I must have a present. My men have been killed, and my house burned.' 'All right,' says Monseigneur, 'you shall have forty tusks of ivory.' 'As soon as I get them,' says the king, 'you shall confess me.' Captain Lugard reached Mengo on December 31st, and we at once felt the position of the Company secure in the country. We had heard news a little before, that the English papers were talking of the probable early withdrawal of the Company from Uganda, and, about the same time, arrived a fresh party of French priests, who, it is evident, gave this information to their people, representing to the king that this was only a trading Company, and that it would be against their interests to fight; and, further, that if they were about to withdraw, and if the Roman Catholic party held out a little longer, they would soon have everything their own way. You will see, as I go on, how this gave great confidence again to the king, and caused him, so far, to defy the power of the Company as to challenge them to fight him.

On Friday, January 22nd, about mid-day, we heard three or four shots fired quite close by, and reports came in to say a Protestant had been murdered by the Roman Catholics. The Protestants immediately went to report the matter to Captain Lugard, also telling him that the Roman Catholics were guarding the body and refused them leave to take it away for burial. Lugard immediately left to see the king, when he was kept waiting for two hours—in itself a great insult to a Commissioner of the Queen. At last, he was taken in to the king, who professed ignorance of the whole occurrence, and asked the chiefs sitting round to tell him the whole story. Lugard said that before he could hear anything, the body must be removed, for it was a disgrace to the king and his country. A Roman Catholic and Protestant were immediately sent off to remove the body. Captain Lugard, too, reminded the king how that, when he had first come to the country, he had told him that, owing to the state of affairs and that a murder would probably cause civil war, any murderer must be executed. The king said he remembered all this, and that the words were very good. Captain Lugard, not feeling well after his long waiting in the sun, left Du Wallah, a Somali in whom he places great confidence, to be present at the subsequent trial. The man was brought in, and told the following story:—His gun had been stolen from him by one of the Katikiro's men, and he had taken his case before the Katikiro, who had promised to see his gun restored, if his story should be proved true. Two or three days elapsed without anything being done, and then this man thought that, as he had not been given another gun, he had better try and take one from the Protestants by force. Accordingly, he made a regular plot. He bought some beer and sat in his gateway offering it for sale—the plan being to take the gun from the first Protestant who should offer to buy it. He had several companions ready to help him, and two men inside his fence with loaded guns. A man presently came by, and came up to buy the beer, asking first to taste it. An argument then arose, and a man slipped behind him, seized his gun, and the whole party rushed into the fence. The Protestant and his friends followed, and were fired on by the two men with guns inside, one shot killing the man. The Protestant fired one shot without effect. The king, on hearing that the thief had been followed into his fence, said that he was, by the law of Uganda, justified in the subsequent murder, and that the prisoner must be set at liberty. It was late before Du Wallah returned, but early next morning he was sent back with a note, asking the king to reconsider this decision, and telling him that, if he persisted in it, he would lead his country into war. For some time Du Wallah was not admitted, but he insisted on delivering the letter into the king's own hand. With the king were the Kimbugwe, the Kanta, and the Musalosleb, all leading Roman Catholic chiefs. The latter read the letter to the king, and when he came to Lugard's words about probable war if this decision was adhered to, the king caught him up, saying, 'What's that he says about war? Let him come and fight, if he will'; and all the others began to laugh at Du Wallah. Du Wallah told the king that he was a Mohammedan, and that he had no leaning to either Roman Catholics or Protestants, but that he had never known such an obviously unfair and rotten judgment given anywhere; and that he could assure the king that Captain Lugard had done his best to avoid war and give justice to all parties. 'What answer shall I take to my master?' said Du Wallah. The Kanta said, 'Tell him that, if he fights, we shall take all his wealth, and wipe out the English from the country.' This was too much for Captain Lugard to stand, and he sent to demand the person of the murderer; if he were given up, the insulting message would be pardoned. Our people went to the king, and asked him why, when, in an exactly similar case, one of the Mugema's men had killed a Roman Catholic, the Mugema had been fined? The king talked about exchanging bodies, and so being quits. No, said our men, we have other grievances besides this for which we have never had justice at all. Captain Lugard, the king and Roman Catholics seeming determined to defy him, resolved at last on stringent measures. On Saturday night, some 500 rifles were served out to the Protestant leaders for distribution, and a large quantity of ammunition; for even then Lugard hoped that it would not be necessary for him personally to interfere.

On Sunday, the 24th, of course services were out of the question. The Katikiro had been told by the Roman Catholics that if the Protestants did not fight they were a pack of cowards; and further, in the morning, as Roscoe had Sembera Mackay and a few others at a Bible Reading, we heard shots, the outcome of which we soon heard had been the murder of a man belonging to the Katikiro. Further Bible-reading was abandoned, and soon our whole place was deserted. We went off to have a short English service together; before we had finished Sembera came, summoning us to go up to the fort, for both sides were all prepared for fighting. We, however, refused unless sent for officially by Captain Lugard, and, even when he did send for us, we said that we could not consent to go and leave all our things. He kindly sent forty men, and, after a quarter of an hour's hurried packing, we were off about twelve o'clock to Kampala. At the marketplace we met Sembera, who, on hearing that most of our goods were still left behind, said he should go off and find a guard for the station. About 12.30 we arrived at the camp, and as we were quietly sitting in the house we heard four guns. Lugard had previously sent demanding the original murderer, the murderer of the morning, and the Kanta, who had sent the insulting message, to be all given up. The man who had murdered the Katikiro's man was sent in, and a soldier of the Company who had been captured in the morning escaped. The Kanta refused

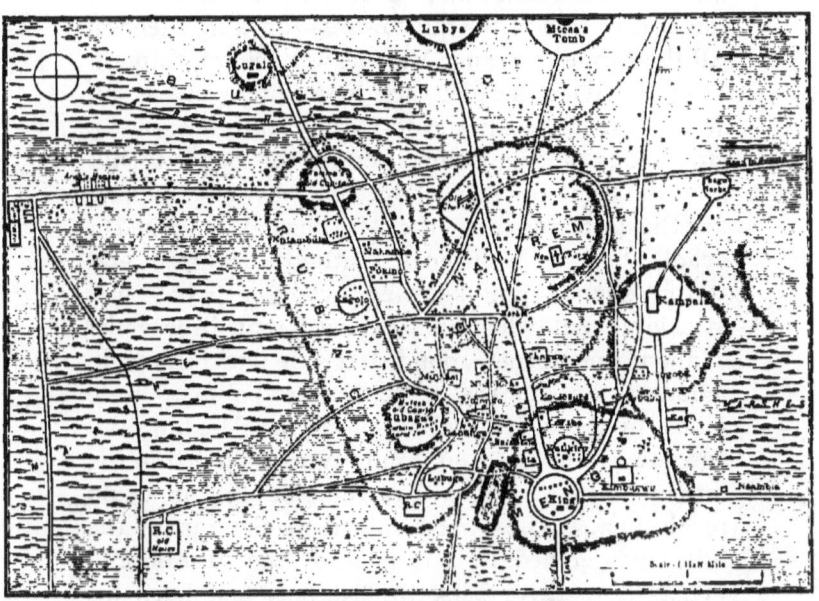

Rough plan of the capital, marking the chief centres.

to come, and the first murderer could not be given up at all. Well, so anxious was Captain Lugard to avoid war that he had sent a further message demanding only the first murderer to be given up, and other affairs would be overlooked, when these four gunshots sent us all flying out to seek the cause.

We saw smoke over at the foot of Mengo, close by Mr. Stokes's garden, and soon other shots followed in a regular fusillade, and we could see the Papists fleeing before the Protestants. On the top of Rubaga Hill was some sharp fighting, and soon the Roman Catholic new church and houses were in one immense blaze, and the Protestants pushing on down the farther side of the hill towards the king's fences. All this while the camp Maxims were silent, Captain Lugard having decided not to interfere unless an attack was made on the fort. Presently we saw a large body of men coming down the opposite hill from the Kimbugwe's at the double, obviously making for the fort, and now the Maxims both opened a deadly fire. The Roman Catholics stopped and stared round, not knowing who or what was attacking, but when they realised that it was the cannon, they turned round and ran like rabbits in amongst the bananas. We hear some forty were killed by these first volleys from the Maxims, and and the Kimbugwe and Kanta were wounded in the former's house, where they thought no gun could reach them. These men rallied at the top of the hill, and, joined by the men of the Musalosalo, managed to drive back the Katikiro and burn his house. Countless houses were now in flames, and one could scarcely see for the smoke. The Katikiro retreated on Kampala, and now Captain Lugard sent out Captain Williams with the Sudanese soldiers, who soon settled matters—the Katikiro's men and Pokino's re-formed behind him, and they went on burning all the Roman Catholic houses and driving the Papists far away towards the Lake. Leniency alone prevented them from driving them right into the water. The Protestants were victorious, the king's flag had been hauled down, but deep sorrow had come to us—the very first guns fired had killed Sembera Mackay, our best and ablest man and most deeply-taught Christian. He had gone to find a guard for our place, and, as he was passing some houses where some of the king's slaves lived, he was shot at and died almost immediately—dear, brave Sembera, whom every one loved, and of whom I never heard a disparaging word, has entered into his reward—and we are left to sorrow over his loss, and to trust our God to supply his place. Two other Church elders have been wounded, and two Protestant chiefs, one badly so. The doctors have their hands full every day now, and I expect never had such work before. Rubaga Hill had been taken by the Mugema and Pokino, together with the Mwanika—they were never once repulsed, but carried everything before them. It had been impossible to bring the priests over to the fort, and their station was manned by Roman Catholic chiefs who made a determined resistance; one of their black Hausa doctors, who foolishly fought in person, was shot dead. The priests were all conducted to the fort the same evening, their place being a total wreck.

We returned the same evening to our station, the whole of the Roman Catholics having fled. The king, with some 300 guns, had fled to the small island of Burungugi, just half a mile from the shore, about two hours from Mengo. Here he had his store and had sent all his wives and wealth, and here it was that the Christians so long withstood the Mohammedans. Here they thought that they were quite safe, remembering the unsuccessful attacks of the Mohammedans. The great object, of course, of the Company was now to get hold of the king and restore him to his throne, knowing that he was a mere puppet, and, if once in their hands, would do all they told him—of course they did not want the old chiefs back again, but the king alone. They sent several messages asking him to return, but he sent back to say that he wished to come but was guarded and unable to escape. Friday morning the French Bishop came to say he wished to leave the fort, but Lugard refused him several times officially. At last he came to say that unless he was forcibly detained he should go, for these were his orders from Rome. Accordingly, he went with all the priests except two, who, however, followed soon afterwards. He promised Lugard to persuade the king to return, and pass on himself to Sesse, and when there do all he could to protect Mr. Bagge, who is daily expected back with the boat, and also to send messages to Budu to his people to protect Ashe, Walker, and Smith, who are there at Masaka. He did none of these things, but went to the king, and he, abetted by Kisali, a blacksmith, a former pupil of Mackay, against the wish of all the Roman Catholic priests and chiefs, refused the king permission to return to Mengo. Does it not seem as if the French Mission is just God's appointed instrument to complete the confusion of Rome here in Uganda? He, moreover, sent to Lugard to come with his Maxim and kill all the Roman Catholics on the island and then he might get the king! Little, I expect, did he think that this would be so literally done. Yesterday, at 10 a.m., Captain Williams marched out with one of the Maxims and some hundred soldiers, together with the majority of the Protestant party; he hid his force on the Lake shore in the trees, watching his opportunity. Presently two women of the king's came off to get food in a canoe, and he sent out two soldiers to take them prisoners; the canoe-men, seeing this, made off to inform the people on the island. Two of the French priests camped on the beach of the island now came out and fired at the soldiers. These shots and the report of the canoe-men soon brought all the Roman Catholics to the shore, and some entered some of the canoes to come across and recover the women, evidently thinking that only a few peasants had seized them. Meanwhile, Williams had his Maxim brought into position, and I expect they were surprised at the warm reception they met with—the people on shore were quickly fleeing, and eleven canoes were sunk. On the first noise of firing, the French Bishop went to the king, and when he ascertained that it was really the camp soldiers, he got into the king's one canoe, and they made off together, and we hear are now in Sesse Island. The paddlers, on the first noise of shots, had all made off, and thus the Roman Catholic party were left absolutely without canoes. Many tried to make rough rafts of reeds and leaves, which quickly sank. The Mujadi, one of the principal Roman Catholic chiefs, fought furiously, and finally hid himself amongst the trees, and has not yet been found. The Kangoo was killed, and a great number of the Roman Catholics, but not one man of ours was so much as wounded.

The camp and people are making every exertion to recover the king, who they feel sure is kept back against his will. If it should prove impossible to get him, the Mohammedan King Mbogo, Mutesa's brother, will be invited in as king. The people are very strong on royalty, and would prefer Mwanga back to anybody else, in spite of all his failings."

A letter of Pilkington's, dated April 1st, tells of the King's return, "having given the Roman Catholics the slip," and so he says, " there is a prospect of peace and security and firm government." With regard to the result, he continues in the same letter, "the rejoicing here is tremendous. I hope the work won't suffer for all this political success; however, it has been God's doing. You know very well that this is not the sort of thing we count success, or care for, except in so far as it opens the door for the Gospel. . . . The English flag at last is really hoisted on Mengo."

Reference has already been made to the serious loss to the Mission caused by the death of Sembera Mackay.

Pilkington's letter about him furnishes us with such a beautiful instance of his power of sympathy, and of the brotherly relations existing between him and his African colleagues, that with it we may fitly close this sad story of civil war in Uganda.

"Namirembe, Uganda,
25th January, 1892.

DEAREST MOTHER,—

I must write to you to-night, though I can hardly see for tears, and my heart is bursting with sorrow. Our faithful friend, our dear, dear Brother, Sembera, was shot yesterday; awful day. The very first to fall; fittest for death; God took him. Praise to His Name, but we are left bereaved. Oh, Mother, you don't know how I loved him, and love him still with all my soul; everyone loved him; the best, the bravest, the noblest, the wisest. Never to see his kind face in this world again, or hear his cheery voice, and I was safe in Kampala; I couldn't even bid him good-bye for the last time. But good-bye or no, God was with him, for he walked with God.

Our joy, our comfort, our right hand is gone; praise be to God who gave us such a treasure for a while, and now has taken it to Himself; but it is hard to flesh and blood. He is a loss greater than any almost I can think of to our work here; he was respected by both parties, and his humble, useful, consistent life has been, and will be, an eloquent sermon on the grace of God. God will not suffer His Work to suffer,

'But O for the touch of a vanish'd hand,
And the sound of a voice that is still.'

His is the joy of meeting with his Lord; ours is the

pain, and the sure and certain hope of glory. His dear name is written for ever on my heart.

He leaves a wife and a baby girl—one of his boys has asked to be with me. His last words were: 'God is taking my soul.' I won't in this letter, or now, write of the other events of that sad day. This letter is, alas! heavy enough, when it has this one burden to bear, that 'a prince and a great man has fallen to-day in Israel.'

Your loving son,
G. L. Pilkington."

CHAPTER X.

LANGUAGE STUDY.

The war over, the next few months afforded splendid opportunities for working at the language. As, however, the strain of recent events had been rather great, Pilkington was persuaded to take a holiday, of which he gives the following realistic description :—

"It was on Saturday, 26th March, that I started for our 'country seat' by the Lake (if I may so call it); it is called Kuilwe, and is a peninsula running out into the Lake, pretty well due south of Mengo.

As I was going partly for change—except for my visit to Sowe, you remember, I've been in the capital for fifteen months—I didn't intend to rough it more than I could help, and so I took, not only our donkey (ours is admittedly the best in the country, his only rival, also ours, had to be left, alas! to the tender mercies of the Roman Catholics in Budu), but also one of my cows and its calf; for, in this country, a calfless cow is unmilkable; I wish, by-the-way, father would send me directions thereanent (as John Paton says in his most delightful book, which I've been again reading with renewed pleasure) when and how should a calf be taken from its mother?

You will like to hear what I took with me exactly. Let me tell you, by way of loads. My porters consisted of a Muganda, whom I asked from his master, James Kabuga, late Mission servant; three boys of Ashe's, whom he was kind enough to lend me; and two boys of my own—six in all. The loads were: (1) a large bag containing blankets (three of them, Jaeger's), a mattress, a mosquito net, a change of clothes, pyjamas, towel, soap, brushes, etc.; this was carried by the Muganda. (2) My tin writing-desk, which contained besides writing materials, tea, coffee, sugar, saccharine, quinine, pills, anchovy paste, a little cheese, a little fresh butter in two small Liebig pots, some needles and cotton for use and also for presents (a fine needle is worth twenty shells, a coarse one fifteen; by-the-way, I'll try and send you some Uganda needles in this letter), and some fish-hooks. (3) A bucket, containing knife, fork, spoon, cup, jug, with some home-made bread, wheat and Indian corn mixed, made into a kind of toast or biscuit by a second turn in the oven (you know my oven is a large native pot inverted, with a bonfire of grass on the top), and some broken biscuit of the kind that, at Uppingham, we called 'dog-rocks,' but which are a considerable luxury out here. (4) An iron basin, containing a kettle and a saucepan, with a folding chair; the two remaining boys carried my three water bottles (which I filled with milk), and looked after the donkey and cow and calf. I actually started from Ashe and Walker's place; they are living in what was the place of a Roman Catholic whom I knew well, and in whom I was, and am, rather interested. He told me that he was a Roman Catholic because it was they who followed the teaching of the New Testament, *e.g.*, ' Where was the cross that we took up in following Jesus?' I told him that, if he convinced me of that, I, too, would become a Roman Catholic, as there was no other authority we followed but the Word of God. We have had a little correspondence since the war, and, in his letter, he asks me where our Fold is, and where is our Shepherd? However, this is a digression.

Walker, as I started, proved himself a true prophet of evil, when he warned me that my newly-cobbled boots would not hold out. (I've turned cobbler of late; mended my dear old Jaeger boots with buffalo hide, only the soles of them. Jaeger boots are the best for Africa; this would do for an advertisement!)

At last, we are off—loads in front, cow and calf, donkey, boy, and, last of all, myself. It was a lovely walk through a sort of country lane, sweet smelling trees every now and again making the air very pleasant; then up some hill-side, from the top of which a splendid view of Lake, creek, and island is visible; then along the side of a valley, with the rich banana plantations crowding up on each side from the wooded valley below; then down into the valley, where there is a scrap of what I suppose a tropical forest is like on a more extensive scale; and then through a river, or rather a marsh, which stretches, perhaps, half-a-mile in width, and for which the donkey comes in very useful, unless some strong and not too lazy Baganda happens to be at hand to take one over; it is really amazing how these men carried me, who am no light weight—I expect I'm as heavy now as ever I was. I mount on the shoulders of one, who kneels down to receive me; with the help of a second, he stands up, and then up to his middle in water, and up and down banks three feet in height, he carries me alone.

I stopped half-way, and had some refreshment in the way of milk, bread and butter, and cheese. Then on again, not waiting for the mid-day sun to go down at all, for I wanted to be in early, that a house and some sort of a bed might be got ready for me. I was now going along by the Lake shore, and in a couple of hours, it was evident that we were on a peninsula, about a mile broad, running out into the Lake. It was like a park, the soil was very rocky and sandy; in consequence the grass was short and light for this country, and not unlike a rather poor meadow at home; clumps of trees were sprinkled about in a very pretty way, some of the trees rather like laurel (a thing which I hate), which greatly increased the artificial appearance of the place; the Lake that bounded it added to the effect. Here, I rode the donkey for a bit, while my boy Serukwaya, quite of his own accord, carried the tired calf; we were the only two who needed either milk or a lift.

At last, we have reached our destination; it is not yet three o'clock, I should think (a watch that will go has long been a thing of the past with me). Kudumusinayi, one of the two tenants, though each

LANGUAGE STUDY.

has several under him, and underlings of underlings also abound, gives me a warm welcome. I knew him as our tenant at Natete.

My boys and I are allotted a small round house, not as big as an average Irish cabin, and yet the seven of us slept and lived there very comfortably for three days. I found the house with a hole in the roof, the floor deep covered with ancient grass and dust, and a very suspicious bed in the corner! Suspicious, in that I fancied that many creatures other than human slept in it.

However, when I came back from a short exploration of our property, I found the hole mended, the floor swept, and a very nice bed in the course of erection. I also found quite a crowd collected to see me; I tried to make friends with them, and invited them to a Service in the morning. Then I had food—coffee, plantains, potatoes, fish, and bread and butter. They also cooked in profusion for my boys. Next morning, about fifty, nearly all men, came to the service. I read and explained and made them say the Ten Commandments, and then pointing out how we could not establish our own righteousness, tried to show them what Jesus had done for us; then we had the Commandments as in the Communion Service, and a few Prayers.

I was told that many of the fishermen still believe that if they take a fish in their hands, immediately all the fish will die; I told them of the quantities of fish I had seen caught on the North Sea; was it only the Uganda fish that dreaded hooks?

I had another little Service in the afternoon, and then went coasting along for a bit in a canoe, and visited a remarkable cave on the end of a long, low-lying, narrow peninsula: the rock which formed the cave was twenty feet high, and covered with trees and creepers, making a very pretty object as seen from a sandy piece of beach, near which I want to get a house built, that will receive any of us who might go to teach or for a change; of course it would be part of the people's business to build for us, either there or at the Capital.

The trees on the island were, some of them, magnificent; three kinds of fruit grow there—empafu, something between plums and olives; ensali, something like a very acid cherry, and eroyidu, not unlike sloes; there is also some coffee. I saw lots of monkeys, crocodiles, and hippos.

On the Monday, I visited each house in the place; men, women, and children, might reach, perhaps, 200, if the ground were full cultivated, 1,000 might be supported there.

If only the reading sheets and other books would come soon; among all these people, five only, I think, had books at all.

I came back on Tuesday, just in time to see the king return, to inaugurate, I hope, a new era in his strange and eventful reign. In writing in detail as I have done, I have this special object: I wish, when the country is quiet, to undertake some itinerating work, in Kyagwe especially, which is the province between this and the Nile; possibly in the Islands too. You will, from this account, be able to understand a little better how I am likely to live while engaged in this sort of work, which, however much I appreciate the privilege and the need of translational work, is what I came for most of all, and which is, moreover, indispensable if the translation is to be done properly."

In April, news was received of the death of Mr. de Winton, son of Sir Francis de Winton, in Toro. Pilkington felt his loss keenly, as the following words shew: " We were all of us here, I know, very fond of him; he was a most delightful companion. He brightened many an evening in this house, and I spent many a pleasant hour with him when he was alone at Kampala. I was the invalid then; and he would keep me interested for hours together with stories of his American and other experiences.

It is hard to believe that I shall never hear his cheery voice again in this world. . . . . He didn't hide his light, but was known by the others at Kampala, and, indeed, by the Christians here, as a Christian man; he sometimes came to our Luganda service in the morning, and often to the Lord's Supper."

It is hard to over-estimate the value of such a man holding an official position in the Mission Field.

On his return to the Capital, Pilkington devoted himself once more to his translational work, and on June 2nd, 1892, he wrote at some length to Mr. Lang, giving some description of the progress of his work, and offering some valuable suggestions as the important subject of Language Study:—

"I have two or three matters connected with translation and language, that I have for some time wished to write to you about, and I take this opportunity, as, having had fever twice lately, the Doctor recommends me not to do so much translation as I have been doing, and so I'll write this letter instead. The first point is about the translation of the New Testament in particular; in ten days or so, if nothing occurs to hinder my work, I should finish Corinthians. Hebrews is finished,— the New Testament will then be all translated. Gordon took the Gospels, and Acts. Ashe, I believe, translated 1 John; and I shall have sent the rest, when Hebrews and Corinthians shall have gone. I am afraid you may think that the work has been too quickly done to have been well done. I want to explain to you how this is not really the case. There never was anyone who more than I entered into other men's labours. I found several men, H. W. Duta far ahead of them all, with a good knowledge of the whole New Testament; they knew Swahili, and were thoroughly practised in translating from Swahili into Luganda; there were none of the ordinary difficulties of searching for words to translate the important terms and phrases of the Gospel; these were not only at hand, but so far stereotyped by extensive use, that any radical changes, had I wished to make them, could hardly have been justifiable. This fact made the work possible, and it also makes me hope that the translation (thanks not to me, but to my predecessors and to the Waganda themselves), is a better one than a first translation into a new language generally can be; it has been, really, beaten out during many years by the best brains among the Waganda themselves, with the help of Mackay, Ashe, Gordon, Walker, and the others who have been here. So you see there were exceptional facilities. I think there was also an exceptional need, for I should think there was hardly ever so large a body of Christians, in modern days, so eager to learn, for so long a time with only one book of the Bible in their own tongue, and that in such limited quantities. There is a special reason, too, which makes me long for Luganda books: the idea has gained ground that—as no can know much of Christianity without being able to read, and knowing Swahili—therefore, reading, and a knowledge of Swahili makes a man a Christian—nothing will quite eradicate this motion, I think, but books in Luganda. There is one defect in the translation, which is at the same time, I think, a merit in a first translation: I have not always translated, or tried to translate, the same Greek word by the same Luganda; I preferred, in the present state of my knowledge, to leave the question open by translating it variously; better leave the decision till the time when we shall be in a position to be sure that the selected translation is the best. There is another defect which, I'm afraid, could not and cannot be remedied—the use of one Luganda word for two or three different Greek ones; for, of course, Luganda, though a very rich language, may happen to be weak just where Greek is strong; we have used one word for the Greek πνεῦμα, ψυχή (in sense of soul), and καρδία—the word for 'spirit,' was one of those stereotyped words I spoke of, and I never thought of changing it (Ashe, however, the other day, said it was still not too late—but I think it is)—otherwise, I think I should have preferred a word meaning 'air' or 'wind,' to the word chosen, which simply means soul or spirit in a metaphysical sense, and has no material meaning. Again, the word for '*to love*' and '*to will*' is the same in Luganda; hence, 'according to the will of God' might mean 'the love of God.' Again, for 'to accept' and 'to believe,' there is only one word. I had intended not to attempt much of the Old Testament, until I had gone home and read Hebrew, but lately, I have started at the Psalms and Joshua. Joshua is finished (but I want to go through it with Henry), and about fifty of the Psalms. About half of Genesis and Exodus is done, too; but I have to go over this again. Before I get an answer to this letter, I am likely, if the Lord will, to get the Pentateuch and a good deal of the Historical Books translated. I should like to know what you think of this, *i.e.*, my doing it without the Hebrew. There is another even more important matter that I wished to write about. I don't think the Committee can realize how much difficulty most men have in learning these African languages, else I don't think they would send men, not specially qualified, into a country where the language is not known. I believe that it's, in most cases, worse than useless sending a man who has not had special training in language and the theory of it, to such a place ; it is awfully trying to himself, physically and spiritually ; at the same time, very discouraging ; and I cannot but strongly suspect that it would account for a good many promising careers cut short. The long period that must elapse, before such a man can express to the natives the object which has brought him there, must surely cause a host of misconceptions on their part ; his apparently luxurious life—as it is to them—must surely give them very misleading ideas which for years the Missionary can't correct. It isn't enough to send a man of ordinary all-round education ; he ought to have made a special study of language—that is, thoroughly compared the structure of any two languages ; and, besides that, he ought to know Steere's book (except the vocabularies) absolutely, so as to know the skeleton of a Bantu lauguage. I beg to respectfully suggest to the Committee to appeal specially for such men—Cambridge men, *e.g.*, who have at least got a Second in Classics ; and, further, that Stations, where a new language has to be learnt, should not be opened till such men be forthcoming, as otherwise great expense will be incurred and perhaps more harm done than good. The language once mastered and a grammar written, men with less aptitude for languages, but, perhaps, far better Missionaries can step in and, without unnecessary loss of precious time and health, begin work. But to send such a man up in the first instance, what a sad waste! I assure you, the majority of the men whom I've seen in the field closely, wouldn't learn a new language without help in twenty years. If you doubt this, write a circular to the Missionaries, asking them how long they they suppose they would be learning a new language without any sort of help from books. I expect the average would put down ten years. I hope I don't seem to be puffing the facility which I have in learning a language: after all the years I've spent on the subject, I should be a duffer if I hadn't profited at all by it; what have I that I haven't received? But I assure you I am prompted to write this by the earnest desire to see the Gospel preached to all nations, an object which I am convinced will only be retarded by sending men not specially trained in language to new stations in the first instance. If men, interested in language, knew what a magnificent field this is, they might come for that reason; but I had rather they came for the Gospel's sake—but the other reason might do as a counterpoise to fever, journeys, and other annoyances."

Commenting in another place on the need of trained men for language work, Pilkington writes—

"Let those who are sometimes inclined to feel that the years spent on Greek and Latin were partially wasted come out here, and in one short year I venture to say they will have 'redeemed the time' so spent. Do any such think they are too good for Africa? If so, may God forgive them a thought so presumptuous and silly! They will get no higher returns on any abilities, spiritual, intellectual, physical, which God has given them for investment, than they will get in Africa, and, perhaps, especially here. Every qualified worker might be the means, in God's hands, of sending out in a few years time, say twenty, well-taught, spiritual, zealous Baganda as missionaries to the surrounding nations—each one of them in many ways far superior to an English missionary. Would not this repay any labour, any loss? The evangelization of Africa is visible from Uganda. How long it is to be before it shall be an accomplished fact Christian England must decide."

At this time he was working at a Root dictionary, of which he writes as follows:—

"I aim at 20,000 words. I don't think I shall find this difficult. Luganda is a very wealthy language. I think it will be necessary to go in for a little Luyima (or Kituse) and Lusoga to do the root work perfectly. These three languages are barely more than dialects and throw enormous light on one another. So does Swahili, but to a much smaller extent. I have also written, some time ago, for a Zulu grammar, as I have reason to think (I have a Zulu Prayer Book) this language very closely allied to Luganda.

I am very hopeful—from the slight investigations I have been able to make into Lusoga and Luyima—that a single Bible will do for these two countries, and Uganda, as well as Unyoro (I expect). The idea (once entertained, I believe) that Swahili would do for these countries is a mere dream. It would be about the same thing us trying to introduce German into England. Luganda is entirely different from and superior to Swahili. Out of a considerable number of Lusoga words I have got, five, I think, in every ten, are identical with Luganda, four the same root, modified, perhaps, and with a different prefix, and one a totally different word, although often a word which also occurs in Luganda but in a different sense. In the Root dictionary, I hope to be able to include (by a simple system of signs that won't, I think, interfere with its usefulness and handiness for Luganda) a good many Lusoga and Luyima and Lunyoro words—the roots being identical in so many cases, this will not be difficult in a Root dictionary; and where they differ they do so by regular changes.

It would be well still to have a Vocabulary on the old system, as in Steere's book, for beginners, containing the words in everyday use only.

My own belief is that a thorough knowledge of the language must be gained if Uganda is to be the great centre of civilization and teaching which I cannot but suppose the Committee expect it to be. . . . In order to give you a better idea of what I propose to do in the Dictionary, I give a couple of roots worked—good specimens of course; you mustn't suppose that all roots are equally prolific, but I think you will admit these to be very pretty.

Three thousand such roots would give a very ample vocabulary." (For specimen quoted above see p. 199.)

A little later he describes the eagerness of the people to obtain books.

LANGUAGE STUDY.

BON-(see).
 Boneka, v. Become visible (used only of moon).
 Bonesa, v. Exhibit.
 Akabonero, s. 7. Sign.
 Kabona, s. 1. (Seer); priest. Olwakabona, s. 7. Priesthood.
 Emunye, s. 3. Pupil of eye. (cf. Luyima emboni,
   and Lusoga emuna; and manja for mbanja,
 [cf. Swahili bona, see; and Lusoga, bona, see.]

TIK-(top).
 Tika, v. Place on head (of another person).
 Etika, v. Place on one's own head; carry (a load.)
 Tikira, v. To put the pointed top on a house, etc
 Ekitikiro, s. 4. The pointed top of a round house.
 Katikiro, s. 4. The greatest chief next the King.
 Entiko, s. 3. The top of a hill.
 Akatiko, s. 7. An eatable fungus; (so called, no
   doubt from its shape).
 Omwetisi, s. 1. A carrier, a porter.

Specimen of Luganda Roots.

"We have been selling books (Matthews. Prayer Books, and reading books. 130, 180, and 600 respectively) to-day and yesterday. How shall I describe it? Feeding the lions at the Zoo, a scramble of street boys for coppers, perhaps a distribution of food in famine time, these are the things suggested.

The people who came with shells to buy and went away empty were twice as many as those who received books, and then this is only one place in this large country; and further, it is not easy to collect shells on one day's notice. What we want are books, not thousands, but millions of books. I should like to see £5,000 spent at once on printing and sending up of books; this would be a glorious way of advancing God's Kingdom.

All day long the place has been crowded with people who refuse to believe that there are no more books. How would you feel if at a Christmas party the tea and cake ran so short that only one in every five got anything at all? I feel something like that. And yet these books are of more value to these starving souls than are tea and cake to a starving child. I wish you could run a long pin into every one at home who's asleep and won't wake up to help us. It's disgraceful the way we've been left without books—simply dreadful. I trust and hope and pray that better times are coming. In other places, money and energy is spent in trying to get people to buy and read (or even take) the Bible; but here, be the reason what you will, the wild desire to read and possess a book has seized the whole country. If we don't supply the demand the Roman Catholics will."

Two letters from George to his mother, written in August and September, besides giving some account of the progress of the work in Uganda, deal with some interesting questions which came before him at this time.

"Namirembe, Mengo,
Sunday, 7th August, 1892.

In Buganda itself, things are going on quietly. The new Church—really a magnificent building that impresses you like a Cathedral—was opened last Sunday. The king came, and a vast congregation, enough to fill the Church twice, not much short, I think, of 10,000 people. I read the Bishop's letter, Henry and Nikodemo preached. This morning there was a congregation of 3,000 or 4,000, I think; Church not quite full, and I preached on Matthew 22, and we had Communion to which about 100 people stayed. . . . .

However, the news from Busoga is very alarming. Wakoli (where Smith is), was shot by one of the Company's coast men (originally a Musoga), whether by accident or not nobody knows. Smith had the narrowest possible escape with his life; forty Waganda, we are told, were murdered. Captain Williams, on hearing of it, immediately set out with the Maxim and 170 men, on the day that I came back from the Islands, 28th July. No news from him yet.

. . . . One of the elders told me the other day that we should never satisfy the demand for books. More people begin reading day by day, and month by month, than books come. Oh for books! However, Ashe's printing press is doing a great work.

. . . . I quite agree with you about distinctions between secular and religious. To a Christian man nothing *should be* secular: he is a soldier on duty always (or neglecting it—never off duty); to one who is not a Christian nothing, is religious; in this, as in everything, not that which 'entereth into a man' from without, nothing external 'defileth the man,' but that which comes out of his heart, that 'defileth a man,' and a man's heart is not visible to us. To his own master, each servant stands or falls. I am no priest to usurp that which is God's alone.

If a man wants to go in for what are called worldly pleasures, I can't see what good it would be to hinder him; if he tastes the pleasures which God gives, the others drop off, as a dog drops a bit of potato when you offer him a bone. There isn't time for both. I say, let every man do according as he is disposed in his heart. A man *is* what he is disposed in his heart to be; what he does is only a symptom of what he *is* and of very trifling importance comparatively—except *as a symptom*. The Devil chained would be a Devil still. Even when he appears as an Angel of light, he's still the Devil.

At the same time, when I see a chap raking in a muck heap, it's only common charity and common sense to ask him what he finds there worth looking for, and point to the crown. Not that I would venture to say that I don't often have a rake at it myself. When I do so, I hope I should be grateful to anyone who showed me what a fool I was.

Don't imagine that I suppose that nobody does God's will who is not a missionary or a preacher or a 'professional Christian' of some sort. Very far from it. 'Let every man be fully persuaded in his own mind.' 'Whatsoever is not of faith is sin.' Good-bye for to-night."

"9 p.m., Thursday, 18th August.

Mail goes to-morrow. Captain Williams back from Busoga. Smith is all right; is at Luba's now."

"C.M.S., Namirembe, Uganda,
3rd September, 1892.

. . . In spite of a good deal of fever lately, I've been wonderfully strong and well; able to go up every morning to the great church on the hill, where, after the regular reading and prayers, I have a class of seven elders; then, while they teach seven classes of candidates for baptism on the lines just given them by me, I have a class of some twenty boys, the most promising ones; then I sing with a sort of choir, which I have started. You will be surprised that I should teach singing, but, as nobody else does it, and they sing awfully badly, I do what I can. In the afternoon, I translate with Henry — Exodus, at present; also I am writing, at the request of our Committee here, a little book in Luganda of outlines of Christian doctrine, which is meant to be a help to Baganda teachers. . . . Luganda is ten times as hard as Swahili; true, Swahili is the easiest language in the world to get a superficial knowledge of, but Luganda is undoubtedly difficult.

My beans are growing splendidly. I have two little broods of fowls (four and six respectively), one hen sitting, and another laying; six goats, nine sheep, a ram, three lambs, a bull, fourteen cows and eight calves. I think this a better way of keeping my cloth (investing it in beasts) than keeping in my house, where the dangers to it are so many.

The produce of my flocks and herds supports me. Leopards are my bugbears.

The rennet powder works beautifully; milk in various forms is my chief food; the other men despise skim milk—I think it *the* thing for this country. Whey is a great thing, too. . . . Don't be afraid of my not taking care of my health; I am a perfect old woman, awfully afraid of a draught or anything damp, over-exertion, or anything else—one learns to be careful here—that is the most important part of acclimatization, though, I believe, one does get to some extent acclimatized besides. I am too much interested in the work here to do anything that might force me to leave it. I hope to live to see the whole of Africa evangelized. If only Christian England made a honest effort, it wouldn't take many decades to do it. But England, I'm afraid, is in earnest about one thing only—making money.

By the way, my flocks and herds above-mentioned are altogether worth only about a load of cloth, costing about £3 at the coast, and £7 for carriage—total £10. Besides, four of the cattle and three of the goats were presents. About 100 lbs. of common washing soap would buy the whole lot."

A little later, he speaks of receiving some wheat from the Katikiro, which he ground in a coffee mill, and made brown bread with it, "besides first-rate pancakes; cakes and puddings occasionally!"

Another trip down the lake gave him another change, and in November, 1892, he writes:—

"Uganda,
November 23rd, 1892.

I have just returned from a trip to Nassa, about which I wrote to Mr. Lang, undertaken by the advice of the brethren here. I am glad to say that it has done me a great deal of good and I feel as well as possible. I got back on the 18th. I was interested to find that the languages spoken all along the West Coast of the Lake and on the Island of Ukerewe are very close to Luyima (Kituse), the language of the Wahuma, as Stanley, I think, calls them. My Mwima boy could talk fluently with them all and understand them. I felt this as an additional reason for extension into the countries of the Bayima, to the West of Uganda, Toro, etc. I believe that this language, in different dialects, is spoken over a greater area than Luganda. But, at present, the miserable reinforcements of which we hear, make me despair of extension even into Busoga, where, as you know by this time, the work was temporarily given up. I do not think that either the Christian public or even the C.M.S. Committee have grasped how great the need is here. There are vast *arrears* of work to be done here; vast numbers call themselves Christians, and are regarded as such by the people generally, who have not only no heart religion, but not even a knowledge of Christian morality. What I fear is a widespread misconception of the meaning of Christianity, if this state of things continues. This calamity can be averted only, I venture to think, by an adequate supply of teachers, and also of books; at present, we have neither in anything like the numbers needed. We already see many sad instances of inconsistency, and, what is worst of all, they are evidently not regarded as anything very bad by the great bulk of the people; I am afraid that this will spread and corrupt the Church. 'Reading' is getting, it seems to me, to be less and less regarded as inconsistent with drunkenness and fornication. Naturally enough, for now great numbers are 'reading,' and few have renewed hearts and therefore renewed lives. Individual work is what is needed here, and this takes such a time.

It is wonderful, and yet, perhaps, not really so when you consider that we are foreigners here, how the Gospel, when preached to numbers even in the simplest and plainest way, seems to be not understood, or at any rate not realized, as a personal matter.

I have quite failed to express how urgent, how terrible seems to me the need of men."

It is clear from the above that the Missionaries fully realized the dangers of a rapid spread of Christianity in Uganda, and, if there have been exaggerated ideas abroad of the progress of the work, it has not been the fault of the Missionaries who have all along told of discouragement as well as success.

Just a month after the writing of this letter, Bishop Tucker arrived for the second time in Uganda, and his testimony as to Pilkington's gifts as an interpreter, and as to the progress of the work in Uganda, form a valuable commentary on much that has been already mentioned in this chapter. The Bishop writes :—

"At about 4 p.m., to our great joy, our long and weary journey of eighty-nine days was at an end, and we were with our dear brethren at Mengo. A heavy storm of rain had prevented people coming in any large numbers to meet us, but, as the weather cleared up, we were soon besieged with visitors. To see the friends and brethren who, two years ago, had travelled up from the coast with me was indeed a great joy. Mr. Pilkington was looking the very picture of health. Mr. Baskerville, too, was looking very well, and enjoys, I am glad to think, excellent health. After some refreshment, we went to see the houses in which we are to live. They have been built for us by our Native brethren. My house astonished me. It is one of the largest in Buganda. It has six rooms in it.

Christmas Day dawned, and verily it is a day never to be forgotten. The thrill that went through me when, two years ago, I addressed a congregation of 1,000 souls in the old Church is still fresh in my memory. If I was thrilled then, I was simply overwhelmed yesterday when I stood up to speak in the name of our Master to a congregation numbering over 5,000 souls. I wonder whether, in the whole mission-field, such a sight has been witnessed since Apostolic days. The perfect stillness as I stood up to speak, and indeed throughout the service, was almost as awe-inspiring as the sight of the great multitude itself. Mr. Pilkington interpreted for me, and it was quite evident that he performed his task to perfection. In the afternoon, a second service was held, and I suppose between three and four thousand people must have been present. At this service about thirty women were baptized. Mr. Baskerville preached in Luganda. Later in the afternoon, an English service was held. At this service a larger number of Europeans were present than have been gathered together before in Uganda. Christmas Day was a trying day, but an intensely joyful day—a day worth coming to the ends of the earth to enjoy.

I have brought with me from the coast more than 8,000 portions of the Word of God. The delight of the people is indescribable. Daily my house is besieged by would-be purchasers. Last time when books arrived, the eagerness to possess them was such that there was danger of the house being knocked down. It has therefore been decided to sell them at different centres at one and the same time. Those who come for books are therefore turned away until the arrangements are complete for the sale to go forward. Many more loads of books are coming up by the old road, and I trust, by our friends at home keeping up the supply, to pour a constant stream of God's truth upon the land."

CHAPTER XI.

THE FIRST MUTINY.

The early days of 1893 were great days in Uganda; six natives were ordained deacons on the understanding that they were to be supported by the Native Church, and ten others were licensed as lay evangelists. In February, the Bishop held his second Confirmation in Uganda; of this he writes:—

"Seventy-five were confirmed, all adults. This was the first Confirmation in the new Church, or, as I think I must call it, the Cathedral. For Central Africa it is as wonderful a building as Durham Cathedral is for England. There are nearly 500 trees used in it as pillars; some of them were brought five and six days' journey and needed several hundred men to carry them. The order and decency of the services is most admirable. The Confirmation was a much more reverent ceremony than many which I have been at in England."

In March, Sir Gerald Portal, Imperial Commissioner to Uganda, arrived in Mengo, and, on April 1st, the Company's flag was hauled down and the Union Jack took its place, in token that Uganda was now to be regarded as part of the British Empire. This was intended, in the first place, to be a temporary measure, the final arrangement being announced to Parliament in April, 1894.

During his stay in Uganda, the Commissioner was chiefly occupied in seeking to arrange terms of agreement between the rival factions in Uganda. With the assistance of Bishop Tucker and Monseigneur Hirth, an arrangement of territory was made which, it was hoped, would be satisfactory to all parties. On May 30th, Sir Gerald Portal left for the coast, Bishop Tucker leaving three days later by the Southern route. He then wrote: " The position of our friends is absolutely secure in our opinion."

How soon these hopes of peace were to be disappointed is shown by the following letter from Pilkington, dated Kampala, June 20th, 1893:—

"You will see that something is up by the address, Kampala; we have had exciting times again these last few days, but I am thankful to say that things are, I think, all right again now; they might easily have been anything but all right. First of all, so that you may understand the events of the last few days, let me explain the state of affairs. Captain Lugard, you remember, brought some 500 Soudanese soldiers with their ' Colonel,' Selim Bey—who had mutinied at Wadelai under Emin Pasha—from the North. He also brought in the Mohammedan party, and gave them three small provinces lying close together to the North-east of Budu. Since they came into the country, they have done no work for the king, as in duty bound.

Sir G. Portal, when here, insisted that they should do their proper work, and told them that, if they

THE FIRST MUTINY.

refused, they would be driven out. They demanded an increase of territory, as they saw that the Roman Catholics, who also, hitherto, have done no work, had received so large an increase. This was refused by Sir G. Portal, and the attitude of the Mohammedans had been threatening. However, Captain Macdonald, who was left in charge on the Consul's departure, made them promise to work about ten days ago, and they sent to their country places for men to come and work. However, our people assured us that they did not mean to work, and were only making this a pretext for getting up their guns, as they said that Selim Bey (of course, the Soudanese are Mohammedans and very thick with the Baganda Mohammedans) had promised, and, indeed, we hear now, sworn on the Koran, that, in case of war, he would help the Mohammedans. This fort was garrisoned by some 100 of the Soudanese; some 200 more, with Selim Bey, were at Ntebe, on the Lake, some twenty-five miles from here; and another 150 with Major Owen, away in the Toro forts. On Saturday morning, 17th June, Captain Macdonald came round to tell us that Selim Bey had sent him a message, the night before, that nothing must be done respecting the Mohammedans without consulting him, and that if the king (Mwanga) fought against the Mohammedans, he would be fighting with him (the Bey). Captain Macdonald had, he told us, decided to take the bull by the horns: he had sent for Messrs. Gedge and Reddie to come up at once with their 100 Swahilis from Ntebe; they would be in that afternoon. He intended, at three o'clock, to parade the Soudanese at the Fort as usual and tell them that the Bey had mutinied, and ask those who were for him (Captain Macdonald) to go off to one side and those for the Bey to the other, when he proposed disarming the latter; also he intended to tell the Mohammedans that they must give up their four leading chiefs as a pledge of their peaceful intentions, by that evening, or he would order the Protestants to attack them next morning. So he wished us to go up to the fort at mid-day, that the presence of a large number of Europeans might overawe the Soudanese. He then went to the French, who also agreed to come up.

So we went up; the Soudanese all protested their loyalty, and Captain Macdonald got the Mohammedan chiefs and we thought it was all over. So we went back to our places that Saturday night.

However, first thing on Saturday morning was a note from Captain Macdonald, asking us to go over at once. Gedge and Reddie had come in in the night, and the Bey had told the latter that, in case of war, he meant to help the Mohammedans. When Reddie suggested that this might mean fighting against the Europeans, he shrugged his shoulders. So Captain Macdonald, considering the circumstances very serious, had decided to disarm the Soudanese. As soon as we reached the fort, Captain Macdonald asked me to translate the following into Luganda, and to explain it to the Katikiro:—
'Whereas Selim Bey has mutinied, and whereas the common law is not sufficient for the emergency, I hereby declare that martial law is in force through-

THE FIRST MUTINY. 213

out this country of Uganda until further notice.' I have missed out a few words defining the common law, but this gives the sense.

He then armed all the Swahilis, 150 or so, and us Europeans, and put the Maxim gun in position, and marched the Soudanese down below, and, after explaining things to them in a speech, ordered them to lay down their arms, which, thank God! they did at once.

Meanwhile, the excitement among the Baganda was increasing; the Mohammedans had brought up 300 or 500 guns in the night, and had already beaten their war drums. I interpreted for Captain Macdonald when he was speaking to Mbogo (the late Mohammedan king, who had been kept at Kampala all through), and the Mohammedan chiefs, who had been given up on the previous day, so I can tell you exactly what he told them. He told Mbogo that all his men, with guns, must go off at once to Natete, the Mohammedan quarter; that if all had not gone by noon, he (Mbogo) would be responsible. They all went, so Mbogo has saved himself.

He then told the three Mohammedan chiefs to send to their people and order them back to their country places, and that, if the Mohammedans fought, he should shoot all three. They said that, if one of their number went, the Mohammedans would listen to him, but that they would not mind a mere message. So one of them was allowed to go on promise of return, but he never came back. During this interview, Mbogo came, and in great fear and almost with tears, upbraided Juma, the chief of the Mohammedans, with writing to his people to come up and fight, saying that he had been against it all through.

About one o'clock, the Katikiro sent a message that the Mohammedans were not going, so Captain Macdonald sent a message to them by one of Mbogo's men that he would be there in an hour with the Maxim gun, and if he found them there he would attack them. Twenty minutes later, we heard the guns firing, in the Natete direction, and we knew that war was inevitable. A few minutes later, a message came from the Katikiro, that the Mohammedans had attacked them, and Captain Williams sent back the message, 'Dispose of them all.' The next news was a wounded man, whose boy told me that the Mohammedans were in flight, and the pursuit was kept up right to the boundary of the Mohammedan country. At midday on the Monday, the Protestants (all the Roman Catholics, led by the priests, had flitted on Saturday night) came back to ask whether they should drive the Mohammedans right out. Captain Macdonald had intended and expected that they would do so, but, as they had spared them of their own accord, he told them to leave them and he would go down and see their chiefs when he had finished matters at Ntebe.

Messages were accordingly sent to those who had not fought to stay quietly where they were, and the Europeans would go down and see them and arrange matters. I heard the Katikiro saying yesterday to the king that they must do all they

can to save them. I think that in this they have
showed themselves no unworthy disciples of their
God and Saviour; in judgment, they have
remembered mercy; in the flush of victory, with
the enemy running before them and all their
property in their mercy, they voluntarily refrained;
the first time, perhaps, that such a thing has
happened in the history of Uganda.

However, I've not finished my story. Captain
Macdonald asked us to stay at Kampala till the
trouble was over, as our presence would, more than
anything, intimidate the Bey and the Soudanese; so
we stayed, and some of us took a couple of hours
at night going round to see that the Guard was
all right. Yesterday (Monday), about mid-day,
news came in that the Bey was on the move,
intending, apparently, to skirt the capital and join
the Mohammedans. The Protestants had just
returned, 3,000 guns, and they were told to go out
and intercept him, and kill them every one. But
it proved to be a false alarm; the Bey had sent up
ten men with guns, and twenty others to say that
he was ready to obey Captain Macdonald in everything, and to explain away his messages to the
Captain and his words to Mr. Reddie. This
morning (Tuesday) Captain Macdonald and four
other Europeans with the Maxim, and 500 Baganda
with guns, and, of course, innumerable spearmen,
have gone to Ntebe to settle the Bey. They
anticipate that the Soudanese will all be loyal and
lay down their arms, and I expect that the Bey,
who was the real cause of all this trouble and

Sunday's bloodshed, and who, but for Captain Macdonald's prompt action, might have had all of us in chains—as he once had Emin—will be shot.

Juma, the Mohammedan chief, is in the chain gang; Mbogo is here, very cheerful apparently, because he is exonerated from blame; I hope it will be possible to spare Juma's life: he is quite a young man and he has had a terrible lesson."

"Namirembe,
Saturday, July 12th.

The Soudanese laid down their arms all right and the Bey was court-martialed and condemned to be degraded and sent away to an island on the Lake, Nsagi by name. Last Monday, all the Protestants went off to drive out the Mohammedans. No news yet except that half the Mohammedans want peace."

I have not yet mentioned the death of Captain Portal, by sunstroke, about a month ago. He was buried up at the Church by Hannington and De Winton.

In all this, Captain Macdonald has acted in the promptest, bravest, and wisest manner. God gave the right man for the right place."

Few will doubt that the English Missionaries were right in standing by the British authorities. They were not asked to take arms against the people of the country, but to help to overawe by their presence the mutinous Soudanese troops who were foreigners to the country. Had they refused, it is possible that the British administration would have been swept away, and Mohammedanism, with its slave-raiding and cruelty, have reigned supreme. Pilkington's story of these events is a clear one. It may, however, be interesting to give Captain Macdonald's account of his appeal to the Missionaries.

"I visited the Church Missionary Society in Namirembe, where I saw Mr. Pilkington, who at once summoned the Head of the Mission, the Rev. J. Roscoe, at that time engaged at the church in superintending classes. To these two gentlemen the situation was explained. I told them my hopes that a rapid initiative would defeat the proposed combination in detail, and that the best chance of success appeared to be in all the Europeans showing a united front, irrespective of creed or profession At the same time, should they prefer to do so, they were free to withdraw to the Eastern provinces while there was yet time; but I explained that such a proceeding would necessarily have a very dispiriting effect on the Protestant Waganda and might lead to their flight from the capital. Other members of the Mission were called in, and it need hardly be said that, in an assemblage of Englishmen confronted with a crisis like this, there was no dissentient voice, but one and all decided to stand or fall by me as the representative of British authority.

I then went to the Roman Catholic Mission Station, at Rubaga, and explained the situation and proposals, in almost the same words that I had used at Namirembe. Here, too, the Missionaries resolved to stand by the Government. Both Missions having thus decided to support me, it was arranged that the Missionaries should come to Kampala in the afternoon—not in a body, so as to create alarm, but dropping in by twos and threes."

After all was over, the Consul wrote thanking the Missionaries for their "valuable services," and adding that "the record of their invaluable services will be laid before Her Majesty's Secretary of State at the first opportunity."

One of the most striking points in connection with the suppression of the mutiny was the part played by the Protestant Baganda. Captain Macdonald particularly mentions the Sekibobo, the title by which Nikodemo, one of the most important Protestant chiefs, was known, who was with him when he went to arrest Selim Bey.

Writing of this incident in his recent book, Captain Macdonald says :—

"The Sekibobo managed his men excellently. When I went to arrest the Bey, several small columns were drawn up concealed by a fold in the ground, but ready to rush into the Soudanese quarter had the Bey's private following offered any resistance; and when, before nightfall, a European inspected the Sekibobo's arrangement of pickets and sentries, there was really nothing to alter. With this stern old Waganda chief, it was like a return to the ancient Covenanting days in Scotland: for, every evening, the day's work closed with a prayer-meeting conducted by the Sekibobo in person, and always largely attended by his followers.

The discipline he maintained in his contingent was particularly good and he carried out my orders in the spirit, not merely in the letter."

Pilkington, referring to his death nearly two years later, speaks of him as follows: "We have had a great loss; our dear brother Nikodemo, kind, good, earnest, Christian man (the Sekibobo, *i.e.*, chief of Kyagwe), also one of those ordained deacon, has been taken from us. As great a loss as Sembera's personally to us and to the work: the Lord who gave him can fill up the vacant place."

The great change is all the more remarkable when it is realized from what degrading superstitions the heathen of Uganda have been delivered.

The nature of this is described in a letter from Pilkington, shortly after the mutiny, as follows:—

"You ask about the religion of the people here. They had an elaborate religion; each county or province had its tutelar god (lubale); each god had several shrines, where there lived the priest and the 'Mandwa,' *i.e.*, a man supposed to be possessed by the god; people gave offerings which priest and Mandwa shared, besides which a great many gardens were given up to the lubale.

People came and enquired of them as at an oracle the priest was the medium, the Mandwa gave the answers. Besides this, the spirits of dead people were supposed to possess the Mandwas in the same way as gods, especially the spirits of dead kings. Mutesa, before he died, told the people that if, after his death, anyone professed to be possessed by his spirit, they were to tell him to read an Arabic book, and, if he failed, they would know he was an impostor as he (Mutesa) knew how to read it; and this actually happened, and the Mandwa was well beaten for his pains.

The same king had a favourite dog which died, and a man professed to be possessed by its spirit, and would do nothing but bark!

When a man is possessed in this way, and some beer is brought in, they all drink, and the spirit leaves him; then the Mandwa is sure to upbraid his friends for not leaving any for him, and when they are surprised, he explains that he didn't drink any, it was the god. The great rivers or marshes, too, were regarded as gods, and, before crossing, they would throw in coffee-berries, or human beings, to propitiate them. Periodically, they sacrificed human beings to both river and other gods, 500 at a time. There were special places where these human sacrifices were made till only a few years ago."

The mutiny having been thus vigorously dealt with, peace was speedily re-established, and Missionary work, which had been suspended for a short period, was carried on with redoubled energy.

Selim Bey was sent away from the country, but died on his way to the coast.

CHAPTER XII.

A REVIVAL.

HITHERTO we have dealt chiefly with the Uganda Mission, and the part played in it by the chief character in our story, from what may be called the external point of view.

We have watched him as he first took his place in the Missionary circle at Mengo, daily gaining in influence over the natives as he grew more and more familiar with their language; his counsel increasingly valued by his colleagues, in many a difficult problem connected with the work, and appealed to by the British authorities to act as their interpreter on every occasion when accuracy and secrecy were particularly needed.

In his hands, during this time, the translation of the Bible had made rapid progress, and the number of readers became so great that their eagerness for books could not be satisfied.

These external results, the only thing which the world looks for, might have satisfied some, but they were not enough for George Pilkington.

It is true that there were outward and visible signs which betokened prosperity, but was there in proportion the inward and spiritual grace? It was this for which he sought, but the dearth of spiritual results was to him and his fellow Missionaries a keen disappointment. Pilkington himself was so much discouraged, that he spoke of giving up Missionary work altogether, unless some change took place. For a time, it is said that he used to absent himself from the prayer meetings held amongst the Missionaries.

In this state of mind he went alone for a visit to the Island of Komé, and it was there that he learnt the great secret of the indwelling power of the Holy Spirit, which transformed his whole life.

Speaking of this at a great gathering of students in Liverpool, in January, 1896, he said :—

"If it had not been that God enabled me, after three years in the Mission field, to accept by faith the gift of the Holy Spirit, I should have given up the work. I could not have gone on as I was then. A book by David, the Tamil evangelist, shewed me that my life was not right, that I had not the power of the Holy Ghost. I had consecrated myself hundreds of times, but I had not accepted God's gift. I saw now that God commanded me to be filled with the Spirit. Then I read, 'All things whatsoever ye pray and ask for, believe that ye have received them, and ye shall have them,' and, claiming this promise, I received the Holy Spirit.

Another verse which impressed me was, St. John xvi., 7—'It is expedient for you that I go away; for if I go not away, the Comforter will not come unto you ; but if I go I will send Him unto you.'"

But perhaps the clearest view of the influence on

his life of this remarkable experience, may be gained from a letter written by him to his mother on May 30th, 1895. He writes:—" Next Sunday is Whit-Sunday. Oh, for another Pentecost here, and at home. 'He that believeth on Me out of his belly *shall* flow rivers (not a stream or a single river) of living water. Greater works than these shall ye do, because I go unto the Father.' Where are these rivers and where are these mighty works? We must ask rather, where 'is he that believeth on Him?' Surely He is not unfaithful to a single line of His promise. What wonder that infidelity abounds, when the worst infidelity of all is in our own hearts. What wonder that Popery increases, when we have dethroned the Holy Spirit from our hearts. What wonder that Mohammedanism defies us, and still occupies vast fields once held for Christ, when Mohammed's successors can still ask as the false prophet himself did, 'Where, but in Mohammed is the promised Paraclete?' Even the Mohammedans here, ignorant as they are, ask that. Praise be to God, many of our people here can answer, 'In my heart and life.' May abundant fruit of the Spirit in our lives prove our witness true.

The people here are hungry and thirsty for the Holy Ghost, they are searching the New and (as far as they have it) the Old Testament to see if these things which we tell them be so. I am looking for a wonderful outpouring of the Holy Spirit on them. 'I will pour water on him that is thirsty, and floods on the dry ground.' (Is. 44, 3.) From God has this thirst come in our souls here for the Holy Spirit, and He who gave the thirst is also satisfying it, and will satisfy it to the full.

It would be an easier thing for the Church of Uganda to evangelize in twenty years all unevangelized Africa than it was for the Primitive Church to evangelize as far as she did in the same period. The Waganda are born Missionaries, they are splendid travellers, and in ability, a good deal above, so far as is known, the nations round them; their country is an island in a vast sea of ignorance; they have been brought in contact with, and have learnt to contend with, the three forms of darkness which they will meet in Africa: Heathenism, Mohammedanism, and Popery. What we want first, middle, and last, is the Holy Spirit. The Holy Spirit is Christ in the heart. See Rom. viii. and Eph. iii.

This reminds me that you once wrote as if you thought that I had meant to say that, till eighteen months ago, I had not had the presence or the help of the Holy Spirit in my work. I never meant to convey that impression. I distinguish between the presence of the Holy Spirit *with* us and *in* us; our blessed Lord said to His disciples, ' He *is with* you and *shall be in* you.' John xiv. It is the birthright of every Christian to have the Holy Spirit in him, to be full of the Holy Ghost as St. Paul commanded the Ephesians to be, but I believe that my unbelief and other sins was a hindrance to the Holy Spirit in my own heart till about eighteen months ago, when God Himself, I humbly believe, opened, or enabled me to 'open the door,' and He came in, according to His gracious promise, to sup with me, even me, and I with Him. Amazing condescension and mercy to such an awful, awful, awful sinner as I know myself to be."

On December 7th, 1893, Pilkington returned to Mengo from Komé, and everyone noticed the wonderful change in Him. His very face told of the reality of the change. His boys noticed it, the Christians of Uganda were conscious of it and all who came in contact with him, and that not only from his words but in a thousand little ways which speak more forcibly than the most eloquent sermon. But it was not only Pilkington who was thus blessed, others of the mission party had been led to seek a special blessing from God, and thus they were able to rejoice together.

Of this Baskerville writes on December 8th:— " Pilkington got back yesterday from Komé about 5.30 : he came over to dinner with us at Roscoe's, and told of the glorious times he had had on Komé. He told us, too, how he had definitely, while away, received by faith the Baptism of the Holy Ghost, and manifestation of His power had followed. People had testified to the saving power of Christ, including Christians of some standing, I mean some who had been baptized but who as yet had not really accepted Christ. One man, a genuine native of Komé, stood up and said, ' You see me a native born, not a Waganda, not a native of Komé, do not call me any longer by my old name, for I have been born anew.' Others said,

'I was blind, now I see.' Praise to God for His goodness."

Baskerville continues: "It has been our private wish for some time to have some mission services here. We can scarcely hope for special missioners until a railway comes, and it occurred to us that God wants to use us. We all, in prayer, dedicated ourselves to Him, and asked Him to baptize us anew. This morning we began; we had not told the people but went up after prayer at the usual time, believing for a blessing. Pilkington conducted the meeting. We began with our version of 'Have you been to Jesus for the cleansing power,' and then Pilkington prayed. He began by speaking about a man, a very sad case which has been the indirect cause of these meetings. A certain Musa Yakuganda has come to us and told us that he gets no profit from our religion, and wants to have his name given out as having returned to the state of a Heathen. Asked if he knew what he said, he replied, 'Do you think I have been reading seven years, and do not understand? Your religion does not profit me at all. I have done with it.' Pilkington pointed out what a cause of shame this was to us. . . . I cannot on paper describe every detail of the meeting. On two occasions, some hundreds were all praying for forgiveness, others praising in the simplest language. . . . We left the church at twelve, having been there since 8.30. Roscoe is now with some of the teachers, and Pilkington has some boys in the next room. We go up to the church directly to another service,"

The Rev. J. Roscoe writes of the services on the next day, December 9th :—" We have had another day of great spiritual blessing. At each service God was present, and souls were brought into union with Jesus Christ. The beaming faces of some who found peace yesterday were sufficient testimony to their changed state, and words were unnecessary. The Katikiro wrote his testimony ; in September he found peace, but has now entered into fuller blessing. Each morning we have had fully 500 present at these meetings. This afternoon, we had a specially solemn service for those who had the assurance of salvation, about 200 being present. We expect from the Lord showers of blessing to-morrow, and await the outpouring of His Spirit in faith.

10th (Sunday). We are in the midst of a great spiritual revival. To the Lord be praise and glory and honour ! Our joy is beyond expression. After the morning service, fully 200 stayed to be spoken to, and I believe the majority went away rejoicing in the Lord."

Baskerville adds : " Musa has come back. It is grand. He was in the Church when Pilkington told the people about him, at the first meeting, on Friday. No one dreamt of his being there. The Lord had brought him."

The Rev. Ernest Millar gives the following account of the mission :—" The majority of those converted could read a little, but some could not read at all, and, on being converted, at once wished to learn to read. One of Pilkington's *bayima* (cow boys) came out very brightly, and told the others about God's love, the consequence being that on the next day one of our Bayima, whom we had previously not thought much of, came to me, and said he had accepted the gift of God, eternal life, and now wished to have a reading book, that he might learn to read. Needless to say, I gave him a book at once, and we can see the change in his life—he is quite a different man, and full of joy; since then, another cowboy has come forward. This is the more wonderful, because the Bayima are generally very backward in learning to read. (The Bayima are the tribe whose especial care is that of looking after cattle; there is a proverb to the effect that you can more easily kill a Muyima than you can take his cattle.) The Mission only lasted three days, but the effect will, I trust, last for ever. One remarkable feature of this work, in the eyes of outsiders, is that the great chiefs in the land were not afraid to confess that they had not hitherto accepted Christ, and that they wished to do so. At the service at the king's, on the last day of the mission, one chief, who had been one of the leading teachers, but had been suspended for misconduct, confessed, in front of the king and his boys, that he had not previously accepted the Lord Jesus as his Saviour, but did so then. We had special meetings for the deepening of the spiritual life during the week which followed the mission, and we trust that many were helped."

One other missionary, Mr. R. H. Leakey, gives his impressions of these wonderful three days; he writes:—

"You will have heard from other Missionaries of

A REVIVAL. 229

the special services here, on December 8th, 9th, and 10th, and of the wonderful blessing we had. Many, who had long been looked upon as leading Christians, realized a new force and power in their Christian life. Some said to us, 'Why have you been here so long and never told us this glad news before?' All we could say was, 'You have been been told, but have not believed it.' May God forgive *us* for any lack of power, or of faith, or of prayer on our part. . . . Before the services we prayed with power to God, and then went to them, expecting great blessings, and we got more than we had dared to expect. I never in my life so realized the power of the Spirit of God present to save and working in our midst as I did at those meetings."

The reason why it was necessary to hold the Mission, without time for preparation, was that the Baganda army was about to start for Bunyoro, to fight with King Kabarega, and Pilkington elected to accompany the Baganda troops, as their chaplain.

Of this, Baskerville writes :—

"13th.—Pilkington has gone. On Monday night he told us that God was calling him to go out to the war with the Baganda. We all felt it to be the right thing, and all has been arranged well, and he left this morning. He will be thrown in contact daily with hundreds of people, who never come near the capital, drawn from every corner of the country, many of them Roman Catholics and Mohammedans. He is not travelling with the white men from the Fort, but with the Baganda. He wanted at first to go without a tent, but the people would not hear of it, nor indeed would we. They have given him about ten porters. The people are all delighted that he has gone—their joy was very touching. In fact, we are all about as full of joy as we can hold, and the people are particularly rejoiced that Pilkington has gone. All say what a unique opportunity he will have. He has two cows with him, and he will, I am sure, be well looked after by the people. Last night we had a very solemn service as a farewell, the Colonel, and all the men at the Fort came, but one. Pilkington preached a short sermon, and several of them particularly thanked us."

Captain Villiers, speaking of Pilkington's presence with the Baganda army on this occasion, remarks that it was "the cause of their abandoning all their former ideas of warfare, and behaving as well as civilized troops." It may be well to add that Pilkington was strictly a non-combatant on this occasion. News received from him by the Missionaries in Mengo is given by Mr. Baskerville, who writes:—

"Two letters have come from Pilkington since he left for the war, the second from Kadoma's, ten miles over the Buganda frontier and their first camping-place in Bunyoro. In his first letter he says, 'Some twenty-five have professed salvation since we left Mengo'; in his second, he says, 'The Mohammedans are listening eagerly, even their chiefs come to hear. I have preached to great crowds four times, numbering from 1,000 to 2,000, and on Sunday Zacharia preached a capital sermon to some 2,000 people.'"

A REVIVAL.

On returning from the expedition against Kabarega, Pilkington paid a visit to Singo, where Mr. Fisher was at work. Here he was greatly struck with the plan, adopted by Mr. Fisher, of erecting reading houses, or, as the people called them, "Synagogi," where they could be instructed by native teachers under the direction of more experienced workers, these in turn being supervised by the European in charge of the district.

On returning to Mengo, Pilkington proposed that this plan should be adopted much more widely, and he and Baskerville decided to delay their return to England until this new movement could be organized.

Thus it became possible to bring the more distant places into closer touch with the centre of the work, and the revival, which had started in the capital, spread in the same year far and wide through the outlying stations of the Mission.

A letter written by Pilkington on the 1st of April, 1894, gives some account of the sending forth of new teachers. He writes:—

"A good many teachers—between thirty and forty—have offered to go out and teach in the country parts; we had a sort of 'dismissal' last Sunday, when thirteen were sent, and another seven are to be dismissed this afternoon, including a very faithful boy of mine called Musa (Moses), who will be a great loss to me, but, I believe, a great gain to the work.

Leakey came back yesterday from South of Lake with 120 loads of books (a load is 70 lbs.), i.e, three and a half tons, 800 New Testaments, only I wish it were 8000.

Captain Macdonald is going home. We owe him a great debt. He saved this country. He has won the confidence of all the people by firmness, good sense, and kindness. We are very sorry indeed that he is going; we shall hardly see his equal again.

We hope very much that he may come back here again.

I hope before long to pay a visit to the Islands; we hear there has been an enormous increase of 'reading' in them lately: and so I hope to find large congregations to whom to preach the Gospel, and I expect many will be saved through the mercy of God and the outpouring of the Holy Spirit."

At the end of July and during the month of August, Pilkington visited the Islands in company the Rev. Ernest Millar. In most cases they were received with the greatest enthusiasm. Mission services were held with splendid results. Candidates for baptism were examined and baptized, and a great impulse given to reading. One serious interruption to the work at Mengo occurred not long after his return from the journey, which he records as follows, writing on 4th of October, 1894 :—

"Last Tuesday I was sitting in this room when my cook, a woman, rushed in, saying, 'The Church has fallen, and I don't know whether people haven't been killed in it.' There was at the time a tremendous storm of wind and rain. Thank GOD no people had been killed. Walker was last out of the Church. He refused to believe that it was falling, till he saw the great poles actually coming down on him, and only just got out when down it came. The poles apparently sound, and not leaning in the least, had rotted inside and broke off one after the other under the great pressure of wind, aided by the enormous weight of the grass roof, drenched by the downpour of rain.

It seems a calamity, but we believe that God's hand is in it; I daresay, as in Acts viii., he wants to scatter our work more in the dark surrounding country.

They are going to build another with a different kind of wood, palm trees, and we hope on a somewhat improved principle. But it is difficult to make so vast a building safe without mortar or ironwork.

. . . . We have had great encouragement among the Mohammedans lately. Two of them, friends of mine, converted I believe, and two others, leading men among them, intending to come out.

I believe that there is a Spirit of enquiry among the Roman Catholics such as I have never seen before. Not less than three or four of them daily, often more, come to see me to talk about things, in ones and twos. They are on the most friendly terms with me.

Before the Church fell, 2,000 at least were coming every week-day morning, besides, I should think, at least 7,000 more in the 200 country Churches. On Sunday not less than 20,000 in the various Churches. Of these, 6,000 were under regular instruction in classes; and this vast work extending right down to Koki and Toro on one side, and Busoga on the other, 200 miles in one direction and 100 in the other, has to be directed by twelve Europeans, often down with fever, and knowing the language very imperfectly. The natives can't yet organise; they are good when led, they seem unable to lead yet. Oh that they may be led by the Holy Ghost! They are improving, one of them is doing a grand work about ten miles to the north of Mengo, really organising, I think. May GOD give us many like him. He used to be a strong opponent of present salvation, but thank GOD, no longer so.

I want to finish translating the Old Testament, and that, with seeing after the teachers, who have been sent into the country, teaching daily a class of would-be teachers in Romans, and holding a service, half in the open air, in the neighbourhood every afternoon, leaves me but little time for correspondence.

The Mohammedans here tell me that they believe and love the Lord Jesus, and I believe that, in a sense, they do; but it is not the same Jesus that I know."

Writing again on Sunday, 4th November, 1894, he continues:—"The work goes on wonderfully; our reading sheets have run out; we are anxiously expecting more. Every afternoon I am now going for an hour or two, to the Mohammedan quarter, Natete, the C. M. S. Station in Mackay's days, and have a sort of friendly discussion, consisting chiefly of reading the Scriptures, with the Mohammedans; they have themselves invited me, and we are great friends, they are not like the bigoted Mohammedans of India, and still they are quite bigoted enough. They ask me questions such as: 'Is Jesus the Son of GOD?' 'What about Abraham?' 'Why don't you keep the law of Moses?' Which I answer by reading, *e.g.*, Heb. i, Mat. iii., 16, 17, Rom. iv., Acts xv., and they listen with utmost attention. But their most interesting question is about Him whom Jesus said was to come (the Holy Spirit— they say Mohammed), and it is glorious to have such an opportunity of testifying to the reality and the power of the Blessed Spirit. This is the lost Truth, the loss of which gave Satan the opportunity of introducing both Mohammedanism and Popery. Of course, you know that in the Koran (of which I have a translation) is mentioned the Trinity, as Mohammed supposed Christians to believe, the Father, Son, and Mary!

We have seen during the last year many hardened and notorious sinners (baptized though they were) definitely brought to Christ, and openly professing to be saved (one of them the other day, just after his conversion). When we told the Church Council that he wanted to go out as a teacher, the proposal was met with uncontrollable laughter as they didn't know about his conversion; and he is now living a life which shews to all the world, the reality of the change.

The Roman Catholic version of St. Matthew (with copious notes from the Fathers) is expected in a day or two. Thank God for this."

The work of that year, which had been a most

eventful one in the history of the Uganda Church, is thus summed up in Pilkington's annual letter for 1894 :—

"Mengo,
December 12th, 1894.

Since my return from Unyoro—where I had wonderful opportunities of preaching the Gospel to many who probably would not have heard it otherwise, and of getting into closer touch and sympathy with the Waganda—my work has been chiefly that of looking after the rapid extension of the work into the country, which has been one of the most marked features of the year; in fact, I have acted, I may say, as secretary to the Church Council, as far as this special work is concerned. I have also done language work, especially the revision of the New Testament, with Henry Wright Duta; but I propose, in this letter, only to review the work of extension into the country parts and neighbouring countries during the past year.

At the beginning of this year, there were not, probably, more than twenty country churches (or reading-rooms or 'synagogues'); there are now not less than 200, of which the ten largest would contain 4,500 persons; the average capacity of all would be, perhaps, 150. In these there now assemble every Sunday not less than 20,000 souls to hear the Gospel; on week days not less than 4,000 assemble (these numbers are exclusive of the capital). The first teachers paid by the Church Council were dismissed in April; there are now 131 of these teachers, occupying eighty-five stations, of whom just twenty are stationed outside Uganda proper, and may be regarded as more or less foreign Missionaries; those in Usoga and Uvuma are supported by the C. M. S. This by no means represents the whole of the work that is being done in the country; there are some places, notably Jungo, some fifteen miles south of Mengo, where a splendid work is being done, and there are probably not less than twenty teachers at work under Henry's able superintendence, and not one of these teachers, nor Henry himself, is reckoned in the above. At Bu'si again, an island near Jungo, there are only two of these regular teachers, and yet there are three churches and about 2,000 people under instruction. This extension into the country has produced, as might have been expected, visible fruit in the enormous increase in the number of those under definite instruction for baptism. At this time last year the catechumens numbered 170; during the year some 800 (I have not the exact number at hand) have been baptized, and there are now 1,500 catechumens.

A blow has been struck at the numerous and absurd slanders current about baptism by the work of the Native deacons, who have, whenever possible, taken baptism in the country churches. While writing this letter I have received a note from Zachariah Kangao, who went to his country place some days ago to baptize some candidates; he says that a great number collected to see the baptisms, and went away saying, 'It was all lies they told us about eating snakes' tails and human flesh,' &c.

One slander he mentions, which I think is not only interesting but most encouraging—that baptism consisted 'in making an incision in the head and rubbing in a powerful medicine which kills the old heart, and then there comes in its place a new religious heart that does not lust for anything,' a glorious Heathen testimony, I take it, to the renewing power of the Gospel of Christ.

Then, further, the work is being extended by the fuller organisation of the country churches. It has been decided to elect six churchwardens whenever the number of baptized men is not less than ten; this organising has only just been begun, but we have seen enough of resultant activity to lead us to hope that the effects, when the scheme is complete and in full working order, will be most important.

To sum up, the year's work has been by far the most encouraging that I have been privileged to witness, and I venture to think that the Church here is only just beginning its course of testimony and victory. I anticipate that next year will see an enormous accession. Is the C.M.S. prepared for the calls upon its resources which the rapid increase of the work here might mean? What if we should require a hundred thousand copies of the New Testament in the course of the next two or three years, and say a million reading-sheets? this would make about 1,500 loads; how are they to be brought here in addition to everything else?

Let me add one word about reinforcements. Is it not obvious that our present staff is not nearly sufficient? There are, thank God, several most able Natives, real soul-winners too ; but they are not yet fully qualified to organise and keep books, nor to train people for this work. Europeans are needed for a few years in considerable numbers; men of ability and education and spiritual power are needed. Such then would, as far as one can foresee, be the means in God's hand of putting into the field here, say, each of them, ten Native Missionaries in a few years, each of the ten in most ways equal, in many ways superior, to any European ; therefore, I venture to say, that one European of the kind required now is worth ten, five years hence. May the Lord of the Harvest open the eyes of those at home to see it ! "

CHAPTER XIII.

ON FURLOUGH.

IN the summer of 1895, Pilkington and Baskerville came home on furlough. They travelled by the northern route which passes through British territory, and it is by this route the railway is being constructed, the commencement of which has proved the most certain indication of the intention of the British Government to maintain the Uganda Protectorate. Mr. Baskerville gives a graphic account of the difficulties of the march and the sufferings of the porters, which will be at an end when the railway is completed. He writes:—

" Though the north road has been proved to be far more healthy for Europeans, yet it is a far more terrible journey for the native porters. There are the waterless districts near the coast, and the long stretch of foodless country, stretching from Kikuyu to Mumia's in Kavirondo, a three weeks' journey, for which food has to be carried in addition to the ordinary load. This foodless district is very high ground, rising over the Mau escarpment to 8,500 feet, and is consequently very cold, and the porters suffer much. Then, too, man-eating lions seldom leave any caravans alone, and highwaymen are always on the look-out for stragglers.

ON FURLOUGH.

Let me recall a few facts connected with our home journey last summer. We laid in our food supplies in Busoga and distributed them between all members of the caravan. The ordinary African does not look far ahead, and it is not an uncommon thing for a man to throw away a large portion of his rations, keeping just enough for his immediate need, or some will eat up three weeks' food in one, and then tell you they are starving. The Government provide all their porters with a blanket and waterproof sheet for crossing the Mau escarpment; the men constantly sell these to natives of Kavirondo, and then die of cold. One day we had just come to a river, when we saw on the opposite bank an up-country caravan approaching. We waited and watched it go by. Many of the men looked greatly emaciated, some mere skeletons. Some were offering things in sale for flour. We had not gone more than a mile when I noticed a man by the side of the path. He had no earthly belongings except a rag of cloth round his loins. We asked him who he was. He said he had been carrying the head man's tent, but that morning could not manage it, so his load had been given to another, and he had been left. That night he would have been eaten by hyenas. He had dysentery and a bad cough. We gave him brandy and milk, and helped him along that day, feeding him at night in camp with arrowroot. The next day he started walking, but arrangements had to be made to carry him. By no force of argument could we persuade our Swahili headman to leave behind a load of drums he was taking down to a friend. We would give him double the price. No, his friend wanted the drums, not the money; fortunately our provision boxes were getting light, and by putting two or three loads together we managed to get two bearers. The next day we were detained by two more sick men. We had passed many corpses of men and donkeys, some only recently dead. When we found these two men by an old hut in a camping place in a very wild spot just by a marsh, one had been there nine days without food. He had bad feet, an old sore had become poisoned by wading through marshes. He had been under the care of a headman, who had thought it less trouble to leave him, and probably reported him dead. We learned the headman's name and reported the matter at Kikuyu, and I trust our friend will get a warm punishment. Thus abandoned, he was found by another caravan, and robbed by them of all he had, food, cloth, and water calabash. A few days before we found him, he had been joined by another, and the night before a third man had crept in to die, and there we saw his corpse lying close by. Strange to say, our friend seemed quite cheerful, and only asked for a fire and some water. We made a fire and drew water for him, and fed him and his companion with some cooked food we had with us. He said, 'If when you get to the Ravine (a Government Station, two days' march away), you tell the white man to send for me, he will find me still alive.' Of course we could not leave him thus, and his companion was evidently dying. We managed to carry them on, one on a small donkey we had; and by giving some light loads to our boys, we set free two men to carry the other. Had we met more sick men, we could not have carried them on, except by leaving behind food, or tents, or clothing, and thereby endangering the lives of ourselves and our own men.

The horrors of the road for these poor porters can only be understood by one who has travelled on it. All this the railway will change, and also it cannot fail to check what remains, and that is a good deal, of the slave-trade."

It may be added that the railway, so far as it is at present completed, as far as Kibwezi, is marked on our map of Eastern Central Africa, as well as the survey up to the Lake.

On arriving at the coast, the missionaries were most hospitably received by the Rev. W. E. and Mrs. Taylor.

Mr. Taylor's reminiscences of their visit furnish an interesting review of this period. He writes:—
"The arrival of Baskerville and 'Pilks,' as he was familiarly called by his missionary comrades, caused quite a stir among us, his friends at the coast, when in August, 1895, they came to Frere Town, with their Waganda porters and boys. We were very curious to see men whose doings and labour had been so wonderfully honoured of God in Uganda. We found them very modest and retiring, which natural trait was further heightened by the shyness they felt to appear before the lady workers at Frere Town in their rough, up-country rig, now very much the rougher for an 800 miles journey on foot, without

the possibility of a renewal of their travelling kit through such deserts as those they had traversed. However, I think a deposit of European clothes, &c., that was awaiting Mr. Baskerville at the Accountant's Office, was divided between them, and they forthwith became more presentable; and so in Pilkington's case also, the way-worn garments and 'clouted shoon' were soon discarded for a more conventional, if not a very well-fitting, garb, although he need not have minded, for he looked well in anything. One odd little matter as to his person struck me—a thick pile of short hair that came well down on the side of the neck. It struck me that this formed a covering to the neck where it otherwise would have been naked to the bitter rays of the oblique morning and evening sun, which are much more dangerous, because more insidious, to the European than are the vertical ones. This may in part account for what I thought an uncommon tolerance of glare, and, therefore, I think it may not be amiss to mention it. Also he told me, in regard to his precautions against sunstroke in itineration and travel, that before going out he would give his headgear—a pith topee—a good soak in water, and also place a fresh banana leaf within the helmet, further to protect his head, and then he was ready for anything, and would suffer no inconvenience in this way for as long a time as the headgear retained its dampness, when, if possible, he would repeat the process.

Very soon after his arrival, we had a walk through Frere Town—he was staying with us in the Bishop's House, which Bishop Tucker had loaned to us, to afford us a change from Mombasa, and Baskerville was resident in another, and boarded with Mr. Binns—and one of the first things that struck one, was the way he could enjoy a *walk* with his blistered feet because of the *talk !* We found in the languages, in fact, a most absorbing topic. We had several such walks, which were to me full of instruction, as we compared notes concerning our respective language studies, and their bearing on our work.

He told me practically what he repeated in a letter which I received only shortly before his death, of his great indebtedness to Sweet's 'Primer of Phonetics,' which I was privileged to have recommended Millar to take out to him in 1892. He said that that book had been the means of making things in the language clear as daylight to him, where all before had been like groping in the dark. He attributed to this book his discovery and fixing the *rationale* of the most important phonetic feature of the Uganda tongue — the longs and shorts in consonants and vowels. He also traced to my little book on the Proverbs of the East Africans ('African Aphorisms, or Saws from Swahili Land,' S.P.C.K.) his beginning the study and collection of the Uganda proverbs, which he turned to such good account in his Tractate on Roman Catholicism and Mohammedanism, and in his Evangelistic and Pastoral work in Uganda. He said justly, that without the study of the National Proverbs, one could never properly know the workings of the African mind. In almost all these things we had come by different ways, to the same, or nearly the same, general conclusions. He was good enough to be present at the weekly Swahili lectures I was giving at that time to the candidates for the Language Examinations, and would give excellent illustrations of the matter in hand from his own experience in the language of Uganda; and I used to call upon him for a demonstration of various African sounds, compared with those sounds as uttered in Irish brogue, with which he was conversant. He was surprised at the similarity thus emphasized.

Pilkington was no half-an-half Protestant, but withal there was no *personal* bitterness imported into his uncompromising statement of opinion in the Romish controversy which he had had to wage while in Uganda." Reference is then made by Mr. Taylor to some special lines of argument which were afterwards developed by Pilkington with great effect in the little book "ANONYA ALABA," which will be referred to later on. There is little doubt that his knowledge of Ireland and the Irish gave him a keen insight into the difficulties of Roman Catholics, whilst at the same time he knew how to deal with such questions in a way calculated to attract, rather than to repel those with whom he came in contact. Mr. Taylor continues:— "He would give one in private, as also he and Baskerville did in a meeting convened for the purpose, the stirring account of God's dealings with the Uganda Mission; which, in leading the Missionaries and Teachers to just views of the absolute necessity for personal consecration and the direct and supreme work of the Spirit of God, so happily brought about the vivification of the Church in Uganda. He had conceived a great respect—and surely he was a judge, as capable as he was conscientious—of the abilities and graces of the Uganda converts, and especially of those who had become teachers, and he would relate anecdotes in support of his opinion, some of which I took notes of as he told them. A preacher at Mengo said in his sermon, that to form a judgment of a man's deserts, *man's* way is to put his evil deeds into one scale, and his virtues and religious observances into the other; whereas God's way, in such a case, would be to put both these into the debit scale. Another similar pulpit utterance, was a determination the preacher made between the spheres of faith and works, or rather of inward holiness and heart religion on the one hand, and outward observances on the other. Said the preacher: 'Religion may be compared to a banana.* The real heart religion is the juicy pulp, the forms and ceremonies are the skin. While the two are undivided, the banana keeps good till it is used, and so it is with religion. Separate the forms from the spirit, and the one will be of no more value than the banana husk, while the latter will speedily decay and corrupt apart from the outward expression.' Observances, the preacher pointed out, had their value in protecting the holy germ within, and fostering the feelings of the heart. This was called forth by the arising of a certain spirit of insubordination to the ordinances of the Church, and

* The banana is the national food of the people of Uganda.

had its effect. What European teacher, Pilkington asked, could have used such a simile? He was always insisting on the necessity to true progress of *the African for Africa*. Another wise saw was: , No poisoner gives poison *neat,* if he would remain undiscovered. The devil knows that.' Again : ' The devil has two devices ; he will do one of two things—first he will try and deprive you of the food; and if he cannot deprive you of it, he will corrupt it.' These were spoken by the native preacher in reference to the Romish teaching, which was then, and is now, combating the work of our Missionaries so keenly and so persistently. One man (I think Samwili), in a prayer for the blessing of God on the Evangelists, used an expression which had greatly struck our friend : ' We have the line, Thou hast the hook ! ' When the Mohammedans of Mombasa had heard him proclaim the conversion of *three* known Mohammedans in Uganda, which I asked him to attest at our open-air meetings in Mombasa, —for the reason that the Mohammedans at the coast had said that the conversion of a Moslem was a simple impossibility,—they characteristically explained it away by saying, ' Oh, the Waganda were written down to the *English* from eternity ! '— by the English meaning ' Christians.' "

On reaching England, at the end of October, 1895, Pilkington stayed for a few days with Mr. Bushell, at Harrow, before visiting his Irish home.

He made his first appearance at the Annual Meeting of the Gleaner's Union, on November 1st, and he created a great impression as he told of the change which had come over the lives of many of the Uganda converts, not to speak of the Missionaries, as the result of the great revival at the out-pouring of God's Spirit. At the same meeting he made an earnest appeal for men to devote themselves to literary work in the Mission Field.

But he had not returned home in order to go from place to place, seeking to rouse the home Church to her responsibilities to the unevangelised world, as in the case of most Missionaries. His mission was a very definite one—to see through the Press the revised Luganda New Testament, to complete the translation of the Old Testament, and thus to furnish for the Uganda Church, on his return, a completed Bible in one volume. But, if he did not often appear on the public platform, when he did speak an impression was made in many cases which will never be effaced. In no case was this more remarkable than in his visits to the Universities of Oxford and Cambridge. At Oxford he spoke at Canon Christopher's Annual C.M.S. breakfast—that remarkable annual gathering, when so many distinguished graduates of the University, as well as undergraduates, gather year by year to meet some Missionary from abroad. On this occasion the gathering was a particularly representative one. Pilkington's review of the history of the Uganda Church was unusually comprehensive, and his illustrations most interesting, and, in conclusion, he made the following stirring appeal to Oxford men:—

"Surely there must be many," he said, "who longed for opportunity to show their devotion to Christ in some more adequate way. There were thousands and thousands of miles in the Soudan waiting for self-sacrifice, and let them not suppose the Soudan would be won for Christ without sacrifice. Surely it would come from somewhere, and why not from Oxford? They could not choose for themselves the sacrifice—that would be no real sacrifice—but when God called them, when God opened the way, when God gave them the privilege, surely they would not shrink from it. Might he end by giving them a message from a Mohammedan in Uganda? He was speaking to him about the riches of Christ, and he replied, 'Do you think we should ever leave this religion of ours which has cost us so much suffering?' He loved his religion because it cost him so much, and he believed it was true that most things were worth to them what they had cost them. If God gave them the opportunity, and opened the way and called them to it, he begged of them not to shrink. He believed they could do a work in Uganda, such as could be done in no other part of the world, because in no other part of the world was there material lying waiting as in Uganda. Here was the opportunity. He challenged them to accept it."

Among the senior members of the University present at that gathering was Sir Henry Acland, late Regius Professor of Medicine, and he rose to express the thanks of the audience to Mr. Pilkington, and, in the course of his speech, he said:—

"They saw before them a man of strength, a man of heart, a man of education, who went forth among the millions of their fellow creatures to teach everything that mankind required to know for their progress, their well-being, their happiness here and hereafter. What more was to be said? They were aware that the study of physical science had, within the last half-century, become an essential part of the curriculum of the University of Oxford. He wondered whether the time would not shortly come when their able, thoughtful, excellent undergraduates, who studied in that department of human knowledge, would qualify themselves especially to go as highly accomplished, medical advisers to assist Missionary work throughout the world—(hear, hear). He spoke from knowledge of some of their young scientific men that he believed, if that idea was put into their minds, they would be proud and anxious, on behalf of God's work, on behalf of their Queen, to go and faithfully join under the instructions and guidance of such a man of vigour and goodness and sympathy for his fellow creatures as they had heard address them that morning—(applause). He would only presume to add one word. Was it not a blessed thing to hear so much that was so deeply, scientifically, and intellectually interesting as was Mr. Pilkington's account of the people of Uganda, without one single word of politics or of the quarrels and disputes of party men all over the world? They had set before them the high object of elevating these poor people, so that they might be even teachers in England."

But, perhaps, even more interesting than this meeting at Oxford, was the breakfast held in the hall of his own College, Pembroke College, Cambridge, at the invitation of the Master. It was an unique occasion, and Dr. Searle's account of this gathering, given in the course of a chapel sermon after Pilkington's death, is a valuable record of that day. He says:—

"His appearance in our hall about two years ago made a great impression. The majority at the breakfast in hall at that time had never met him, or heard him speak. One was the present Bishop of Rochester, Dr. Talbot, who kindly wrote to me to condole with me on the loss of my friend, and adds: 'I see him standing at your high table that morning, and his manners and words made a great impression on me, as strong as any that I have received for some years.' I can recollect how intently the Bishop followed him, and took notes of his address.

Others were greatly impressed. The Master of Trinity referred to his choice language and exquisite delivery, and remarked, though ignorant of his classical distinction, 'it is like the address of a scholar.'

All this can be remembered, and serves to show how precious all natural gifts can become when consecrated to God. His fine person, his rich voice, his linguistic ability, his classical knowledge, all told. But there was something more; he kept back nothing of the Gospel, and as he spoke of the deepest things with a holy reverence, I know our hearts burnt within us, and we felt that we had a prophet amongst us, a man young, indeed, in years, and though not a doctor of theology, who could, notwithstanding, lead us to a high wisdom and instruct us in the way of God more perfectly.

So do teachers learn from their pupils, and must not disdain to confess it."

Previous to these meetings, Pilkington was present at the historic Conference of the Student Volunteer Missionary Union, at Liverpool, in 1896. Here there were 717 student delegates from the Colleges of the world, 77 being foreign delegates including representatives of 19 foreign countries, and at this conference the motto 'The Evangelisation of the world in this generation,' was deliberately chosen as the watchword of the S.V.M.U.

We have seen something of the work of Christian men at Cambridge during the time that Pilkington was an undergraduate, and at the same time a similar work was being carried on at Oxford, though amid greater difficulties, and even then there had been organised year by year for a considerable time, an annual Conference of members of the Oxford and Cambridge Christian Unions for their mutual help and encouragement.

Meantime, owing to the visit of the "Cambridge Seven," already mentioned, under the leadership of C. T. Studd and Stanley Smith, a revival was taking place in Edinburgh University, fanned to a flame by the work of Professor Henry Drummond and by other Christian Professors.

It was some years later, however, that the idea

borrowed from the Student Volunteer Missionary Union of America, laid hold on British students and resulted in the formation of the Student Volunteer Missionary Union, which, with its sister organisation, the British College Christian Union, has drawn together students from all the chief Universities and Colleges of Great Britain and Ireland, and through the World's Students' Christian Federation, is uniting in one great bond of brotherly Christian sympathy, the National Students' Christian organisations of Europe, Asia, Africa, America, Australia and Japan.

The Liverpool Conference was the first outward demonstration to the churches of this country of the wide-reaching importance of this movement, though even that was only an imperfect forecast of the development which has taken place since that time.

This was the first time that Pilkington had been brought face to face with the work of the Student Volunteer Missionary Union, and this Conference was an inspiration to him, whilst his presence was an inspiration to the Conference.

The evangelisation of the world in this generation was a possibility which he had already contemplated, and he threw his heart and soul into the working out of this great ideal, contending that if only the natives of Uganda were used as they might be, Africa at least might speedily be evangelised.

No one, however, must suppose that Pilkington was a mere theorist; he did not encourage others to high aims and expectations without giving them the most practical suggestions as to the methods of work to be adopted, and the qualifications needed for it.

His remarks on this subject at the Liverpool Conference were of so great value that we may reproduce the main part of his address.

He said:—

"I wish to speak to you first of all about the methods of directly evangelistic work, and secondly, about the main qualifications needful for it.

1. *Methods*:—It is most needful to seek to understand the ignorance of those with whom you have to deal. If you speak to an African of God, he does not know what you mean, and your words convey no meaning to him. If you would win him, you must give him *the testimony of a Christian life*. These people must see that the Gospel will meet their needs ; they must be made to realize that it is a power in your life, and can be in theirs. They must know by your life that your profession is a true one. See that your words of preaching come naturally and freely. Never speak to a soul to salve your own conscience, but only when impelled by the Holy Ghost.

To gain the heathen we must live with them. *Get close to the hearts you would win for Christ*. Let your heart be entwined with their hearts ; let no barrier of big houses, or clothes, or custom come between you and the souls you would reach. See that you suffer no barriers of national prejudice to mar your work, nor any pride or daintiness. God can take all these things away from us. Let us become all things to all men ; become, not pretend to be. We need not necessarily dress like the natives, nor make any external change. It is our hearts that must be one with the hearts of those we seek. We must love and sympathise with them, ever remembering that each soul may be made like the Son of God.

Two practical hints as to method. In Uganda, we have found after-meetings of great service and very successful. It is just the outcome of the principle, that there is no salvation save by the dealing of the soul with God. We point the people to God, and say, 'We cannot save you; God can and will.'

The power to read the Bible is the key to the Kingdom of God. With the exception of one case, I have never known anyone profess Christ who could not read.

2. *Qualifications.* There are four things essential for the work of evangelisation.

    1. Physical qualifications.
    2. A knowledge of the language.
    3. Love and Sympathy.
    4. The Power of the Holy Ghost.

The first two are, of course, possessed by natives in far greater measure than by ourselves; the third we share with them; the fourth is free to all.

If this be so, then the natives are more qualified to evangelise than we are. The evangelisation of Africa must be carried out by Africans, and it will be accomplished when we have a hundred native evangelists to every European missionary.

Physical Qualifications. I was speaking once to a

man of the world, and he said he believed that success or failure depended on this, that some men do, and some do not, realize the importance of physical care in the matter of food and sleep. The best training for a missionary is to be able to live on the simplest food, and never to *indulge* in sleep. It is a most important thing that a man should have perfect control over these things. It was in the matter of food that the Israelites were first tempted, and in the matter of sleep that the disciples failed in the hour of their Lord's need.

Knowledge of the Language. Learn the native language till you can read the hearts of the people and get to understand their thoughts. Do not be content to speak as a European, but aim at perfection, for on this may depend immortal souls. Do not let English come between you and the people. Do not study the language before you go out, but study the sounds of spoken language—that is, phonetics. Study not only the Bible and the hearts of men, but also their throats. *Now* is the time to do it. Get Sweet's Primer of Phonetics, which will teach you to combine sounds and get control of your vocal organs. When at length you are learning the language, seek to associate sounds with objects. Let each object bring some native sound ringing in your ears, so that the sound brings the object before your eyes.

Love and Sympathy. Now and here is the time and place for preparation in these essentials. Take every opportunity of exercising love and sympathy towards all whom you meet.

The Power of the Holy Ghost. I would urge every man to accept the power of the Holy Ghost to change his life *now*. It is only by the fulness of the Holy Spirit in our own hearts that we can really get at the hearts of the people. Let us each one maintain by any means, and by all means, and at all times, the fulness of the Holy Ghost in our lives."

Considering the success which Pilkington attained not only in his Bible translation, but in his knowledge of the colloquial, his hints on the methods of acquiring a foreign tongue may well be laid to heart by those who would follow in his steps.

He frequently stated that, in his opinion, it was not so much an essential to be possessed of rare abilities, as it was to follow definite methods of study, such as those mentioned in his Liverpool address.

In a letter to his sister at the time she was working as a Missionary in India, he writes:

". . . I think you will find that the real and most stringent test of knowledge of a language is, whether you can understand the natives speaking among one another.

I believe we must learn like children, through the ear, not by books much; rather the office of books is to enable us to make up and understand when we hear spoken words and sentences, which only constant hearing (whether by repetition to ourselves aloud, or by hearing others say them) will teach us to know in that instinctive way which is necessary to real speaking or understanding. To know thoroughly by book is an utterly different thing from knowing by ear."

But it is not all who are ready to adopt the methods which he adopted. He never cared what anyone thought of him, and did not mind how ludicrous he seemed to others, as he copied even the grimaces of the natives, if only he could achieve his object of speaking like a native. Nor was he disappointed, for we are told that the natives spoke of him as "a true Muganda."

But he was not satisfied with a mere knowledge of the sounds of the language, and the ability to produce them. If he was to be understood, he felt that he must master the native idiom, and be able to use their similes instead of European ones, which would be utterly unintelligible to the African mind.

It is strange how often this is forgotten by those who go to work in foreign countries, and it is largely owing to this, that so much of the knowledge gained, even in mission schools, is superficial, because the books used in teaching have been based, not on the customs or even the objects seen in the country, but upon things which the children have had no opportunity of understanding, owing to the land in which they live.

Pilkington therefore devoted himself to the study of the proverbs and similes of Luganda, and he describes his plan in a letter to his mother from Uganda, dated April 5th, 1895.

" I am learning every day, and am daily realizing my ignorance more. It is a beautiful language, and most rich and expressive, but with very little in common with English; it is necessary to know their similes and metaphors as well as the mere words;

what European would talk of having ears as 'sharp as an elephant's,' or being as thin (not as a poker), but 'as a blade of grass'; or of being afraid (not of your shadow), but 'of the breaking of a blade of grass,' etc., etc. These are the things that make one intelligible and interesting to these people, but to get to use them naturally, without effort, is extremely difficult. Then their proverbs! Half of our English ideas are only translatable by means of proverbs into Luganda—*e.g.*, the words 'impartial or partial,' 'interested or disinterested,' would have to be turned by using the proverb, 'In matters that concern the forest, is the monkey judge?' or to translate the expression, 'he's only got himself to thank, your own fault, etc.,' you must use a proverb about sores, that come from self-inflicted cuttings in the flesh for ornamentation; and nothing else would be really intelligible to these people in that context, except that particular proverb. So we are still a long way from being masters of this language."

Such was the great burden of his conversation when he met with those who, like himself, felt the paramount claims of the unevangelised world, and who desired to gain from him some hints as to the great secret of his success during only one term of service on the mission field.

At the same time, his earnest devotion to this great work of his life did not in any way act as a depressant upon his naturally buoyant spirits, and he was just as ready as ever to enter into the interests of those around him, and to have a game with some boys, who always seemed to be to him the most congenial of companions.

Mr. Hyslop writes of his impression of him at this period:

"In personal appearance he was, I thought, unchanged. But in the place of the young University man there was, I might almost say, the mature veteran missionary, whose heart seemed to be 'bound in the bundle of life' with his beloved Baganda, and whose mind was intent on giving them the Bible in their own tongue. Anything 'Ugandese' (if I may venture to coin a barbaric word) attracted and interested him, and I can remember how inexhaustible was his patience in answering all importunate questions on his favourite subject. He was equally at home whether he discussed the phonetics of the native languages, or detailed the varieties of plantains to be found in Central Africa; whether he enumerated the vagaries of King M'Wanga, or described the customs of his people."

At the Keswick Convention, in July, 1896, his testimony to the work of the Holy Spirit in his own life and in the Uganda Church was a stimulus to many, especially to the young men who were there in large numbers.

One special meeting, at which he took part, was held, during the time of the Convention, of workers on behalf of Africa. It was felt to be most desirable that African Missionaries should have greater opportunities of benefiting by one another's experiences. and at this meeting it was suggested that some paper might be started which would embrace all African Missions, and form a means of knowing how far the work of evangelization was being carried on in different parts of the continent, and by what agencies. The idea of having an African Year Book of missions was also mooted, and the need of a text-book for students of African Mission-work was mentioned. This latter has since been drawn up by Mr. Douglas Thornton,* who was one of the conveners of this meeting.

From Keswick, Pilkington went for a few days to one of the Universities' Camps for Public School-boys, at Bexhill, where he was in his element. He had his bicycle with him, and had some splendid rides with parties of boys, but even during his time under canvas he was revising the Uganda Bible, and he would press boys into the service by getting them to read out to him from the English revised version, whilst he had the Luganda before him.

Afterwards, he took one of the elder fellows, whom he had met at the camp, to have a bicycle tour with him in Ireland near his home.

This was good preparation for his great ride, especially as he had one or two minor accidents, which tested, to some extent, his powers of endurance, He is said, for instance, to have ridden for the greater part of one day, with only one pedal, having damaged the other. We have dwelt at considerable length on some of the occasions when Pilkington had the opportunity of taking part in public meetings

* "Africa Waiting," by Douglas M. Thornton. Published by the Student Volunteer Missionary Union, 22 Warwick Lane, E.C.

and conferences during his furlough; it must be left to another chapter to speak at greater length of that which was his first work, Bible translation.

CHAPTER XIV.

BIBLE TRANSLATION.

"God's revelation on the one side, its breadth, its depth, its height! On the other, a heathen nation, heathen ideas, a heathen language! How can the gulf between them be bridged?

First, we must understand that a translation of the Bible can, in the nature of things, be adequate only in so far as the ideas therein contained have been transferred to the native mind.

Love, joy, peace, forgiveness, God, worship—such ideas as these cannot be adequately represented in any heathen language at first; because they are conceptions unknown to heathendom. The words which are used to translate them will gradually assume a new, and deeper, and purer meaning; but only in so far as the native mind grasps these new conceptions. Therefore teaching must go hand in hand with translating. This was markedly the case in Uganda.

The Swahili language was first used as a temporary bridge, so to say, on which to stand to build the permanent one, a translation in Luganda. This Swahili version we owed to the work of Krapf and Rebmann, and Bishop Steere and others.

For a long time the Swahili New Testament was the text-book of Uganda; day after day the most intelligent of the Christians translated from it into their own language; day after day they discussed among themselves the proper rendering of terms, appealing to the European as to the exact force of the original; for years they were thus occupied in hammering out a version on a native anvil.

Then a tentative translation of St. Matthew's Gospel was made by Mackay and Ashe; this was printed in the country, eagerly read, and criticised, and revised; reprinted, again revised, and again printed; and so on, until a version was produced which was faithful to the original and idiomatic, a splendid piece of work, and a grand basis for future translation."

So wrote Pilkington in "The Gospel in Uganda" of the first steps of Bible translation in that country.

The difficulties of first committing to writing an unwritten language is naturally a task of very great difficulty, and this had been chiefly carried out by Mackay, who in the first place had printed reading-sheets from wooden type cut with his own hand.

Assisted chiefly by Ashe in the way just referred to, some progress had been made in the translation of the Gospels; this work was taken up by the Rev. E. C. Gordon on the death of Mackay, and at the time Pilkington had arrived in Uganda, he had translated the gospel of St. Mark and commenced St. Luke, having as his helpers Henry Wright Duta and Sembera Mackay. He also completed the translation of St. John's Gospel which had been left unfinished by Mackay. Pilkington then took up the work of translation, and, with Henry Wright Duta as his chief assistant, he translated the rest of the New Testament, and later on revised the whole, carrying it through the press when in England.

He had translated, also, a considerable part of the Old Testament while in Uganda; the minor prophets being contributed by the Rev. W. A. Crabtree, and the remainder, Pilkington carried out in Ireland with the help of notes made in Uganda, in association with Henry Wright Duta.

How he actually did his work, whilst on furlough in his Irish home, is told us by his sister, Miss Pilkington, who writes of this as follows :—

"George reached Tore for his furlough in November, 1896. He had set before himself the translation of the Bible during that time. With this in view, before leaving Uganda, he went over the untranslated books with Henry Wright Duta, taking copious notes.

He had not been at home many days before he began to work systematically. He first calculated how much translation he ought to do daily, in order to finish the whole, leaving a margin of time, and then set himself a task for each day.

He had no type-writer at first, nor could he discover any way in which he could be helped. His progress was thus very slow, and each day he fell very far short of his appointed task. Soon, however, he found that it would save him much time to have the portion to be translated read aloud. I read from the revised version, with the authorized open beside me for reference, and also a French Bible, in which he found delicacies of expression which do not appear in the English. The writing was very fatiguing to him—it was with great joy that he received a present of a type-writer. At first, he could not accomplish as much with it as with pen and ink, but soon he learnt to write so fast that the amount of work got through in the day was almost doubled, and with much less fatigue. We now secured the services of a lad in the neighbourhood, who shared the reading aloud with me.

The type-writer was placed on an erection at which he could stand, without being compelled to stoop as in writing; he could now work for hours without being over-tired, and thus standing surrounded by commentaries, Greek Testament, and the parts of the Bible already finished, and his notes, he translated and wrote as I read. As a rule, he was able to write off quite rapidly; sometimes there were long delays while a word was hunted up to ascertain how it had been translated in a former passage, or an obscure portion looked out in the commentaries. As well as I remember, 'Proverbs' was the book he translated with the greatest ease and rapidity, that book seemed specially to be adapted to the Luganda mode of expression and way of thought, while the long lists of proper names in 1 Chronicles, each of which had to be spelled, were by far the most tedious parts.

He generally worked on without much pause for conversation, but now and again some verse suggested a thought, and a talk or discussion ensued.

or some idiom or beauty in the language was too interesting to be passed over in silence ; then would follow a comparison between Luganda and Hindustani, with probably a digression on the characteristics of the Waganda and the natives of India, and the best methods of reaching these different peoples. But, as a rule, we worked hard without interruption ; I used often to be reminded of our more youthful days when play was more absorbing than work, but his keenness was just the same, and in a game of lawn tennis, whether as partner or opponent, he never would allow one to grow slack for a moment—as boy or man. Not only was he himself whole-hearted in whatever he undertook, but he inspired others to be so ; it seemed as if half-heartedness could not exist in his presence.

He worked generally for six or eight hours a day, and for three weeks, when we had the house almost to ourselves, the rest of the family being away, he reached an average of ten hours a day. At this time especially his bicycle was a great help, for half-an-hour's run on it refreshed him so completely that he could start with new energy.

He always worked with the window of his room wide open, he being stationed near it, his brain refused to act without an abundance of fresh air !

When a book was translated it had, of course, to be carefully revised, then sent to the Printer, the proofs received back, revised, and again sent to the Printer, then once more carefully looked over before the final printing took place.

He was sometimes away for a few weeks at a

time addressing meetings, but in order that he might have time for the translation he was not called upon to do much deputation work. He spoke at a good many meetings in our own neighbourhood.

When not at work he was generally talking over plans for the extension of Christ's Kingdom all over the world, especially in Uganda and its neighbouring countries, but Arabia, the Soudan, and all the Mohammedan world lay very near his heart; the great problem of how to bring the Gospel Message home to the hearts of the Mohammedans was a most frequent topic of conversation.

He liked to talk over anything that he was about to write, such as articles for Magazines, and 'The Gospel in Uganda,' which Mr. Baskerville and he wrote while at home.

During the last months of his furlough, his thoughts were much occupied by the three years enterprise for Uganda, he was constantly making plans and calculations as to how the European Missionaries might move on to new ground, leaving the work already established to natives. The evangelisation of the whole world was always before him.

He was one of those who longed to impart a new idea to others, and sometimes at a very early hour in the morning, unable to wait any longer, he would seek me out full of eagerness to tell of some new plan that had struck him, or calculation he had made as to how many heathen could be reached in a given time; he loved to work out his ideas in a mathematical form, and to illustrate them with diagrams, or sometimes it was to put forward some fresh argument in a discussion which had been cut short the night before.

Notwithstanding the fact that so much of his time was devoted to work, his interest and share in the family life was very keen. He entered into all our plans for amusement with boyish zest, and was always the life of the party, bringing fun and good humour wherever he went.

He left us for Uganda in October, 1897, deeply happy in having accomplished the task he had set before him."

Besides his translation of the Bible, Pilkington also revised the Prayer Book, and the Rev. T. W. Drury, Principal of the Church Missionary College, Islington, who came in contact with him in connection with this work, bears witness to the clear grasp of Christian doctrine which he possessed. This is all the more remarkable, seeing that Pilkington had not in the ordinary way been trained in Theology, yet no doubt the close study of God's word necessary for the translation had been in itself a Theological training.

But in addition to translational work, Pilkington was the author of one important original pamphlet in Uganda, as well as a number of hymns. This pamphlet, under the title of "Anonya Alaba, He who seeketh findeth," dealt with the teaching of the Church of Rome.

The title of the first chapter, "Love," is suggestive of the spirit in which he entered into the discussion of controversial questions with those who differed from him, and it was this which gained for him the respect in which he was held by all parties.

The basis of his argument was, as he said, "the book of the Apostles of our Lord." He referred to this as the source from which both parties professed to derive their teaching, at the same time illustrating his remarks by references to Church History.

One chapter is headed with the extraordinary title "Mr. Eat and put back." In this he alluded to the way in which the Church of Rome had taken away much from the Word of God and inserted her own traditions in its place; this he compared to the action of the white ants who eat out the inside of a log of wood and put earth in its place.

By such similes as these he was able to gain the attention of the people, and what is more, to make his words intelligible to them.

CHAPTER XV.

THE CHURCH IN UGANDA: A RETROSPECT.

THE story of the Uganda Church, whether we think of it as the wonderful cathedral on Namirembe Hill and all the work connected with it, or as the body of Christians gathered out from heathendom in the centre of dark Africa, was often told by Pilkington during his furlough. But he did more. He has furnished us with a vivid picture of the work in Uganda, in the shape of four scenes, which are published in pamphlet form,* but which we are enabled to reproduce here as we believe they form the best permanent record of these addresses.

"A HUNDRED thousand souls brought into close contact with the Gospel—half of them able to read for themselves; two hundred buildings raised by native Christians in which to worship God and read His Word; two hundred native evangelists and teachers entirely supported by the Native Church; ten thousand copies of the New Testament in circulation; six thousand souls eagerly seeking daily instruction; statistics of baptism, of confirmation, of adherents, of teachers, more than doubling yearly

* "The Gospel in Uganda." Church Missionary Society, Salisbury Square, E.C.

for the last six or seven years, ever since the return of the Christians from exile; the power of God shown by changed lives; and all this in the centre of the thickest spiritual darkness in the world! Does it not make the heart reel with mingled emotions of joy and fear, of hope and apprehension?

Well may Christian hearts rejoice with trembling as they hear of it! Well may they 'labour in prayers' for such possibilities, either of magnificent success or heartbreaking disaster!"

The following is an attempt to describe what the writer has seen of these things:

Scene I.

"We are in the great church in the capital on Namirembe Hill. It is a week-day, any week-day but Monday, about eight o'clock in the morning. As we glance down the aisles of poles, we see that the whole building is filled with groups of learners, sitting most of them on the floor, but the teachers and some others on chairs or stools; some dressed in robes of snow-white calico, others in bark-cloth knotted over the right shoulder. What is this large group, fifty or sixty in number? This is a class for St. Mathew's Gospel, and this teacher with refined and intellectual face is Thomas Semfuma, and he is teaching St. Matthew's Gospel. There are two or three other classes for this one Gospel, which, as it was the first translated, is still the most popular. And who is that keen and energetic little man who is organizing those elementary classes for reading near the end of the church? That is Wambuzi,

God-gifted for that, to us, tedious and trying work. No hound keener after game than he after every soul that can from Heathen be transformed into a seeker after God; none more unwearied than he in hammering into dull heads the letters and syllables which are to be the means of letting in the Gospel light. Come out for a moment from the church, and from the high vantage point of Namirembe's summit, look out at that cluster of bee-hive huts on that hillside opposite. That is an encampment of Wasoga, come from their homes across the Nile to make noisy music with the blare of their horns and the monotonous twang of their harps for Mwanga's royal ears. If you go there this afternoon, you will be not unlikely to meet indefatigable Wambuzi as he passes from hut to hut, trying to coax these wild and untaught, but good-natured and easily-led Wasoga, into giving heed to the things of God. Many and many a Musoga has gone home with the first beginnings of Divine knowledge instilled into his mind by Wambuzi's persevering efforts. May God give many like him!

There are many other classes, forty or so in all, with an average of thirty or forty in each class. Each of the four Gospels is represented by more than one class; and some of the European Missionaries are teaching the Epistles, while one organizes and supervises the whole.

But what is that sound that recalls us to the church and its congregation, nearly forgotten as we gazed across the hills into far-off Kikabya and Bulemezi, and thought of the millions lying behind those hills to north, and east, and west, and wondered when, oh, when——!

But the loud, rhythmical beat of the great drum calling us to prayers, heard for some four or five miles round, disturbs our reverie, and we return to the church as the classes break up and gather in the front while one of the native readers or deacons gives out a hymn; then the Apostles' Creed is recited as by men who believe it: then prayers, some from the Prayer-book, some extempore. And then the assembly breaks up, and we watch them dispersing, the bright sun gleaming on the snowy robes of the chiefs, and less dazzlingly on the humble bark-cloth of the poorer folk, as down the hill they go to pursue their various avocations—chiefs to decide disputes or pay their respects to the king; women to cultivate and cook; boys to dance attendance on their lords or run messages; some to the market, some out to their farms in the country."

SCENE II.

"It is three o'clock one Friday afternoon, and again we climb the hill and enter the great church; it is not full, but perhaps a thousand or more are gathered on this first Friday in the month to hear what God has been doing throughout Uganda and in some neighbouring countries, and to bid prayerful farewell to those who are being sent out with the Gospel message to needy places, and to bring offerings to God for the support of this work.

Who is that young fellow who is pleading with

tears for more labourers for that dark spot where he has been working against great odds for some months? That is Nathaniel. As he speaks of the need and the encouragements he has met with, and the difficulties, we are encouraged and depressed by turns.

And who is this who is telling of a great work in Koki, far away to the south-west? Defiant opposition, slander, misunderstandings, and then prayer answered; charms brought to be broken or burnt; a weekly congregation of two or three hundred souls, besides others in the country; books bought in considerable quantities, and sixty able to read a Gospel where not one could read before. This is lame Michael, who, in spite of his lameness, result of a bullet in the Mohammedan wars, undertook the journey to Koki, one hundred and thirty miles away, and with the help of half a dozen other teachers, bore a bright Gospel testimony in that interesting country, befriended, it is true, by the King, Kamswaga, whose handsome and intelligent features and quiet dignity of manner have greatly impressed all Europeans who have known him. This young ruler decided a year ago to be instructed in the reformed Christian religion, in spite of the great pressure brought to bear on him from more than one influential quarter. He spent a few weeks in the capital, and at that time declared his intention of being a Protestant by attending services on Sunday in the big church; after his return to Koki with Michael, and when he had by his instruction learnt more of the Protestant religion, he wrote a letter to the Church at Mengo declaring his fixed intention of persevering in the course he had entered on, in spite of opposition. The possibilities of service offered in Koki are unique.

Or perhaps we have the privilege this afternoon of listening to the story of evangelisation in Toro, two hundred miles due west from Mengo, and therefore within only a trifling distance of Stanley's Great Forest and the dwarfs. Perhaps it is Noah Nakiwafu who is telling about the trials and encouragements there; how Kasagama, the King of Toro, welcomed them, and how presents were sent and efforts made to induce him to profess a less pure form of Christain faith—in vain. How, imitating the example of the native evangelists, although they never spoke to him about it, he became a total abstainer, strange novelty for a great African chief; and how now (if we may project into past time what we now know to be the case) he has asked for baptism. How a church was built in some still more remote spot, and application made for teachers, and how none were forthcoming; how the two churches in Toro were filled each Sunday with congregations of two or three hundred; how the King of Unyoro, Kabarega, sent an army and broke up the work in the more northern of the two stations (where Japheth, long ago baptised, is chief), but only for a time; and how the natives with their teachers were in hiding until the army retired; and how afterwards Lwabudongo, Kabarega's prime minister, wishing for peace with the British, came to Kasagama and became his man, and is now, with many of his followers, desirous of Christian instruction.

But we must pass on from Noah's most interesting story, and listen to the accounts from nearer home: from Kyagwe, where some sixty churches have in a year sprung up, under the fostering care of the central station at Ngogwe; from the Islands of Sese, where more than twenty churches on as many islands testify to the wish of the sailors and fishermen of Uganda to hear the Gospel, in spite of the foolish belief that no Christian or reader ever can be a successful fisherman; as soon as the fish see a book in the angler's hands, either they will all die, or, at any rate, refuse to be caught.

But at last the various speakers have finished, and a hymn of praise has been sung, and prayers have been offered for further blessing on the work. And now a list of names is being read, and as each name is called out, we see a young man rise from his seat, till some eight or ten are standing up; these are evangelists who are being sent out to some of the country churches. And now an address is being given, urging, probably, on these young messengers of Christ, their duties and responsibilities, and on the Native Church their part in the work, their duty of prayer, and the privilege of giving in support of their evangelists, for all the native teachers are supported by the natives: 'It is more blessed to give than to receive, and we Europeans cannot rob you of your blessing by supporting your teachers,' so we have often told them. And so, when the address is over, we shall see them coming forward with their offerings to God—shells, which they deposit in a large native basket placed in the centre of the aisle; calico, bark cloth—the beautifully prepared bark of a kind of fig tree, torn off in strips, scraped, beaten with grooved mallets, and sewn together with plantain fibre; mats; fowls; goats; cows sometimes, and even ivory; and then comes a long stream of women and girls, each carrying a bunch of plantains or a bundle of sweet potatoes on her head, till the pile of offerings grows to an alarming size, though its money value is not great; and then a prayer of dedication is offered, and we ask the Lord to accept and make use of these gifts which He has allowed us to give Him; and then the benediction, and the service is ended.

These monthly Missionary Meetings are now being established in other centres too.

Do these evangelists do good work?

A Missionary visited a small island in the Lake two years ago, and found one person only there who could read at all. Two teachers were sent, and after nine months sixty were able to read a Gospel. Two teachers were sent to another island: in a year one church, or rather hovel, capable of containing a hundred by crushing, had become four churches, one of them holding seven hundred souls, and the congregation of a hundred had become a thousand, and some fifty or more had been baptized, and many more were catechumens; its name is Busi. You can see it on the map.

The teacher whom God chiefly used to produce these wonderful results is a man of spiritual power; on fire with love to God and man. 'Oh, Lord, we have only the bare line, Thou hast the hook,' so he prayed one day as he asked that souls might that day be saved. And God has proved that hook sharp and barbed to His servant who has counted upon Him.

The work done and being done by these teachers has opened our eyes to marvellous possibilities for Africa and the World. 'The World to be evangelised in this generation'—can it be done?

Kyagwe, a province fifty miles square, has had the Gospel preached, by lip and life, through almost every village in the space of one short year, by some seventy native evangelists, under the supervision of only two Europeans: more than two thousand square miles and only two Europeans! The teacher, on Busi above mentioned, has by this time probably accomplished his purpose of visiting every house in that island with the message of Salvation on his lips. Soon we may hope that there will be no house left in Uganda that has not had God's message brought thus to its very threshold. What is to prevent the extension of this system two hundred miles in every direction round Mengo—this is the distance of our furthest outpost, Toro—in the course of a few years, three or four? Only the lack of the comparatively few European trainers and organizers needed for so magnificent an expansion! Will they not be forthcoming? 'Let us go up at once and possess it; for we are well able to overcome it.'"

Scene III.

"And now let me transport you to the wooded

island of Kome; for, standing on its centre ridge, we can gaze across the Lake to east, and west, and north—a very lovely sight. There is Ntebe twenty miles away on the mainland, the Government Station, the port of Mengo; we have there a church, in fact, three churches and four teachers, with a promising work. On that bare island of Nsazi, separated by only a narrow piece of water from that on which we stand, and contrasting strangely its treeless hillsides with Kome's rich forests, there is a small church. It is only some two years since a missionary, visiting Nsazi, found there only one soul who could read at all. Two teachers were sent there. After nine months' work there were sixty who could read pretty well.

Then over to the east lies Lwaji, first of the Buvuma Islands, though politically part of Uganda; here is a church and a keen desire to learn. And far away behind Lwaji, we see the large Buvuma Island, dark-wooded ridge bounding the furthest horizon; and about it lie its smaller sisters of the Buvuma group, all still unoccupied by the Gospel, except uttermost Bugaya, the one bright spot in great darkness. On this outlying island a good work seems to be going on; the two chiefs of it seem favourably disposed, and several have learnt to read; a church has been built. The three Muganda teachers sent there showed much real Christian zeal and self-denial, resolutely putting up with food to which they were not accustomed (and little enough of that), a kind of canary seed made into porridge, husks and all; eaten with milk, or with a kind of sour fruit; it is poor stuff after plantains.

A boy from this island of Kome, a slave by old native law, followed one of the missionaries to the capital, and finding that he could claim his freedom, he did so, and was declared free by the Katikiro. A bright idea struck him; he would go and release from domestic slavery a sister, whose master owned her by the same right by which he had owned him, the brother. So off he went—to return crestfallen; he had met only ridicule and contempt. 'What, she, a member of a decent family, take a freedom which wasn't hers! Was ever the like heard!' Like the Irish-woman, who replied to the kind-hearted stranger who, summoned by her screams, rebuked her husband for so cruelly beating his wife, 'And who's got a better right?' A willing slave is a slave indeed.

Turning our eyes a little to the south, we see Bukasa, now a C.M.S. Station, and the centre of the work in the Sese Islands. Yes, let our eyes rest a while on its long ridge; it is a bright spot; had you once seen its tall and hideous (with small-pox marks) but delightful master, you would not soon forgot him. He it was who sent back, unbidden by any voice but that of God and the native teacher, the slaves captured on Buvuma Island, in the war that took place there some four years ago. Those who saw him shoving his way through crowds of book-buyers in the old days on Namirembe, and returning to the fray again and again to purchase reading sheets for his islanders, when dearth of books had caused the missionaries to refuse to sell more than one copy at a time to a single purchaser, will not forget his persistence and jovial good temper.

He and two other island chiefs, when almost all the islands were in the hands of the Roman Catholics, stood firm in spite of much opposition, and that, though their own knowledge at that time was only trifling. Would that we had as good reason to believe that the other two are the Lord's as we have of him!

The large Island of Sese is not generally visible from Kome, but we can imagine that we see it some ten miles beyond Bukasa, rising high above all its satellites, twisted like some great snake upon the Lake's bosom. All its chiefs are Roman Catholics; yet on it are some three hundred and twenty Protestants, nicknamed, we are told, 'the people of the Holy Ghost,' and enduring some persecution and opposition for the truth's sake, ignorant as they are. The Native Church has sent them two teachers and a plentiful supply of books; and they hold the fort there, despite the presence of three French Missionaries; the latter have had a station there for years. Pray for this little struggling church.

On that Sese group of islands, and on those in the midst of which Kome lies, there are some twenty churches; and in no part of Uganda has a greater desire for 'reading' been shown than on Sese. May the holy fire be passed on to Buvuma and Kigulu, and on through the islands that lie along the Kavirondo coast to Ukerewe, and there mingle with the flame that is already glimmering at Nasa, from which bright reports have reached us lately of the

Gospel preached each Sunday in six different places round; and where the Gospels are rapidly being translated into the Sukuma language and being printed. And may it also spread down the western side to Bumbide, most northern of the islands in the German sphere, and along the southern shore of the Lake to Nasa again."

Scene IV.

"It is Sunday afternoon, and some eighty souls are just about to be admitted into the visible Church by baptism. They are arranged—men on the left, women on the right—in a great semicircle by the font near the door of the church. One by one they answer the solemn questions, and are baptized into solemn covenant with the Triune God.

It is a solemn scene, and yet the truth must be confessed, that familiarity has taken much of its solemnity away. How solemn must have been those secret baptisms ten years back, when baptizer and baptized must have felt that before long the baptism of water might be sealed by a baptism of blood! But, now, when fifty baptisms take place on an average every week, and when, alas, a profession of Christianity is sometimes made for the sake of social advantages, the service is often not what it might be.

How have the candidates been prepared for admission to this solemn rite? Probably some two or three years ago they began to learn to read, taught in their own homes by their friends, or, perhaps, by teachers in the various country churches. It is astonishing what an educational value this reading of God's Word has; their very physiognomy seems to be changed by it, so that it is almost possible to tell a reader by his outward appearance. And in no other way does the reality of God seem to impress itself so forcibly on the native mind as by the daily poring over the pages of the New Testament, at first mechanically, and then with more and more glimmering of meaning, until at last the Divine message of love is intelligently grasped, and perhaps driven home by some sermon, or meeting, or the faithful words of a friend, and another catechumen is added to the roll, and, we trust, another soul to the company of Christ. It is a noticeable and deeply instructive fact that profession of conversion never, or hardly ever, has been made by a Muganda who cannot read, except, of course, a few special cases of blind or old. At the close of some of our services, after-meetings are sometimes held, and those present are asked to signify in some way their acceptance of God's gift of eternal life; out of many hundreds the writer has never known any such profession made by a person who had not learnt to read; the very words are not intelligible to those who hear them for the first time—sin, salvation, love, faith, etc., convey little meaning to their minds. Be it understood, at the same time, that on this very account we take the greater pains to point out to them continually that there is nothing to prevent an absolutely ignorant and utterly sinful soul, the very moment the Gospel message is grasped and believed, obtaining the full and free salvation which we proclaim.

In some such way, with infinite variety of detail and experience, has each individual of the class of thirty catechumens, whom we see sitting at the feet of, say, Samuel Naganafa, now Mukasa, been brought to desire baptism; some, alas, no doubt, have been influenced by worldly motives of social advancement, or by the mere example of others to enrol themselves for admission into the Church.

For two or three months past they have been daily carefully instructed in St. Matthew's Gospel, and are now half-way through St. John. One of them reads aloud a passage, then Samuel makes comments and asks questions, and his pupils ask questions, some wise, some foolish, *e.g.*, 'Why did John the Baptist send disciples to the Lord to ask if He were the Christ?' 'Wisdom is justified of her chldren—what does this mean?' 'What was the name of Peter's wife's mother?' 'and his wife's name?' 'How is it that Herod, whose death we read of some time ago, reappears on the scene?' and so on.

When four month's instruction or so is complete, they will be examined, and some tears shed, probably, if they 'fall' (*i.e.*, are 'ploughed'); then if no reason appears, on inquiry made, to prevent their baptism, they will be brought forward the next Sunday afternoon. And so the Church grows."

CHAPTER XVI.

THE FUTURE OF UGANDA: A FORECAST.

WE have glanced at the past, how about the future? Time was, when Uganda was regarded as a mere isolated centre in the mission field, a land of romance but little more. But that day is gone. Africa is no longer looked upon as the special preserve of the explorer, the scientist, or the Missionary. We need fields for the development of our commerce, and an outlet for the energies of our race. A great part of our British Empire lies in Africa, and we must see to its development. We have had put before us the ideal of a great highway from Cairo to the Cape, with its two most important junctions, Khartum and Uganda, and whilst we owe the conception of this project to one well-known living Englishman, we must not forget those to whom, as much as any, is due the interest now being taken by Great Britain in this splendid scheme.

Gordon from the north, Livingstone from the south, advanced along this line, each to die alone, though under very different circumstances; yet each was fully convinced that some day Christian England would awake to her responsibility to these regions. "I beg to direct your attention to Africa," said Livingstone in the Senate House at Cambridge in December, 1857. "I know that within a few years I shall be cut off in that country which is now open; do not let it be shut again! I go back to Africa to try to make an open path for commerce and Christianity; do you carry out the work which I have begun; I leave it with you."

"An open path for commerce and Christianity" was that for which these great pioneers lived and died, one in purpose with the men who laid down their lives for Uganda, the chief connecting link between the north and south of the new World's highway.

It is not for naught that Mackay pleaded for helpers to help to bridge the chasm between civilization and savagery, that Hannington lost his life ere he reached Uganda, furnishing by his death a trumpet call to the Church, more eloquent even than his life, or that Pilkington gave to the Uganda nation a completed Bible, in itself the best bridge from heathenism to Christianity. These African graves do not breathe to us the language of despair, keenly though we feel the loss of leaders such as these, are they not an inspiration to others to follow in their steps? There has been some talk of revenge as our brave soldiers step by step approached Khartum, and when the great victory of Omdurman was an accomplished fact we have been told that Gordon is avenged. But is it so? Gordon's death calls for something more than that, above all it is a **challenge** to Christian England to carry the

THE FUTURE OF UGANDA.

blessings of Christianity thoughout that land which has been desolated by the scourge of Muslim fanaticism. How, then, is this to be done? The answer which Pilkington would have given may, we think, be summed up in one word, "Uganda."

It has ever been the aim of British administrators to employ the peoples of savage or semi-civilized lands to be the chief agents in the development of their own country, and to this fact may largely be attributed the success of British colonisation. In no part of the world is this so important as in Central Africa. Whatever is to be done there must be done by the native races, and our first efforts should therefore be directed to learning the native languages, studying the characteristics of different peoples, bringing to the front those who are qualified to be the leaders of others, rather than attempting to do all by European agency.

Pilkington realised this most fully, and in his plans for the development of the Uganda Mission, he regarded Uganda and its people as the great means by which East Central Africa at least should be evangelised.

With this in view he put forward what he called "A three years' enterprise in Central Africa," to correspond to the celebration of the last three years of the first century of the Church Missionary Society all over the world.

In this he said :—

"The Church Missionary Society is entering on a Three Years' Enterprise. The key-note is Extension. New supplies of men and means, it is hoped, will be forthcoming. How are they to be applied to the best advantage? May God Himself guide!

With great diffidence, conscious as he is of only partial knowledge of the World's needs, and conscious also of the bias that must attend all strong affections; with great diffidence, therefore, but none the less with great earnestness, does the writer put forward a Three Years' Enterprise for Central Africa, asking for it the calm, and balanced, and prayerful consideration of all friends of the Society and especially of those who directly control its operations. Need it be said that the basis of operations for this proposed enterprise is Uganda?

Half of the great country of Unyoro is ready to receive evangelists; there are already under instruction a good many hundreds of its inhabitants; through this country, and by means of its people, lies the road to the Nile valley and to the great forest. Kavirondo is open, Usukuma is open, Karagwe is open, Koki is open. Nkole and Ukedi are within reach and touch, though not absolutely open at present. In fact, for two hundred miles east, south and west from Mengo, the country lies, for the most part, wide open to the Gospel; to the north, seventy or a hundred miles is open. The country is healthy; native help is available as it is nowhere else in the world; the desire for reading has already been carried to some of the extreme points within this radius; in language, and sentiment, and mode of life, the whole region is closely knit together; in a word, there is good reason to hope that, as far as local conditions are concerned, a circle, including

THE FUTURE OF UGANDA. 291

within its radius of two hundred miles the three lakes, the Albert, Albert Edward, and the Victoria, an area (excluding the lakes) of nearly 100,000 square miles, might be fully occupied, if not evangelised, within three years' time!

How would this enormous extension — multiplying by ten at least the present area of occupied territory—be undertaken?

Wanted, first, European leaders for bands of native evangelists. The province of Kyagwe, as already mentioned, more than 2,000 square miles, is being evangelised by means of two Europeans at the central station, directing the work of seventy or a hundred native helpers. At the same rate, a hundred European Missionaries would be needed to lead and organise the evangelisation of this vast circle. Will they not be forthcoming?

Wanted, secondly, an army of native evangelists; it is believed that the raw material for these would be forthcoming, but in order to train them efficiently, a few more European missionaries are needed.

Wanted, thirdly, about ten men to master the native languages, and translate into them.

Wanted, in all, from home, one hundred additional men missionaries and some lady missionaries, full of the Holy Ghost.

Is this too large a demand?

Even judging by the irrational method of a count of heads, it is not much; these men are not needed for Uganda, not even for this circle of two hundred miles only; we plead for the millions upon **millions of souls in Central Africa; and we only** ask for a paltry one hundred missionaries. Area and population alike call for large reinforcements in Central Africa.

But there is another method, a rational one, of distributing missionary workers, and that is, so to dispose of available forces as to bring in the greatest return in the end.

Take an illustration: There are two places that may be occupied. Let us call them A and B. To one or both of these, six missionaries are to be sent. At A, there is a great desire for instruction and a missionary spirit among the converted. At B, there are practically no converts and no missionary spirit; in fact, the Holy Spirit is at work at A but not at B. Although the population of B is ten times that of A, the irrational, but plausible, method is adopted, and five are sent to B, and only one to A, and even so complaints are made that A is receiving more than its fair share of workers.

After ten years, little or no impression has been made at B; the five workers are discouraged and depressed, and their depression has acted on the Church at home. At A the work has progressed, but the workers cannot keep pace with the growing need; and the missionary enthusiam, not having found any adequate outlet, has decreased. But let the other method be adopted, and let all the six be be sent to A, in spite of short-sighted objections. In five years, as one result of their work, a body of twenty well-trained native evangelists invade B; by the end of another five years the fire of God has been transferred to the second centre. The Church

THE FUTURE OF UGANDA. 293

at home and the Church abroad alike are encouraged and strengthened in faith.

But this is a digression.

How would our supposed reinforcement be employed?

Each fresh missionary would spend a year or more at first in Uganda; he would learn the Luganda language, become acquainted with native ways of thought (the same through all that region), gather round him a few native helpers, and open communications across the missionary frontier. To do this he would most probably settle down at the furthest C.M.S. station in the direction of his proposed advance; for instance, for Central Unyoro, Wadelai, and the Nile Valley, he would proceed at first to Kinakulya; for the west and the Great Forest, to Toro; for the south, to Koki; for the east and south-east, to Luba's or Mumia's; for the north-east, to Namuyonjo's. When the time appeared ripe, he would advance with his chosen helpers across the border, and open a tentative station some fifty miles beyond what had till then been our outpost: this new station would in turn become a basis from which to advance still further, as fresh reinforcements came out. There can be little doubt that in places, more numerous than we could even wish to occupy by Europeans, the natives would extend a welcome, and in most cases build a native house for the missionary, and supply him with native food.

Consider (i.) the geographical position of Uganda.

(ii.) The present open doors.

(iii.) The construction of a railway.

(iv.) The suitability of the natives for evangelistic work.

(v.) Their desire to engage in it.

(vi.) Their preparation by contact with two typical forms of perversions of Scripture truth.

(vii.) Their former leading position in the Lake Region.

(viii.) The past marvellous history of the country.

(ix.) The abundant 'seed of the Church' sown (martyrs, Bishop Hannington, Mackay, and many others).

Are not all these leading up to a future worthy of such a past?"

Pilkington, as will be seen by much that has been already said, was a firm believer in the evangelisation of Africa by Africans, and in support of this he furnishes us with the following contrasts:—

"An European is on a journey in Central Africa: how laboriously he trudges along, followed by a train of porters, who carry his tent, his clothing, his camp bed and bedding, his cups, plates, knives and forks, his box of provisions, his cooking utensils, his chair and table; notice how eagerly he avails himself of the shade of any tree that he is fortunate enough to find at his mid-day halting-place; see him carried over that great papyrus swamp, half a mile broad, on the shoulders of the strongest of his porters, themselves up to the chest in water. Observe the elaborate preparations for his meal; the tent pitched, the table laid, the cloth spread on it, the plates, the tea, the meat, the potatoes, the rice; and when all is done, it seems to him a rough and hard life, calculated to produce fever, or send him home, prematurely worn out, to a more congenial climate and surroundings.

A Muganda is on a journey: how gaily he trots along; his head, it may be bare, it may be covered with a turban of cloth or bark-cloth, not for fear of the sun so much as for appearance sake; or perhaps he is carrying all his luggage on a plantain leaf, twisted in turban shape, on his head. It is twelve o'clock; he has had no food since the previous evening; but he thinks nothing of that—he is prepared to march on, if need be, till sundown, fasting; but probably he will turn into one of the houses in the garden just ahead, and make an ample meal of steamed plantains or potatoes. He needs no table, table-cloth, or plates; the plaintain leaves which have helped to cook the meal, pressed down in the mouth of the huge earthen cooking pot to keep the steam in, will supply the place of all these three European necessities. Spread on the grass-covered floor, they receive the mass of steamed and steaming plantains; and the guests sit round, on mats if they have them; and the master of the ceremonies divides the huge lump into chunks for each guest, using his hand, covered with a piece of plantain leaf, as a carving knife: and so they fall to, with their fingers for knives and forks; they have previously carefully washed their hands with plantain fibre or with water. And so the lump disappears, as bit by bit they roll it in their hands, push in their right thumbs to make a sort of spoon, and dip it in the gravy (if they have any), and so convey it to their mouths. The meal done, the hands are washed again; and off goes our traveller, prepared to travel, should that prove necessary, for another twenty-four hours without any further meal, though he will be disappointed if he does not reach some hospitable roof that evening where similar refreshment will be provided. When night comes, no elaborate preparations are necessary; no camp bed, no mosquito net, he simply undoes his pack, takes out his mat, lies down on it, and, wrapping himself up, head and all, in a barkcloth, he sleeps till day-break. Is it surprising if we sometimes feel inclined to envy their simple lives?

Another picture: an European is teaching a class; how slowly come his words, how painfully sometimes; how he struggles to express himself! Do you see the lurking smile on those faces that good manners would fain hide?—but the struggle is a hard one; some mispronunciation, some solecism, some mistake has provoked it. How flat some of his illustrations seem to fall! And yet this is not some young missionary in his first attempt; for years he has endeavoured to master the native language, and not without success; but it is a partial success only.

Beside this class is another, taught by a native. How the words flow from his lips; how quickly question and answer and exposition follow one another! If there is a smile, it is at some apt illustration or some apposite proverb: 'Does the monkey decide forest cases?' *i.e.*, 'Is it reasonable to appeal to an umpire who has a personal interest

THE FUTURE OF UGANDA. 297

in the point at issue?' or another of that infinite store. Africa must be evangelised by Africans; surely this is the obvious moral that we are forced to draw.

Africans are fitted for the work, because they are better adapted to the country. Especially are they better travellers than Europeans. Then they are better adapted by their knowledge of the language and native modes of thought. An illustration which appeals to a European need not impress a native, and *vice versâ*. Arguments which are conclusive to us prove nothing to a native, and again *vice versâ*. Most important of all, it is impossible, too, in this case, to attribute the effects of the grace of God in his life to a white skin or to his bringing up. A native can say to a native with a cogency that no European's words can have, ' The Lord and Saviour who saved and saves me, can save you too.'

Where are Africa's evangelists? God must have them somewhere. Let us find them, and train them, and use them. The promise of the fulness of the Spirit is as much for the native as for the European, for the promise is ' to all that are afar off, even as many as the Lord our God shall call.'"

But there is another contrast to which he would draw our attention, which shows to us the wonderful change which the Gospel has wrought in Uganda. He writes:—

"The work that is going on in Uganda is mainly carried on by natives; the Sunday services, the preaching, the teaching, all are done by men who once were heathen. Do you know what that word means? Ask old Isaiah, 'the good-natured giant,' how three hundred brothers and cousins of the king were penned within the narrow compass of the dyke, that still may be seen by the roadside some two or three miles north of Mengo, and left there by their brother's orders to starve to death, a six days' misery of nameless horrors.

'Oh, a goat I was herding got lost, and so my master cut off my ear'—so a boy of fifteen answers, as if it were the most natural thing in the world, when you ask him how he became so mutilated.

Ask Sezi, jovial Sezi, in spite of the loss of both his eyes, who it was that gouged them out, and why? Ask any of our people what Heathenism means; for they have seen and can tell you; they know (better than many a wiseacre at home) what Christless humanity (black or white) is and always will be, when the salt taken away: it is left to itself, and relapses to its native corruption—inevitable consequence!

In those days, if some unfortunate courtier accidentally trod upon the king's mat, death was the sure penalty.

In those days, none dared raise a protest when the king, to maintain his royal dignity, commanded the slaughter of all who happened to be standing on his right hand or on his left; or of all whom a band, sent for the purpose, should meet in the streets. 'Why kill the innocent?' we innocently ask. Their innocence is their doom. 'If I only kill the guilty,' so would the king have replied, 'the innocent will not respect me.' They have no word in their language for respect, except fear.

In those days, no protest was heard when women and children were sold into the hopeless misery of Arab slavery. Now, even domestic slavery has been abolished, at least, its legal status. And in this matter the Protestant chiefs were the movers and imitators, so much so that Sir Gerald Portal, who was in the country at the time, considered that perhaps their movement was premature. To-day it is the law of the land that any slave may claim his or her freedom, and that it must be granted as a matter of course.

Not that the Waganda had no religion of their own. They were very religious; they worshipped and propitiated the spirits of ancestors. These spirits were believed to possess mediums, who uttered oracular sayings with foaming at the mouth, a close reproduction of the Delphic prophecies. There was the priest, too, who acted as go-between for the inquirer and the spirit-possessed medium. Many of the gardens of the country were set aside for these priests; hence their bitter opposition to the Gospel, continued to this day.

Once a man professed to be possessed by the spirit of the King Suna's dead dog, and went about yelping. By the king's orders, a fine house was built for him, and he lived in ease and luxury all his life!

Then charms were worn, and are still worn, and implicitly believed in. Horns (either actual horns or imitations in pottery) were filled with various substances, supposed to have magical powers

—for instance, blood or earth—and sold as certain remedies for various diseases.

In old days, woman was but a beast of burden; how wonderful to see her now in many places begin to take her rightful place by man's side! It will be a gradual work—the elevation of woman; but we do see it already proceeding. The arrival of the five ladies who accompanied Bishop Tucker last autumn will, no doubt, greatly accelerate it. Cultivation is woman's work in Uganda, and too often the heaviest work is still left to her. The men are lazy; the Gospel not only shows them the duty and nobility of work, but also provides them with motives for working.

But it is in individual lives that the greatest and most marked change is apparent. A slave of drink, a big chief, was converted. He had been baptized long before, but had no strength to conquer this vice; he had often prayed with one of the missionaries that he might be saved from this curse; he had even prayed with tears; the will was there, but not the power. He was converted, and was enabled to win the victory.

A Mohammedan began reading our books: he was convinced of their truth, and gave up Mohammedanism; a month later, so he told us, he accepted God's gift of eternal life. 'In old days,' he said one day, 'I was like a bird trying to fly without wings; I thought my fastings, my prayers, and ceremonies would save me. I now know that Christ is the way.'

Another, a teacher, told how, long ago, when he

first became a nominal Christian, he had hoped to be saved by his works; as he read God's Word he found this would not do, and then he hoped he would be saved by a combination of faith and works. 'But now I know that Christ is all.' Many have given up the vicious habit of smoking Indian hemp; the Christian Church will not permit any hemp smoker to be baptized, so utterly inconsistent is it considered.

Could you come and see some Sunday morning while men and women, brought up as heathen, gather round the Lord's table, and reverently eat and drink those 'pledges of His love,' there would be a joyful echo in your ears of the Apostle's words—'These have been washed, these have been sanctified, these have been justified in the name of the Lord Jesus Christ, and by the Spirit of our God!'"

CHAPTER XVII.

BY BICYCLE TO UGANDA.

OWING to the length of time occupied in carrying his work through the Press, Pilkington did not leave England until two months after the party with whom he expected to travel to Uganda. He, however, managed to reach Frere Town in time to accompany them, as the following letter indicates:—

                Frere Town,
                     Friday, 27th November, 1896.

I arrived, after a delightful voyage, on Wednesday, to find the party still here, hoping to start to-day. We are now hoping to start to-morrow. Goods, including bike, here, all right. Europeans and Waganda boys all well, so there is much to thank God for. . . .

We are really to start, it seems, to-morrow morning—it is now nine p.m., so I suppose we shall.

I rode up and down the road here on my bike. A sort of light case, easily detachable, has been made for it; I propose to ride it where possible.

There has been much rain lately, and so the dry part of road near the coast ought to be much better than usual."

The early stages of the journey are described in a letter to Mr. G. A. King, dated :—

"Kibwezi
(190 miles from Mombasa),
Monday, 14th December, 1896.

I came on here last Friday on my bike from Ndi (called seventy-eight miles, but eighty-one and seven-eights by my cyclometer). The caravan, which I propose to meet to-morrow about half-way and come back with it, will probably be here on Friday, perhaps Thursday. I started at 5.5 a.m., and got here, not much fagged, at 3.55 p.m.—the first time, I suppose, anyone, even a native, has come from Ndi to Kibwezi in one day.

I came on to try to settle a serious difficulty about some of our porters who are claimed by a trader. I have every confidence that it will be all right now; no thanks to me and my bike, for I found it settled already, I may say, when I got here, and no wonder, for we have made it a matter of special prayer for a fortnight past. This is the second remarkable, and from the merely human side, most unlooked-for removal of difficulties in answer to prayer, since I reached Mombasa in the nick of time on the 25th to start on the 28th!

We have had a delightful journey—especially we bicyclists; when travelling with the caravan, we reach our camping-place, though we start last, two hours before the rest, generally before eight a.m., and so entirely avoid the sun. We expect to leave this day week; we should be at Nzawi, where are some American Missionaries, for Christmas."

Having once tasted the joys, not unmingled with sorrows, of bicycling in Central Africa, he determined to go on ahead, and our next letter, reproduced as it was written on the journey, gives us his itinerary to the borders of Busoga; it is instructive for intending bicyclists in Central Africa.

"Kikuyu,
Christmas Eve, 1896.

Here I am at Kikuyu, about a hundred miles, I suppose, ahead of our caravan. I came on to fetch Mr. Snowden, of the Railway, who was here till to-day, because his wife, who is travelling with our caravan, is, or was, seriously ill. I left her with the rest at Kibwezi. I shall carry this letter in my pocket (for having come thus far, I shall, if practicable, go on to Uganda), and give it to the down mail men when I meet them, and so you will have the latest news of my movements. I have come on very successfully, a few punctures, etc., and delays, and bad bits of road, but neither I nor the bike are any the worse; and now I am in this splendid healthy country.

Sunday, 3rd January, 1897. — Nandi Station. I arrived here the day before yesterday, Friday; and so am now within sixty miles of Mumia's in Kavirondo, which is 90 miles from our station at Luba's, which is 60 miles from Mengo. The whole journey from this on is inhabited, and so, thank God, the worst part of my journey is over. I propose going on to-morrow to Mumia's, if possible; if not, half way.

BY BICYCLE TO UGANDA. 305

From Kibwezi (from which I started a fortnight ago) to this place is about 330 miles, most of it desert and full of wild beasts; from here to Mengo is 200 miles of friendly country.

Let me give you my itinerary:—

Sunday, 20th December.—Kibwezi to Nzawi, $57\frac{1}{2}$ miles, only half the road rideable; arrived 5.30 p.m.

Monday, 21st.—Kilungu, 10 miles, fearful road.

Tuesday, 22nd.—Machakos, 37 miles, fearful road.

Wednesday, 23rd. — To Kikuyu, 47 miles, good road; $2\frac{1}{2}$ hours delay owing to tyre; arrived 6 p.m.

Thursday, 24th.—Rested.

Friday, 25th.—To Naivasha, 47 miles; tyre broke down three times; should have been there 2 p.m., got there 5.30 p.m., having had to ride on deflated tyre, or should have been benighted; tyre spoiled. I had to go on through Christmas Day, because I knew I should have to go on with mail men, who had left Kikuyu on Christmas Eve. They reached Naivasha on Saturday, and so I had to start on Sunday.

Saturday, 26th.—Rested: tailed to mend tyre.

Sunday, 27th.—Went on with mail men, shoving bike, to Kambi ya Mbaruk, 29 miles: hard work.

Monday, 28th. — To Kambi ya moto, 30 miles through grass 5ft. high; fearful day.

Tuesday, 29th.—To Ravine, 25 miles; bad road. Here Mr. Jackson with infinite kindness put on rope and raw hide on hind wheel as substitute

x

for tyre, and gave me provisions for the road. At all the other stations, Nzawi and Kilungu, the American Missionaries; at Machakos, Ainsworth and De Hinde; at Kikuyu, Hall and others; at Naivasha, Major Smith; here Dr. Macpherson, have been kinder even than I could have expected.

Wednesday, 30th. — To Mianzini, 18 miles; bad road ; had to shove bike nearly all the way.

Thursday, 31st.—To Chini ya kilima, 24 miles ; shoved bike nearly all the way, but in riding one very rough down hill piece cracked my seat pillar—not a very serious damage; when it breaks through, the longer bit of it will do very well. After getting into camp, had a nasty bit of fever, which lasted till I got here.

Friday, 1st January, 1897.—Came on here with some difficulty, 16 miles, pushing my bike because of the cracked seat, which I propose to repair here with wire *pro. tem.*

Saturday, 2nd.—Rested and bound my seat pillar with Dr. Macpherson's kind help. Recovered from fever. So glad of a rest again.

Sunday, 3rd.—Rested and wrote this letter, which I propose to give to the down mail men. I met the other down mail the day I left Kikuyu, just after the final explosion (E—— knows the sound) which convinced me that my hind tyre would carry me no further. It was 1.20 p.m., and I was about 20 miles from Naivasha, and so I had no wish to alarm you by writing a letter under such circumstances ; besides, it would have taken too much precious time. It has been most wonderful how accidents, punctures, etc., have occurred so as to let me reach each station by sundown; and how, in spite of it all, it has been possible to come steadily on : *e.g.*, had the tyre given way ten miles before, on Christmas day, I don't know what would have happened. Had I waited at Kikuyu for Christmas I could not have gone on from Naivasha. Had I had fever on any other of the six days from Naivasha here, I should have failed to get here with the mail men, and could not have come on alone. The mail men left this yesterday ; I can now go on alone, and it doesn't matter whether I catch them up or not. The bicycle goes fairly well on the rope tyre ; it is down hill from here to Mumia's, 2,000 feet lower, I may get there to-morrow.

Now I will finish up this letter, so that if I meet the mail men suddenly, I need only add the place where I shall be, and anything else of importance in a pencil postscript. . . .

I had one accident with tyres at least every day from Kibwezi until the final breakdown ; it's the hot sun.

Tuesday, 5th January. — Safe at Mumia's. All well ; a few more troubles with bike, but all right again. I hope to reach outskirts of Usoga to-morrow, Luba's probably two days later : then two days to Mengo.

Your Homocea (the box you gave me when I had

that bad fall) has been invaluable to me; my left leg has been a little sore, but is healing rapidly.

I came yesterday from Nandi to a place where Corporal Clark of the road party is camped, bridging a river—40 miles or so; thence here only 20 miles.

I leave this letter here, as the mail men leave Luba's to-day, and I might miss them. You ought to get this letter in two months' time."

His next letter is from Uganda:—

"Namirembe, Mengo,
28th Jan. 1897.

All's well that ends well—and here I am, having been here for 17 days, all well. I had a little attack of fever a few days ago, but I'm all right again now. I got here on the 11th January, having been 23 days from Kibwezi where I left the caravan. I shall probably find that I gained more than a month on the caravan. From England two months later—in Uganda one month earlier!

From Ndi here (650 miles) in 19 journeys—a record for Africa; of course I waited at Kibwezi and went back from there and rested elsewhere; and so I did not travel from Ndi here in 19 days; but it took me only 19 days of actual travelling.

I am busy getting my house into order, though, of course, until the caravan arrives (I expect it in another 12 or 15 days) I can't do much; and yet with borrowed and native things I am beginning to be comfortable. I am having a daily class in **Luganda** for the ladies especially, but the others come too. A language examination is to be held as soon as possible.

I propose to devote the greater part of my time for a year or two to the language. I hope to start almost at once on the exercise book I used to speak about when at home; then on an enlarged and improved grammar, and then on a dictionary: or rather the last two simultaneously. I am looking forward to letters from home; they ought to be here in ten days or so.

I took 74 days from London to Mengo—a record, I think; and of that I practically spent 9 days at Kibwezi—I say 'practically,' because I actually rested only three, and then went half way back and returned. I hope when next I write to be able to say that my bike is once more in running order. I am waiting for my extra tyres, and Rowling, who is very good at mechanics, to help me. In the meantime I have taken it all to pieces except the centre crank. I have taken out and cleaned no fewer than 138 steel balls; this is the number the machine contains exclusive of said bracket which has, I suppose 20 more. A couple of the spokes of the hind wheel have given, and one crank is twisted, nothing much wrong besides except the tyres.

I've not had time to look round yet, so I say nothing about the state of the country, but externally all is well."

The impression produced upon the missionaries in Mengo, by Pilkington's sudden appearance among them, is thus described by Miss Chadwick.

"About half an hour before tea time I was in my

room . . . . when I heard a strange voice saluting the children down in the pathway below, and thought 'No one from Kampala talks Luganda like that, yet it's not any of our men that *I* know.' A minute later Tabitha and some of the youngsters came up simply yelling—Pilkingtoni! Pilkingtoni!! and we at first declined flatly to believe them. How Mr. Pilkington, who, when we last heard, had not even arrived at the coast, should have passed and left the others behind, and arrived a month sooner than we expected even to see them, seemed incomprehensible; however, by the aid of his bicycle, he had done so, and arrived absolutely without an attendant, with nothing but a tiny knapsack. . . .

A rather unshaven man in borrowed clothes decidedly too small for him—he beats even Mr. Pike in stature—and about as sunburnt as a man can be. Furthermore, having overtaken the mail men, some little way back, he had stirred them up to such effect that we got, on Monday, the letters not supposed to be due till Friday."

Of the value of his language lessons, already referred to, Miss Chadwick writes:—

"I have already written to mother about Mr. Pilkington's unexpected appearance a month before we were expecting any of them . . . . I had always heard his praises sung so *very* loudly . . . but after a week's acquaintance and two grammar lessons, I am quite ready to join in the chorus of admiration of a truly great and good man. As for his Luganda, it is just *beautiful*. He is giving us a lesson every evening at 6.30, but I fear it will last all too short a time."

On February 26th, 1897, Pilkington writes: " The rest of the party got here on Monday, the 15th, five weeks after me, having come across the lake by steamer, except Baskerville, Cook and Weatherhead. The latter stayed in Usoga, and the other two got here on the 19th, a week ago.

I have chiefly been engaged in getting my house in order, making tables and shelves, &c., and getting boys, and teaching them something, especially to cook. My old boys have got married most of them, or are going to be. Talking of cooking, an exciting incident has just happened. A bottle of barm I was making has burst and flown all over the room in small pieces, but no harm done. Yesterday, the corks flew out, and Hall (who is staying with me, having arrived yesterday from the islands) and I were douched with barm: but I didn't expect the bottle itself to burst. . . . The new men are scattering day by day to their various destinations. I am glad to say that they have been specially requested to devote their first eight months, at least, to the language.

I have been examining some of those who have been one or two years here. Miss Chadwick has done the best of all at present, and Miss Browne very good. Ireland for ever!"

By March 26th, Mr. Rowling's assistance had been procured for the unfortunate bicycle, and a letter of that date describes the method of repair: " My time for the last few days has largely been taken up with mending my bike, or, rather, in giving Rowling some feeble assistance in so doing. He has made a wonderful job of it : soldered and riveted a brass plate into the broken rim, mended two or three spokes, adding a piece on to one with a wire nail, put a copper plate on to the cogged wheel where it was cracked, straightened (and is going to harden by heating and plunging in oil) my crank, and, most remarkable of all, soldered on to the main hub a tiny piece of steel, so that the loose crank now fits perfectly. He has also strengthened the seat pillar by putting into it a piece of hard wood, tight fitting. We stripped my old outside tyre of the rubber, and put it on with the new one (which, to our horror, yesterday, we found a size too large) over it ; and I have this morning been riding about Mengo as comfortably as ever on it."

Apparently the tyres did not last very long, and on April 10th we read : " I am mending my tyres with the sap of a native rubber tree, called ' mulemu,' and I'm inclined to think it is going to prove successful. It takes a long time drying, but we are not in such a terrible hurry in Africa as you are at home.

I'm hoping to go over to Ngogwe (Baskerville's Station) on it for a mission in a fortnight or three weeks' time. It is thirty-five miles—a nice day's ride in this country.

When the rains are over, probably in May or June, I hope to go out a good deal through the country, to try to improve the organisation of the teachers and the native church generally."

By April 23rd, he was convinced that "pneumatic

tyres wont do here," and adds, "I am trying to convert mine into solid ones by stuffing the outside cover with cotton wool."

The solid tyres do not seem to have been a great success, but much later on in the year he writes: "My bike is on the go again. Fresh tyres (pneumatic) have come by post, thanks to the kindness of my friend Mr. G. A. King."

With regard to the progress of the work, he writes on 19th May, 1897, to Mr. Dowse the Vicar of the parish who had adopted him as their own missionary:—

"The increase in the number of adherents is not going on as it was two or three years ago. Why is that? I can't answer, of course, dogmatically, but I fancy there are two reasons. The greater part of the country has now been evangelised, or those who were willing to become readers have been taught a certain amount; those who were opposed are only coming over in small numbers. Then, again, a considerable number who began reading two or three years ago, but were really never converted, have learnt to read, and have read a Gospel or two, and then have got tired and given up reading, and their example is deterring others, for they are supposed to know all about Christianity, and themselves so suppose, and yet they don't think it worth while to persevere.

These remarks apply chiefly to Uganda itself, and not to the surrounding countries.

We are in great difficulties about the self-support of the Native Church. I fear a good many teachers have been sent out too hastily, and we shall be forced to recall them. But I trust we shall always abide by the principle of entire self-support; Waganda teachers supported by Uganda money, and by that *alone*, whatever happens. I notice a considerable growth of independence in the leading teachers and Christians. A great deal of work is now being done by natives, which two years ago was being done, and only could be done, by Europeans. There is a large district between the Capital and the Lake, which is now in the charge of Yairo, who is in priest's orders; very encouraging reports of activity and really independent life have lately come in. We are just going to commit another district to native charge, the district of South Bulemezi, which Buckley is leaving for Toro, to take the place of our dear brother Callis, who has just been taken from us. We hope that this will prove as great a success as Yairo's district seems to be. My own work at present is chiefly that of looking after the supply of teachers in the various country places."

On May 20th, 1897, Pilkington wrote to the Church Missionary Society announcing his engagement to Miss Bertha Taylor, who was a member of the second party of lady missionaries to Uganda.

For some time after his return to Uganda, he seems to have been chiefly occupied in making plans for the further consolidating of the Native Church, and particularly with the subject of self-support. In the course of a letter written from Mengo on June 3rd, 1897, he writes concerning the principle of " Teachers supported wholly and only by the Church of which they are members." " The C.M.S. has come to the conclusion that if this Church were to depart at all from this principle, it would strike a blow to the Missionary cause all the world over.

To support any native with foreign money is to wrong the native Church, depriving it of a privilege and a stimulus to which it has a right.

It is unfair to the teachers, depriving them of a powerful testimony to the Gospel; when supported by native funds, they can appeal to these as evidence that natives like those with whom they plead, have found the Gospel so well worth having that they have been willing to deny themselves in order that others might hear it.

It lays the teachers open to the suspicion that they are the bribed agents of foreigners who desire to denationalise the country for their own ends; it alienates from our side the patriotic feeling, and those men in whom this feeling is strong; the very men we need to build a really independent Church.

If it is objected that an infant church cannot support its own sons who are teachers, it surely seems reasonable to suppose that if the church has had strength enough to produce a genuine teacher sent by God, the less precious product of a few shells for his support will be forthcoming.

On these grounds would it not be better to refrain from sending out teachers than to send them out supported by European money, whether loan or gift?"

At the end of this letter he says "I propose

to go to Budu and Koki, starting some day next week."

On June 29th he arrived in Koki, in company with Mr. Clayton, having passed through Budu, on the way. He found Mr. Leakey in Koki, and whilst there, sent messengers to the neighbouring district of Nkole to find out if there were opportunities for work there, but without any satisfactory result. A few days later, Mwanga revolted and fled from Mengo, having done his best to rally round him people from the various countries round Uganda. Some idea of the state of affairs may be gathered from a letter written by Miss Chadwick on July 24th, 1897.

"It has really been an anxious week for everybody, and, of course, all kinds of rumours came up to us of people deserting to Mwanga. However, the native chiefs as a body, seem to have been splendidly loyal to the English, and their people, as a whole, to them.

This is, I think, the most hopeful thing we have seen in this people yet, as, after all, we have to remember we are foreigners, and personal loyalty to Kampala would hardly have carried this vast body of men to fight as they have done, if it were not that English rule is more or less understood as synonymous with law and order and religion, and we now see, in spite of all our doubts and suspicions, the reality of the friendliness of the Baganda. Practically, all the big chiefs have decisively declared in favour of law and order, and against a return of despotism and heathenism, which Mwanga's victory would certainly have meant for the time being. He meant to turn every Englishman out of the country, I believe. That is pretty widely felt, and it is really everywhere spoken of as a war between religion and heathenism. . . . I have not yet told you what the news really is, for which we feel so much thankfulness. Our last letters went out just when our men had gone off to Budu to look for a runaway king. Then came two or three days of quiet, and then, very disturbing reports that the kingdom of Koki, next door to Budu, was inclined to befriend Mwanga; that the King there, Kamswaga, had lent him 300 guns (an utter fabrication), and that the lives of Messrs. Pilkington, Leakey, and Clayton were in great danger. In fact, Mr. Pilkington sent up a letter to the effect that they had no hope of getting up to Buganda again, but might possibly escape to German territory, and made his will, but this was before they knew how close our party were on the heel of the king, and as a matter of fact, Kamswaga, so far from helping Mwanga, lent Mr. Pilkington and his party 50 guns to protect themselves."

Pilkington's short summary of the rebellion is given in a letter dated August 11th, 1897:

" When I was in Koki, Mwanga ran to Budu (50 miles from us), and raised a rebellion against Europeans, Christianity, civilization, and progress. He and his friends are for a return to heathenism, slavery, polygamy, and all the horrors of the past. Ninety per cent. of the people are probably with him in their sympathies, but, in the body, they prefer the side which musters most guns and holds the gardens. We were in some danger for a time in Koki, but on the arrival of a large native army and Major Ternan with 200 Soudanese in Budu, and after two victories, each of them fought and won 20 or 30 miles from where we were, things became all right, and I came back. Mwanga has been to the Germans, who have taken him prisoner. The French priests in Koki retired to German territory, when it all began. Our staying was useful, we believe, in helping Kamswaga, King of Koki, to stand firm, and indeed Major Ternan, so he told us, wrote to Lord Salisbury to say that our action in staying there had helped the Administration. God will bring good out of it all, as always hitherto."

"August 17th. On Saturday, Daudi Chua, a one-year-old baby, son of Mwanga, was proclaimed King. The two Katikiros (Protestant and Roman Catholic) with Zachariah Kangao, one of the native deacons, form a Council, who will rule the country till His Majesty is old enough. Politically, the Protestants are immensely stronger than they were, which is good for the peace and stability of the country, but a fresh danger to the Church. Still, we can't but be most thankful. The Commissioner asked me to translate into Luganda, and read out for him, the proclamation and a speech to the chiefs."

CHAPTER XVIII.

THE SECOND MUTINY.

WITH the coronation of the new king and the formation of a Council of trustworthy chiefs to admininister the government, it was hoped that peace and quietness had been secured once more, and on the 13th of September, Pilkington writes :—

"Mwanga has been taken to the South of the Lake, and the country is settling down again.

I am working at the Luima language, the shepherd tribe; and also at 'Elementary Luganda Lessons.' I have just perceived how very important a part of a language intonation is (thanks to Sweet), and I am working at that specially now; many words are distinguished only by intonation.

I am having two classes per week with the teachers, to help them with (i) preaching, (ii) reading, and (iii) teaching. I am trying to show them at present how to preach from notes. I go round to different Churches on Sundays, and take special note of the preaching and reading.

Miss Chadwick is doing something at Arabic; I have lent her my Grammar. I am teaching one of my boys to use the typewriter; he can copy fairly correctly now; I hope soon to make great use of him.

We have started football lately! I play most afternoons. It is great fun and good for the boys.

The rebellion is still greatly hindering the work; I hope we shall be able to resume fully soon."

With regard to the football, Dr. Cook writes:—

"September 2nd.

" Archdeacon Walker has got a football out from England, and Pilkington has been diligently coaching the boys. It is very comic to see him, as he enters with great earnestness into it. . . . I, with my boys and about ten others, stood Pilkington and another lot. We got two goals each. We play on a large grass field between Kampala and Rubaga."

Meanwhile a danger was at hand greater than had ever yet threatened British rule in Uganda. In order to understand the situation rightly, it may be well to remind ourselves of the method by which the Protectorate of Uganda was being administered.

At the end of 1891 it will be remembered that Captain Lugard brought into Uganda a number of Sudanese who had at one time been in the service of Emin Pasha. Since then—in spite of the treachery of Selim Bey, which, but for Captain (now Major) Macdonald's prompt action, might have had the most serious consequences—the Sudanese had continued to be employed as the chief soldiers in the employ of the government, and not only was the garrison at Kampala largely composed of them, but they were scattered over the country to form garrisons for various forts under the command of British officers. That their influence upon the people of the country had been an evil one, can hardly be doubted, but, at the same time, they were well-trained fighting men, and served a useful purpose.

During 1897, they had their hands full, going from one place to another, in order to put down the revolution, and in August, Major Ternan left for the coast with a company of Sudanese who had been engaged in the recent fighting, in order that they might join Major Macdonald, who had been commissioned by the British Foreign Office to conduct an exploratory expedition to the north of Lake Rudolph. Major Ternan accordingly met Major Macdonald, as arranged, and the latter was just starting northwards, when, owing to certain reasons, disaffection spread amongst the Sudanese who had come from Uganda, who accordingly deserted him. Of the causes of their disaffection, and the blame which might be attached to one or another in this unfortunate affair, it would be out of place to enter on here, suffice it to say that after unsuccessful attempts on the part of Mr. Jackson to come to terms with them, they made their way towards Uganda. They were joined by other Sudanese from the forts of Nandi and Mumia's, and eventually reached Luba's in Busoga.

With this brief statement we may now turn to the graphic account of the outbreak of the mutiny given by Dr. A. R. Cook.

" In Camp at Luba's,
October 23rd, 1897.

Terrible things have happened in Uganda. About three weeks ago, 300 Sudanese soldiers from the Kampala garrison at Mengo were sent to the Ravine (Eldoma station). Here they mutinied, and looted a large store of the Government Agent's. All the Government stations in Uganda are manned by Sudanese—perhaps 1,800 in all. After revolting, they determined to march back to Mengo, raise the standard of revolt, kill the Europeans, and start a Sudanese kingdom here. They arrived at the station of Nandi and looted it, obtaining, among other things, 3,000 rounds of ball cartridge. Fortified by this and provided with plenty of ammunition (nearly 40,000 rounds of ball cartridge), they marched on to Mumia's. Here Tomkins, though he had only heard native reports, had fully grasped the situation and promptly disarmed all his garrison, armed the few Swahilis he could get, and prepared to fight to the death. He cut down all the bushes round, &c., and, when the mutineers appeared, they were so cowed they failed to attack. Passing on through Busoga, they killed the natives and looted the cattle, finally appearing before the fort at Luba's.

Meanwhile, rumours were brought to us at Mengo of what was going on, and Major Thruston started off at once to meet the mutineers. Though repeatedly warned, he declared he was perfectly confident as to the loyalty of his men, and, being a splendid Arabic scholar, was confident that he could persuade his troops to remain loyal. He crossed over to Luba's and admitted thirty of the mutineers to a conference. They immediately revolted, with the whole garrison at Luba's, and seized Major Thruston and the commander of the fort, Wilson, and tied them up.

THE SECOND MUTINY. 323

They then occupied the fort. Of course, the great danger was a general rising of the Sudanese throughout Uganda and the massacre of the Europeans.

We heard the news at Mengo on Monday night (October 18th). The officers were seized on the Saturday, and we also heard that our two Busoga missionaries, Weatherhead and Wilson, were both in chains in the fort. This turned out to be false. Special messages were instantly sent out to all the ladies and other missionaries to come into the capital. That night we hardly got any sleep, as it was feared the Sudanese garrison would rise. It was decided, on the advice of the native chiefs, not to send the ladies away to an island, as they said they would be probably speared *en route* by the Bakopi. Early in the morning, we made our way to Kampala, and rifles and ammunition were served out to us, the Hotchkiss gun and Maxim were got ready, and then the Sudanese were summoned to lay down their arms, which, to our great relief, they did. Meanwhile, the Baganda were being summoned in from every side, and hurried off to the Nile to prevent the Sudanese from crossing. It was a great answer to prayer that the Sudanese were disarmed so quietly. None of us quite knew if we should go back that morning.

On Tuesday, October 19th, matters were so threatening that Mr. Wilson (the Acting-Commissioner of Uganda) asked for volunteers from the missionaries, as he wanted to give moral support to the Baganda, and they placed great confidence in the missionaries. We at once held a conference of all the male missionaries in Mengo, and it was decided that Pilkington and myself should go— Pilkington to act as interpreter, myself for medical duty. This was the unanimous opinion of Archdeacon Walker and all the missionaries. Meanwhile, the Mohammedan Baganda had joined the rebels, and things looked worse and worse. Fortunately, the ex-Mohammedan king, who is a political prisoner at Mengo, remained loyal to the Government, and actually sent in the letters he had received from the rebels telling him to make himself king and kill us all.

The attacking expedition consisted of fifteen Europeans and 2,500 Baganda, but, at the last moment, all the Europeans — save Pilkington, myself, Captain Malony, and Mr. Malick — were recalled, and also 1,000 of the Baganda, to make the capital quite secure.

We started—i.e. Pilkington and myself—at 3 p.m. on Wednesday afternoon, and pitched our camp with the Katikiro, only four miles from Mengo. After three and a half hours' sleep, we struck camp at 4 a.m., and marched thirty-one miles to Ngogwe. We were not too tired, though my arms were badly burnt by the sun; for, as the sky was covered with clouds, I marched with my coat off and my shirt-sleeves rolled up to the elbow. At Ngogwe we found Baskerville, who decided to stick to his post until we returned, as in all probability the station would be looted if he left. He is now in no danger, as our army is between him and the Nubians.

Meanwhile, we heard the distressing news that

the Government steamer, which had been sent with forty Sudanese soldiers and a Maxim to fight the rebels, had fallen into their hands. These Sudanese revolted and joined their companions, seizing the unfortunate engineer. We had also the good news that Major Macdonald and nine other Europeans had hastily armed 300 Swahili porters, and, with eighteen Sikhs, were keeping one day's march behind the mutineers. Pilkington and I were well ahead of the other Europeans and were able to open up communication with Macdonald.

All the ladies and men, with the exception of the two Koki missionaries and Buckley in Toro, were now in the capital. Weatherhead had a marvellous escape. He was on his way up to the capital for a visit to Ngogwe, when, hearing there was trouble in Busoga, and not understanding that the Sudanese had risen, he at once started back to look after his station. He arrived at Luba's at 4 a.m., Saturday morning, just as the rebels were tying up the officers, and, passing quietly through them, went over the hill to his station and lay down to rest. In a short time, however, Unwa, the faithful Buganda teacher, rushed in and told him of his imminent peril. Groups of Sudanese were then passing the house, and he hurried him away through the bananas and jungle, and crossed the Nile at Jinja (the Ripon Falls), and so on to Ngogwe, carrying him on his back part of the way, and then put him in a canoe and sent him to Mengo, where he is now safe and sound. Of our other missionary in Busoga, Wilson, we have no definite news, but believe he is quite safe, as he is twenty-five miles north.

To return to Pilkington and myself. After a very disturbed night at Ngogwe, we pressed sternly on, and at 9 a.m. sighted the Nile in the far distance. We arrived opposite Luba's, and saw the rebel fort five miles across the Nile at 1.45 p.m., having reached the Nile (fifty-nine miles) in forty-six and a half hours after leaving Mengo. Meanwhile, Major Macdonald had fought a great battle on the 19th, and, though driving off the rebels, was very short of ammunition. One European, Fielding, was killed and two wounded, including the doctor. We had sent back urgent messages for ammunition, and at 10 p.m. it arrived. There were only two small canoes, however, so we sent it on and crossed over with the Katikiro and a fleet of twelve canoes in the morning, and, making a long *détour* to avoid the rebel fort, arrived at Macdonald's camp at noon, where we had a most warm welcome. Meanwhile, (on the 20th) the rebels had brutally murdered the three prisoners — Major Thruston, Wilson (the Government captain), and Scott (the engineer). Mr. Jackson, who was on his way to be Acting-Commissioner until Mr. Berkeley returns, is severely wounded in the shoulder, and thanked us most warmly for coming. Dr. Macpherson was wounded himself, and, though suffering, had all the wounded to look after; he was most grateful for my assistance.

The fight on Tuesday was most severe; Major Macdonald's party managed to arrive at the summit of this hill without the Nubians seeing them. He had with him two Maxims, about 250 Swahili porters armed with Sniders and Martinis, eighteen Sikhs, and nine other Europeans. Next morning, 300 of the Sudanese, who, of course, are well armed and disciplined, came up laughing and chatting, and saying they did not want to fight. Major Macdonald was not a man to be caught napping, and quietly got everything ready. Suddenly the Sudanese crammed cartridges in their rifles, and fired on the Europeans, and for over five hours a fierce battle raged, the men often firing at only thirty yards' distance. At length the ammunition of the Major's party began to fail, and, giving the word to charge, they made a desperate effort and drove the Sudanese back, who then retired to their fort, where they have remained since. They lost sixty-four killed and thirty or forty wounded; our side, one European and sixteen Swahilis, and many severely wounded. The Sikhs fought magnificently.

Some 2,500 Baganda have now crossed over, and the rebels are cooped up. The Hotchkiss gun is expected in to-morrow, and if they do not surrender then, I suppose there will be some desperate fighting. Of course, there are no non-combatants in Centra Africa, and Pilkington and I take our turn at night duty, etc., each having our allotted station in case of an attack. The view from here is superb, thirty miles each way. Through the telescope we can see the rebels walking about below; two or three days longer will settle it. There are still some corpses lying unburied, but the vultures and hyænas are clearing them away.

My hands are very busy with the wounded. I know how much you will remember us in prayer—it is a very serious time for Uganda. We cannot feel certain as to the garrisons in Budu (300 Sudanese and two officers), or in Toro and Bunyoro. The answers to prayer have been wonderful. The camp is pitched about the very spot where Bishop Hannington was seized. If it comes to a fight, Pilkington and myself will stick together. I feel sure we are here in the line of God's will."

"October 24th, (Sunday).

Mail now going—the rebels are hemmed in and cannot possibly escape. The men here are practising for an attack as I am writing. We had an alarm this morning, and all turned out; but the enemy merely sent out a strong picket. There are now most of the big Baganda chiefs with us, and perhaps 3,000 or 4,000 spearmen and guns. Port Victoria and Ntebe are practically abandoned. The capital is strongly manned and quite safe. No one quite knows what will happen, but it will be just right. Of course, Mission work in the country is almost stopped. The ladies behaved very pluckily when the alarm came. All eight are at the capital, and probably Namirembe Hill will be fortified.

Poor Thruston! Only a few days ago he was chatting with me, and showing me his sketches from Bunyoro; and Wilson, too, last time I was here, he so kindly entertained us—and now——.

God has been very good to us and the whole Mission. For a time there was very real danger, but now I trust it is passing over. All of us Europeans (except the sick ones) are messing together. I must now close."

Dr. Cook has already referred to the reasons which led him and Pilkington, after conference with the other Missionaries and with their unanimous approval, to help in quelling the mutiny; but as it is of the greatest importance to understand the circumstances aright, it may be well to quote Pilkington's own view of his position and also that of Major Macdonald.

On November 23rd, Pilkington wrote a letter to be sent home in case of his death, in which he says:—

"We go down to-morrow morning to attack the Sudanese, and, as it is possible that I may be killed, I write this to be sent to you in that case. I hope you won't think my being here and my going down with Capt. Woodward unjustifiable for a Missionary. It seems to me to be my clear duty, and I go without any doubt or hesitation. I may be able to save many lives by maintaining a clear understanding between Woodward and the Waganda: to put it another way, a misunderstanding might cost many lives."

But nothing could make matters clearer than the following letter from Major Macdonald, in answer to a letter from Archdeacon Walker, asking how soon it would be possible to dispense with the services of the other Missionaries who remained with Major Macdonald after Pilkington's death:—

"With reference to your wish to know whether

it would not be possible to withdraw from the army in Usoga the two members of the C.M.S. who are serving with the forces there, I have the honour to inform you that I consider such a step would be highly undesirable and fraught with public danger. Messrs. Lloyd and Fletcher, together with the late Mr. Pilkington, whose death I so deeply deplore, have lent invaluable assistance in acting as interpreters between the Government officers and the Waganda, in carrying orders and in preventing misunderstandings which might so easily occur. Their withdrawal in this crisis would undoubtedly greatly detract from the value of our Uganda levies, who, in the siege of the mutineers' fort, at Lubwa's, have to fight in a way to which they are quite unaccustomed. I have no hesitation in saying that, but for the presence of the members of the Mission with the army in Usoga, the Waganda would lose far more heavily than they have done, as they would not so fully understand the wishes and plans of the officer commanding.

I need hardly mention that the present military operations are quite different from an ordinary campaign in Uganda, as our very existence, whether Government officials, missionaries, or traders, depends on our quelling this mutiny. It behoves all British subjects, whatever their profession, to stand together until the mutiny is suppressed, and, far from agreeing to the withdrawal of Messrs. Lloyd and Fletcher, I would ask you whether you could not spare another member of your Mission to help these gentlemen in their arduous duties.

I am aware that these duties are not those for which they came to Uganda, but when the existence of the Protectorate, and consequently of the Missions, the lives and honour of English ladies, and the saving of bloodshed are at stake, I have no hesitation in calling on all British subjects to assist in these military operations to the extent of their power."

When these circumstances are realised, and when it is understood that the Missionaries were not fighting against the natives of the country, but standing shoulder to shoulder with their own native brethren to help to defend them and their country from what was in effect a foreign invader, who could suggest that they were not in the place of duty?

But to return to the situation in Busoga. On November 4th, Dr. Cook returned to Mengo in charge of Mr. Jackson and others who were wounded. Pilkington still remained on, and on November 12th, 1897, after referring to the battle described by Dr. Cook, which took place on October 19th, he writes:—

"Next afternoon, the friendly Waganda began arriving, and then the position began to change to what it is now; the Sudanese shut into their fort, and getting into a bad way for want of food.

The Waganda have twice fought with them, and inflicted considerable loss, losing themselves, alas, some 25 killed and 80 wounded; five of the killed, teachers of ours. We are waiting now for ammunition before going down to the fort to invest it by making a fort or forts if necessary round it. I am to go with Major Macdonald as 'staff officer!' in order to interpret between him and the Waganda.

We had a night attack the other day: the Sudanese came up in the middle of a great storm and fired 20 or 30 shots; we fired 137, including some rounds from the Maxim. It was 12.30 a.m., and I got wet through. We have night watches, after every second night, at first more frequently.

The Waganda fought most bravely the other day, to the great surprise and admiration of the men here; but their praise is poor compensation for the lives of our friends.

Dr. Cook returned a week ago to the Capital with Mr. Jackson (shot through one lung, going on well) and other wounded. About the same time Fletcher, Lloyd and Wilson, all of C.M.S., came here, so we are four missionaries here; and two Roman Catholics came a few days later.

Captain Kirkpatrick, one of Major Macdonald's officers, is a cousin of Lefroy of Delhi, and met E— at Delhi.

Captain Woodward, also, was at Harrow, and so knows many whom I know.

Major Macdonald, you remember, was in Uganda before, and saved the country from a Mohammedan outbreak, He has saved it a second time now. No man has been in Uganda for whom I have a greater respect and admiration.

The great danger was that the rest of the Sudanese in Uganda and Unyoro, over a thousand in all, would join the mutineers, and that they would be joined by all the Mohammedan Waganda ; or that the rebel heathen party, Mwanga's friends, would seize the opportunity to make fresh trouble. However, up the present all is quiet.

The rest of Major Macdonald's expedition, 400 strong and four Europeans, have been sent for. And 800 Indian soldiers from the Coast are expected in a couple of months. Then things ought to be pretty secure. But, after all, our trust is, and has been, in God, who has always so wonderfully overruled all sorts of evil in this country to His glory invariably."

"Luba's,
26th November, 1897.

DEAREST MOTHER,—

I must write a line to tell you of the fight two days ago, lest you should be anxious. We went down to the fort first thing in the morning, the Wasoga and Waganda on our flanks. However, the Waganda went too fast ahead, and were met by the Sudanese, whom they drove back into the fort, but with frightful loss to themselves, 71 killed 180 wounded, among them one of my friends, Obadiya. who wrote you that letter, shot dead.

We took up a line about 250 or 300 yards from the fort. I was with Woodward, who was in command, about 50 yards further back, but I spent most of the day superintending the making, by Waganda, of a fort which we intended to occupy at night, about 450 yards from the fort. Firing was very brisk at first, and two or three sorties were made, and driven back, but the heavy firing was too much for the Waganda workmen, of whom one was killed and one wounded; but they would run away in parties when the bullets came much over our heads; and so by evening the fort was not finished, and we had to leave it. The Sudanese broke it up next morning.

The position in Uganda is still serious, because more Sudanese may mutiny, or there may be a fresh anti-European rebellion among the Waganda; but these things haven't happened yet, thank God. And the Sudanese here are much reduced in numbers, and can have very little communication left.

The rest of Major Macdonald's expedition (450 rifles) is expected soon, and Indian troops.

It's terrible to see these Waganda being killed in a quarrel not theirs but ours. . . . .

It was some comfort to share a little of the danger the other day. I sometimes half wish that some of us Europeans had been killed, or at any rate wounded, if it weren't for friends at home.

All the Europeans except those on watch and three Roman Catholics came to a prayer Meeting the evening before.

We, and the Country, and God's work here, are all in His hands, and it's all right.

Your loving son,
G. L. Pilkington."

This letter, written in pencil, is actually the last letter received from him.

On December 11th, the following letter was written by Major Macdonald to Archdeacon Walker :—

"Luba's Hill,
11th December, 1897.

Dear Archdeacon,—

I am very sorry to say that Pilkington was killed in to-day's fight. I know what a loss this is to you all and to Uganda, and more especially does my heart-felt sympathy go out to Miss Taylor, as such brave, fine men as Pilkington are scarcely found. I cannot quite express what I feel, as not only have I lost in Pilkington an old friend, but my brother was also killed in to-day's fight. We also lost seven natives killed and fifteen wounded, and the Waganda lost three killed and ten wounded, but the Nubians were completely defeated, and lost more than all our loss together.

The Nubians fought desperately to prevent our cutting the last of their shambas on the right, but it was no use; they were repulsed at every point and driven from the position they took up, and the Waganda, under Fletcher, completed the destruction of the shambas.

So our victory, though dearly purchased, was complete.

Yours very sincerely,
W. R. S. Macdonald."

This letter was accompanied by a detailed account of that sad day from the pen of Mr. A. B. Lloyd :—

"The Fort, Luba's Hill.
December 11th, 1897.

But I must tell you some of the details. It was arranged this morning that the banana gardens from which the Nubians get their food should be cut down by the Waganda. A covering party was to go out to the front, clear the gardens of all Nubians, and the cutting party directed by our dear brother, to follow after. The advance began about seven a.m. Pilkington took up his position with Captain Harrison, who was leading the attack. Presently Pilkington's boy (Aloni), who was by his side, shouted out 'There they are, close to us.' Both Pilkington and Captain Harrison saw men coming towards them, but thought them Waganda, and told Aloni so, but he being quite sure about it, fired a shot into them as they advanced, and this proved, without doubt, that they were Nubians, for they then opened their fire upon our men. One man took several deliberate aims at Pilkington, but missed him. Then Pilkington fired a few shots at him, but the shots went wide, and then it was that he fired again at our brother, shooting him right through the thigh and bursting the femoral artery. He cried out, 'Harrison, I'm hit,' and sat down on the ground. One of Harrison's Nubian officers then shot at the man, who was still close by, who had wounded Pilkington. He missed him, and the fellow returned the fire, hitting the officer in the left arm, breaking his arm, and shouted out to him, 'Bilal, what are you doing here? Go back to Egypt. Have you come here to fight against your brothers?' 'Yes,' said Bilal, 'you are rebels, and we will wipe you all out.' And with his right hand he drew his revolver and shot the man who had killed Pilkington.

While this was going on Harrison had made arrangements for some Waganda to carry Pilkington back to the fort. Aloni knelt down by his side and said, 'Sebo bakukubye,' ('Sir, have they shot you?') Pilkington replied, 'Wewao omwana wange bankubeye' ('Yes, my child, they have shot me'); then he seemed to get suddenly very weak, and Aloni said to him, 'My master, you are dying, death has come,' to which he replied, 'Yes, my child, it is as you say." Then Aloni said, 'Sebo, he that believeth in Christ, although he die, yet shall he live. To this Pilkington replied, 'Yes, my child it is as you say, shall *never* die.' Then they carried him some little distance to the rear of the battle which was now raging most furiously. When they had put him down again he turned to those who carried him and said, 'Thank you, my friends, you have done well to take me off the battle-field; and now give me rest,' and almost immediately he became insensible and rested from his pain.

They then brought him into the camp, but we soon saw that the end was very near. We did all we could to restore him, but he fell quietly asleep about 8.30.

Just before they brought in Pilkington, Lieutenant Macdonald was brought in quite dead, shot right through the spine by Nubians concealed in the long grass. It was awful work, and one's heart seemed to melt within one.

The fight lasted till about 12 o'clock midday. The banana cutting went on ahead and a huge garden was levelled to the ground. Fletcher took Pilkington's place in this work. At midday, the force came back to the fort. The Nubians had fought with more determination than ever before. They made repeated charges down upon our men and poured in volleys of shot. Still, our total loss was comparatively small. I suppose, all counted, Waganda and all, not more than 30 killed and wounded. The Nubians, we think, lost far more than that. We are hoping that they have got through their cartridges, and that they will not again be able to fight with such cruel results. But it is a bad business, and there must be a good deal of fighting yet before all is over."

"December 12th.

Last night another attack was made by the Nubians upon our lower fort, but with little success —not more than two wounded on our side.

We buried Macdonald and Pilkington last evening under a tree outside of this fort. I read the English burial service, and all the Europeans, with the Sikhs, attended. A most solemn time."

CHAPTER XIX.

A LAST WORD.

To give expression in any adequate degree to the sense of the loss sustained by the Church of Christ and the British nation generally, by the death of George Pilkington, would occupy more space than we have at our disposal. The public Press, secular and religious, Committees of Missionary Societies, and individuals of all ranks and opinions, have joined with one voice in lamenting the sudden cutting off of a life characterised by such singular gifts and graces.

But most touching of all are the messages that have been received from the people of Uganda, from his fellow-missionaries, and from Government officials who knew him in the field.

First of all we may give, as representing the feelings of the Christians of Uganda, the letter of the Rev. Henry Wright Duta, Pilkington's chief assistant in the translation of the Bible. He writes to the Rev. E. Millar as follows:—

"Uganda,
December 14th, 1897.

My Dear Millar,—

How are you, my friend? I tell you about the sorrow which has just come to us about our brother, Mr. Pilkington, whom we love very much. He was killed in the Sudanese war in Usoga on December 11th.

When he saw that the Baganda and the Government were going to war with the Sudanese because they had mutinied—you know what his love for us is—he went to the war with Dr. Cook, Lloyd, and Fletcher; and of the Baganda many—110—were killed, but of all the English not one was killed. Pilkington was very sorry, and said, 'I want very much to die. I should have liked to have died in place of those Baganda.' Well, when they fought for the fourth time they killed him and Lieutenant Macdonald, but we were all very much distressed at the death of Pilkington. We all shed tears; we cried our eyes out. Of Pilkington we have only now the footprints; but it is difficult to follow in the footsteps when the leader is not there. Pilkington has died, but his work has not died; it is still with us. He preached to all men the Gospel—Protestants, Roman Catholics, and Mohammedans, all lamented him when he died, because he was beloved by all. He always welcomed both the wise and the foolish. All black people were his friends.

We sorrow very much, beyond our strength; we do not see among the missionaries whom we have anyone who can fill his place and take on his work. I worked very hard at teaching him Luganda; he learnt it very well, and was able to speak Luganda like a native, and could translate any book into Luganda without my help, and I was not afraid of him making any mistakes.

You see this is what makes all of us Baganda so sad. Where is another Englishman to give himself as he did to this work of translating our books?

Therefore, I want you, if you are still in England, and have not yet left, to go to the Committee of the Church Missionary Society and tell them how our brother Pilkington has been killed; tell them the Baganda sorrow very much for Pilkington—that if we could write their language (English) we would have written to them in tears, and our tears would have fallen upon the letter as we begged them to seek for a man of Pilkington's ability, and to beg him to come here and take on Pilkington's work.

His body will be disinterred from Usoga, and buried here in Uganda, near our church, that we may always remember him. If we had known how to carve his likeness on stone we would have done it; but the sight of his tomb will suffice us.

My friend Millar, I entreat you, do not fail to send my message to the leaders of the C.M.S., that they may send us someone to succeed Pilkington; and you yourself, do you beseech with tears those Christians, who have hearts filled with the love of Jesus Christ, to come and pity us and help us.

It would be an excellent thing to circulate this letter among all the English. I know their love for us. They will hear us. I trust so.

H. W. D. KILAKULE."

"Someone to succeed Pilkington," that is the plea of the Church in Uganda, and shall they plead in vain? To our readers we leave the answer to this question.

By his colleagues his loss is very keenly felt, as the following extracts from letters by Archdeacon Walker and the Rev. G. K. Baskerville, clearly show.

Archdeacon Walker, in a private letter from Uganda, dated December 21st, 1897, writes as follows:—

"By telegram you will have heard of the sad loss this Mission has sustained in the death of Mr. Pilkington. We have lost not only a friend, but one who was completely devoted to the work here. Pilkington was always ready to give advice, and to hear patiently any matter that concerned the good of these people. He was a man of very great intellectual ability, and had gained a very complete knowledge of the native language. We had hoped that he would have prepared many useful books for these people. A commentary, and histories, as well as a grammar and dictionary, were all in contemplation, and partly begun. We always looked to Pilkington for advice in any forward movement. He was so fair in all his judgments, and so much respected and beloved by all the people, that his influence was very largely felt. We always felt that Pilkington was so much in sympathy with the natives that he could do almost anything he liked with them. But now he has been taken from us, and we are deprived of all the help and comfort his presence gave us. I trust the native Christians, and especially the ordained men, will exert themselves, and so supply in some measure what we have lost."

Mr. Baskerville, who was Pilkington's companion

on so many occasions, and especially in his journeys to and from Africa, writes :—

"My heart bleeds about dear Pilkington. I cannot see how the gap will be filled in the work. Clear head, sound judgment, grasp of native language, customs, &c. ; universally respected by all creeds, a born leader. I feel as if I ought to write an 'In Memoriam,' but what can I say?"

From the Administration comes the following remarkable tribute.

"Kampala,
December 13th, 1897.

SIR,—

I have been asked by Mr. Jackson and the whole of the staff of this Administration to give expression to the deep and heart-felt sympathy, which they feel with the members of the Church Missionary Society in the loss they have sustained by the death of our friend, Mr. Pilkington.

We join with you all the more deeply, in that we feel that the misfortune is one that falls upon all Uganda, and I am sure that no higher tribute could be paid, nor one which Mr. Pilkington would have esteemed greater, than the sorrow which is expressed by the native population of the country for which he has worked so hard, and for the honour of which, I believe we can say in all sincerity, he has given up his life.

I am, Sir,
Your most obedient, humble servant,
GEORGE WILSON.

The Venerable Archdeacon Walker.
Namirembe."

Captain Villiers, of the Royal Horse Guards, who had known Pilkington in Uganda, bears the following testimony to his work:—"It is owing to the attachment of the Protestant Waganda to men like Mr. Pilkington, that we have been able to hold Uganda so easily up the present time. In Mr. Pilkington's death the cause of civilization in Africa has received a severe blow, and England has lost a most devoted servant."

One more quotation may be given, and that is from the letter of Bishop Hanlon, the English Roman Catholic Bishop in Uganda, who writes to Archdeacon Walker:—"We do heartily condole with you in the deep affliction that has befallen you by the death of a dear friend and fellow-labourer of such ability. I can to some extent realize, dear Archdeacon, what the death of a member of Mr. Pilkington's worth must mean to your mission, and that he has left a void it will be difficult to fill."

From later information we learn that the wish of the people was carried out, and "on Friday, March 18th, Mr. Pilkington's body, which had been brought from Busoga, was buried with military honours at Mengo. The Acting Administrator and Major Macdonald and most of the officials and a large crowd of natives were present. The coffin was covered with a Union Jack, and a party of Swahilis and Punjabis fired a volley over the grave. The Rev. Henry Wright Duta and the Rev. G. K. Baskerville conducted the service. A grave had been dug in line with those of the other Europeans who had been buried on what is called the 'Church Hill.'"

Of the state of affairs in Uganda after Pilkington's death, it is sufficient to say that, after considerable trouble in dealing both with detachments of the mutineers and also with Mwanga and his confederates, the peace of the country seems to have been once more secured. Missionary work has been re-opened in many places where temporarily it had been closed, including Luba's in Busoga, and it is hoped that the future may see a great development from Uganda as a centre for all the surrounding countries.

And now we have told our story, and we may close most fitly by giving Pilkington's concluding message from the little pamphlet, "The Gospel in Uganda," and which is entitled, "A Last Word."

"We have stood together now in fancy on Namirembe's far-viewing summit; we have looked across Unyoro's plains into the far Nile valley and the vast Sudan: we have gazed in imagination across the Albert on into the Great Forest, and wondered when that strange pigmy race will learn that they, too, are objects of the Eternal Love. We have looked across many a mile into wild Kavirondo; we have pictured the great Lake the centre of a united, active Church, sending its evangelists east and west, north and south, to many nations and many tongues.

But now comes the question: Is all to end here?

Oh, let us be real! Emotion is no substitute for action. You love Africa, do you? 'God so loved that He gave—'

God gave—what? Superfluities? Leavings? That which cost Him nothing?

'When ye shall have done all, say, We are unprofitable servants; we have done that which was our duty to do.'

If we are doing less than all, we are robbing God.

What is the present position?

(i.) The Son of God sitting on the right hand of His Father, all power in heaven and earth His, having reached the gift of the Holy Ghost to pour on each yielded, believing soul.

(ii.) The world wide open almost everywhere.

(iii.) Two-thirds, at least, of the human race having never heard the message of forgiveness which is for all.

(iv.) Mohammedanism and Heathenism and Infidelity increasing more rapidly than Christianity!

(v.) Christians (so we call ourselves) satisfied! Is God satisfied?

We salve our consciences by doing a little, and refuse to recognize the fact that the work for which the Lord died is not being done.

A house is being built: the workman, paid by the day, does not care if for each brick he lays two others fall down: he gets his pay.

But is the Master satisfied?

Let us confess that hitherto we have only been playing at Missions. God has given us much more than our miserable efforts have deserved.

Let us begin in a new way.

New prayer; new giving; new going.

The World for Christ, Christ for the World, in this generation!"

INDEX.

Accompanying Troops, Reasons for, 217, 323, 329.
Acland, Sir Henry, 250.
Aloni, 336, 337.
Anonya Alaba, 246, 270.
Ashe, Rev. R. P., 132, 139; Translations, 146, 265.
Baganda, 114, 224, 295; Thirst for knowledge, 121-3, 136-8, 151, 199; Political parties, 121, 168; Evangelistic work, 145-7, 275-280; Baptisms, 284; Ordinations, &c., 209; Spiritual revival, 222-239; Teachers, 231, 236, 273-4; Native church, 272-286, 314.
Baptisms, 284.
Barter, Articles of, 76-7, 126, 148.
Baskerville, Rev. G. K., 63; Ordination, 111; Furlough, 240; Letters from, 160, 225-230, 342.
Bassett, Mr., 4.
Bayima, 228.
Bedford, 51.
Bexhill, 262.
Bible Translation, 264-271.
Bicycle Journey, 302-310.
Binns, Rev. H. K., 65.
Books, 137, 164-8, 193, 199, 200.
Boutflower, Rev. Cecil, 40.
British East Africa Company, 158, 170, 209.
Broadrick, Mrs., 15.
Budu, 317.

Buganda, 114-5; Revolutions, 90, 141, 161, 316; C.M.S. work, 113, 157, 236; The king, 119, 180-2, 316, 318, 324; Country, 120; Roman Catholics, 142, 160-184; Provinces, 147, 152; Civil war, 161-184; British Protectorate, 209; Mutinies, 210-220, 320-338; Native church, 272-286; Missionary meetings, 275-280; Future prospects, 287-301; New king, 318.
Bugaya, 281.
Bukasa, 282.
Bushell, Rev. W. D., 48, 64, 248.
Busi, 279.
Busoga, 145-6, 201, 322-338.
Buvuma Islands, 281.
Cambridge, 20-40, 252.
Cathedral, 168, 201, 273.
Chadwick, Miss, 309, 316.
Chagga, 75.
Children's Special Service Mission, 23, 47, 132.
China Inland Mission, 43, 52.
Christian, The, 140.
Church Collections, 278-9.
Church Missionary Society: Boat, 103-4, 108-111, 116-7; Committee, 60-1, 205; Meetings, 61-64, 159, 248-9. Missionaries, 61-63, 65, 73, 89, 91, 113, 217; Policy, 52-4, 289-294, 315; Secretaries, 58,

INDEX.

65; Stations, 73, 75, 89, 91, 103, 115, 120, 293.
Civil War, 160-184.
Classics, xii, xiii, 4, 20, 21, 35, 38, 41, 42, 50, 195-7, 252.
Clifton College, 44.
Climate, 115, 145, 150.
Clothing, 140, 187.
Cole, Rev. H., 92.
Cook, Dr. A. R., 320-9, 331.
Cooking, 131, 311.
Cotter, J. D. M., 63, 78.
Crabtree, Rev. W. A., 266.
Crawfurd, Mr., 66.
Daudi Chua, 318.
Deacons, 209.
Deekes, D., 107, 110.
Dermott, Rev. J. V., 84, 94, 107.
De Winton, Mr., 139, 191.
Donkeys, 84, 86, 95.
Douglas, Rev. Sholto, 30.
Dover College, 47.
Dowse, Dean, 35, 313.
Drury, Rev. T. W., 270.
Dublin, 4.
Dunn, Mr., 111.
Duta, Henry Wright, 128, 130, 143, 163, 339.
Du Wallah, 174.
East Africa: Description of Country, 70, 73, 89, 91, 94, 115, 120; Fauna and Flora, 70-4, 140, 190; Native races, 95, 114, 228, 319; Religions, 219, 299; British East Africa Company, 158, 170, 209 (See also "Buganda.")
Elwin, Rev. E. H., 47.
Emin Pasha, 82, 103, 149.
Fauna and Flora, 70-74, 140, 190.
Fever, 72, 78, 146.
Fisher, A. B., 231.
Food, 69, 86, 95, 102, 105, 112, 186.
Football, 320.
Frere Town, 64.

Gleaners' Union Meetings, 159, 248.
Gordon, Rev. E. Cyril, 118, 124, 265.
Gordon, General, 288.
Hanlon, Bishop, 344.
Hannington, Bishop, 66, 328.
Harrow, 48, 109.
Heathenism, 219, 299.
Heywood, Rev. R. S., 63.
Hill, Mr., 78, 83.
Holy Spirit, 222-9, 235, 258, 261.
Hooper, Rev. Douglas, 23, 51, 81, 84, 111.
Hunt, Mr., 109.
Hyslop, Mr., 39, 48, 261.
Inskip, Rev. T. J., 44.
Interpretation, 207, 212, 324, 330.
Islands, 205, 232, 281-4.
Itinerary, 304-8.
Jackson, Mr., 321, 332.
Jaeger Boots, 40, 106, 187.
Jungo, 237.
Kampala, 176-8, 191, 210.
Kamswaga, King of Koki, 141, 276.
Kanta, 175-8.
Kasagama, King of Toro, 277.
Katikiro, 133, 174, 214, 227.
Keswick, 261.
Kiganda (Swahili), 114. (See Luganda.)
Kilimanjaro, 73.
Kimbugwe, 152, 172.
Kimegi, 89.
King, G. A., 303, 313.
Kisokwe, 90.
Klein, Arthur, 25
Koki, 141, 276, 317.
Komé, Island of, 222, 225, 281.
Kuilwe, 185, 189.
Kyagwe, 278, 280.
Lang, Rev. R., 191.
Languages—see Philology.
Leakey, R. H., 228, 316.

INDEX.

Literature, Importance of, 167, 200, 206.
Livingstone, David, 288.
Lloyd, A. B., 330, 335.
Lubale, 219.
Luba's, 321-338.
Luganda, 114; Language study, 106-7, 123, 192-208, 258; Translations, 123, 128-131, 144, 192-208, 264-271; General suggestions, 192; Grammar, 125, 134; Dictionary, 197; Specimens of roots, 199; Phonetics, 245, 257; Native proverbs, 259; Intonation, 319.
Lugard, Captain, 114, 121, 157, 170-5.
Lusoga, 198.
Luyima, 198, 205, 319.
Macdonald, Captain (now Major), 211-218, 232, 320-335.
McDonnell, Sir Alexander, 2.
McDonnell, Dr. Robert, 3.
Mackay, A. M., 72, 114, 265.
Mackay, Sembera—see "Sembera."
Mamboia, 86, 89.
Mengo, 115, 152; Plan of, 177; Cathedral, 168, 201, 273; Native congregations, 201, 207, 273; mutiny, 323.
Methods of work, 255.
Mgunda Mkali, 102.
Milk, 105, 185.
Millar, Rev. E., 227, 339.
Missionary Meetings, 61, 249, 275.
Mohammedans, 122, 211-216, 234, 324.
Molony, Rev. H. J., 24, 34.
Mpwapwa, 91.
Muganda, 114, 295.
Mundara, King of Chagga, 75.
Musa Yakuganda, 226-7.
Mutesa, 167.
Mutinies, 210-220, 320-338.

Mwanga, 119, 160, 166-7, 180-2; Flight, 316; Taken prisoner, 318, 324.
Namirembe, 141, 273.
Nassa, 205.
Nathaniel, 276.
Native Agency, 234, 248, 289, 294-7.
Native Church, 272-286. 314-5.
Native Proverbs, 247-8, 259, 260.
Native Tribes, 95, 228, 319; see also Baganda, Wagogo.
Neil, R. A., 41.
Nikodemo—see Sekibobo.
Nile, River, 115.
Noah, 144, 277.
Northern Route, 240.
Nsazi, 281.
Ordinations, 79, 111, 209.
Oxford, 249.
Parker, Bishop, 114.
Pembroke College, Cambridge, 20-40, 53. See also Dr. Searle.
Perry, Mr., 14, 17, 19.
Persecution, 298.
Philology: Methods of Study, 84, 107, 192, 258-9; General suggestions, 192; Roots, 197-9; Allied languages, 106, 197, 205, 245; Phonetics, 245, 257; Dialects, 197, 319; Intonation, 319; see also Luganda, Kimegi, Lusoga, Luyima, Swahili.
PILKINGTON, George Lawrence: Birth, 1; Parents, 1; Boyhood, 3; Uppingham, xi.-xvi., 8: Scholarships and prizes, 12, 14, 18, 20, 43; Tutorship, 15; Athletics, 16, 320; Confirmation, 19; Cambridge, 20; C.S.S.M., 23, 47; Conversion, 26; Christian work, 28, 34; Gospel Missions, 34, 36-8, 43-4; Classical tripos, 38; Testimonials, 41-2, 50; Missionary call, 41;

INDEX.

China Inland Mission, 43, 52; Harrow, 48; Bedford, 51; Accepted by C.M.S., 61; Arrival in Africa, 64; Visit to Kilimanjaro, 65; Fever, 72, 78, 146; Travels, 80-112, 240-3, 302-310; Arrival in Uganda, 117; Early impressions, 120; Language work, 123, 128, 134, 144, 146, 192-208, 245, 264-271; Appeals, 150, 155, 291, 345-6; Love for natives, 183, 340; Spiritual revival, 222-239; Accompanying troops, 229-232, 320-334; Annual letter, 236; Furlough, 240; Protestantism, 246, 270-1; Bible translation, 264-271; Bicycle journey, 302-310; Engagement, 314; Death, 335-338; Burial, 338, 344.
Pokino, 141, 178-9.
Political Parties, 121, 168.
Portal, Sir Gerald, 209.
Portal, Captain, 216.
Prior, Rev. C. H., 40.
Protestants, 121, 160-184, 218, 318.
Rabai, 67.
Railway, 240, 243.
Rawnsley, Mr. 12.
Reading, 121, 143, 206, 227.
Religions, 219, 299.
Revival, 222-239.
Rochester, Bishop of, 252.
Roman Catholics, 121, 142, 151, 160-184, 233, 246, 270-1.
Roots of Language, 197-9.
Roscoe, Rev. J., 217, 227.
Routes—Northern, 240-3, 302-310; Southern, 80-112.
Rowling, Rev. F., 311.
Rubaga, 179.
Rutako, Pass of, 91.
Saadani, 82.
Searle, Rev. Dr., 59, 60, 252.
Sekibobo, 218-9.

Self-support, 314-5.
Selim Bey, 157-8, 210-220.
Sembera Mackay, 143, 161, 179, 183.
Sese Islands, 111, 130, 278, 282-4.
Siegel, Lieut., 96-100.
Singo, 231.
Skrine, Rev. J. H., xi-xvi, 13, 19.
Slavery, 76, 299.
Smith, Rev. F. C., 106, 146, 201.
Stanley, H. M., 113.
Stock, Eugene, 150.
Stokes, Mr., 82, 98, 106.
Student Volunteer Missionary Union, 253-8.
Sudanese, 157, 210-220, 320-338.
Superstition, 76, 189, 219, 220, 278, 299.
Swahili, 197, 203, 264.
Sweet's 'Primer of Phonetics,' 245, 257, 319.
Taita, 73, 76.
Taveta, 74-5.
Taylor, Miss B., 314, 335.
Taylor, Rev. W. E., 243.
Teaching, 164, 273.
Thornton, Douglas M., 262.
Three Years' Enterprise, 289-294.
Thring, Rev. Edward, 11, 14, 40.
Thruston, Major, 322, 326.
Tore, 1, 36, 38.
Toro, 277.
Translations, 123, 128-131, 144, 192-208, 264-271.
Travelling, 87, 93, 186, 240, 294-295, 302-310.
Tucker, Bishop, 82, 137; Letters from, 92, 117, 123, 206-8, 209.
Uganda—see under Baganda, Buganda, Luganda; also under Climate, Political parties, Religions, &c.
Ugogo, 94.

INDEX.

Universities' Camps, 262.
Unyanguira, 92, 96.
Unyoro, 236.
Uppingham, xi-xvi, 8-19.
Usambiro, 103, 107.
Usoga—see Busoga.
Usongo, 102, 106.
Victoria Nyanza, 114, 281 ; see also under " Islands."
Villiers, Captain, 230, 344.
Waganda (Swahili), 114 ; see under " Baganda."
Wagogo, 95-101.
Walker, Ven. Archdeacon, 118, 329, 342.
Wambuzi, 273-4.

Water Supply, 145.
Weatherhead, Rev. H. W., 311, 325.
Webb-Peploe, Rev. H. Murray, 27, 46.
Welldon, Rev. J. E. C., 50.
Wigram, Rev. F. E., 54, 58, 167.
Williams, Captain, 146, 160, 170, 181.
Wilson, Mr. George, 323, 343.
Wilson, Mr (Government captain), 322, 326, 328.
Wilson, Mr. (C.M.S.), 323, 325.
Wolfendale, Dr., 99.
Wood, Rev. A. N., 89.
Zulu, 197.

www.ingramcontent.com/pod-product-compliance
Lightning Source LLC
Chambersburg PA
CBHW032044220426
43664CB00008B/856